About the author

Margaret Clarke, born in 1946, was brought up in Sheffield. Moving to Nottingham in 1973 she studied English at Nottingham University and subsequently taught in Nottinghamshire schools. Her career before retirement was with local authorities advising on curriculum development. She is married to Brian. They have two sons and four grandchildren.

Dedication

To Brian
Everyone needs a Brian in their lives.

To my family
With love

Margaret Clarke

ARE YOU AVERILL?

ISBN-13: 978 - 1508859154

First Published (2010)
Austin and Macaulay Ltd.
25 Canada Square
Canary Wharf
London E14 5LB

Acknowledgements

It was not my intention to write a book when I began my search for Kathleen and Zygmunt but thankfully, my friend Godfrey Kent in asking me to talk to the Rotary Club in Thailand set me on the road to recording my experiences. The rest grew like Topsy as my quest unfolded. I was reading Kate Adie's *Nobody's Child* when I started putting together the notes for the talk and, empathising with her notion that her passport contained a lie was inspired to use this. I drew on her statistics for the numbers of adopted children after the Second World War. Also, I had recently read Nicky Campbell's *Blue-eyed Son* which I found inspirational.

I'm grateful to my dear friend Mary Dunn who having read the first draft of the manuscript made suggestions which improved the work considerably. Thank you for taking the time to read the manuscript and for your insight: shades of nights spent on the WRL Toolkit.

Social workers Stuart in Nottingham and Sue in Sheffield helped ease the way to my first meeting with Kathleen. Their work is essential in bringing together adopted children and their birth parents. A starting point for contact is: The Registrar General, General Register Office, Smedley Hydro, Trafalgar Road, Southport PR8 2HH. They sent me a booklet: Access to Birth Records: Information for People Adopted in England and Wales. A useful website is: www.ukbirth-adoptionregister.com

None of my discovery could have been achieved without my good friends Pam and Alan Craven whose expertise in genealogy guided my search. I am forever grateful for their help. They searched for information using www.ancestry.co.uk; www.192.com; www.192.com/people/electoralrole/?gkw=voters+list+uk They suggested the following websites to research information on the Polish Air Force:

www.305squadron.com/

http://info-poland.buffalo.edu.web/history/WW11/britain/link.shtml

www.geocities.com/skrzydla/300 referred to in chapter 13 gave me information, in the article written by Wilhelm Ratuszynski, on the bomber squadrons that the Polish flyers were attached to in WW11. Interesting information is also to be found on www.polandinexile.com/airforce01

The work done by Colin Mitchell-Smith to keep alive the memories of the Polish 300 Squadron and the contribution to the war effort of the Polish Air Force is amazing. My visits to the airfield at Faldingworth gave me a sense of the reality of those flyers. He can be contacted through: RAF 300 Polish Squadron Memorials, Faldingworth, Faldingworth Parish Council, 12 Ashing Lane, Dunholme, Lincs. LN2 3NN. Two useful websites are:

www.raf-lincolnshire.info/faldingworth/faldingworthmemorials

http://sites-google.com/site/faldingworthmemorials

The help I received from the Ministry of Defence at APC Polish Enquiries, Building 28B, RAF Northolt,

West End Road, Ruislip, Middlesex HA4 6NG enabled me to have access to Zygmunt's service record. The information they provided was valuable in my search as was that from the Polish Institute and Sikorski Museum,

20 Princes Gate, London SW7 1PT. Their respective websites are:

www.mod.uk/defenceinternet

www.sikorskimuseum.co.uk

My greatest thanks are to my family. Dorothy and Ted Kay were the best parents any child could have had and none of my search diminishes that. My wonderful sons and their families are patient and understanding of my needs, especially my daughters-in-law, Debs and Lisa. My mum-in-law, Doris and cousin Margery, too, have supported me. Top of the list is Brian. He knows he's there. I am grateful, too, to my new families. I am indebted to them all. They could have shut the door at my appearance. They didn't need a disruption in their lives, especially my brothers known here as Paul and John and John's wife Lynn, as they have a lot to cope with. I know they are aware of my appreciation and hope that they feel I have treated our coming together with fondness and sensitivity. Grateful thanks are due to Michael and Yoli who have been amazing in their acceptance of my arrival in their lives. I look forward to furthering my relationship with them. And finally, Kathleen and Zygmunt, thank you with all my heart as without you I would have no life or relatives to be grateful for.

Disclaimer

In telling my story of self-discovery I have been dedicated to the recording of the truth of this account as I see it. All the details of my family: husband, children, grandchildren, close relatives and my friends are themselves as are some of my newly found family. There are, however, several family members in the book who have not been identified by their real names in order to protect their privacy. I have also changed some geographical locations for the same reason.

Part 1

The Search Begins

Chapter 1

Talking the Talk

The last thing I expected to be doing during an idyllic holiday in Thailand was to be baring my soul to complete strangers. I was in Patong Beach, Phuket on a balmy evening in January 2006 with a gentle breeze blowing still warm from the heat of the day. The 4x4 pulled into a parking bay beneath the hotel and my husband, Brian, four friends and I scrambled out. The six of us climbed the stairs into the reception area of the Aloha Villa Hotel and taking the lift, were transported several stories upwards.

As we entered a thickly carpeted room the members of the Patong Beach Rotary Club smiled greetings; the President, a quick and vivacious Belgian, introduced himself whilst ushering Brian and I to a damask-covered table set with highly polished silver and glassware. The guest speaker sits with the President and guests from other countries we were told. I looked around the room, a hotel bedroom now doing service as the Rotary Club's meeting room hung at picture-rail height with gaudy satin pennants of Rotary Clubs from around the world.

We began a conversation in English with a married couple from Norway, in Thailand for a holiday, and a quietly spoken, barely audible Swede. I drank water. Too soon for the wine. Food was spread out on two tables on the balcony outside the room and we chose from dishes of delicious spicy Thai meats and fish with delicate flavours of lemon grass and ginger. When the meal was cleared the business of the evening began.

Glancing across at our friends sitting at another table I smiled nervously. Pat and Stuart, with whom we had flown from Heathrow to Bangkok a week earlier, waved encouragingly and lifted their wineglasses in a silent toast. You'll be fine, it intimated. Godfrey was acting Master at Arms at Patong Beach Rotary. We were on holiday staying with him and his wife, Maxine at their home in Chalong, in Phuket. The previous evening sitting together by the pool listening to the chatter of exotic birds and inhaling the heavy scent of frangipani, I began telling our friends about something that had happened to me just days before our flight out. They were quiet whilst I spoke, realising something momentous had occurred then as I fell silent, bombarded me with a barrage of questions. A while later Godfrey took me quietly on one side and asked if I would be prepared to talk to his group the following evening bout what I had told them and after a few moments hesitation, I agreed.

And now here I was, smiling nervously at Brian, as I mounted the small podium to the microphone. Maxine had introduced me but the only thing the audience knew of the subject of my talk was what they could read on the Club's website: 'The Long Search.' Perhaps they were expecting a travelogue. I shuffled my notes, in what I hoped was an encouraging way, smiled out at faces lifted towards me and thought: Dear God what am I doing standing here talking to the League of Nations? Godfrey hadn't thought to tell me that the membership wasn't

English. They all spoke and understood the language, of course, but I was about to tell my story to people from all around the world. Let's hope it was of sufficient interest for them. I breathed deeply to still the butterflies and began:

"*I'm going to start my story with a small confession.*"

My audience looked a little startled, taken aback. Was this the right way to start? I reassured them. "*It's all right. Not that kind of confession.*" They settled back into their chairs, relaxing visibly.

On the flight to Bangkok I had been reading Kate Adie's wonderful book 'Nobody's Child' about foundling children and she starts her book with the dramatic sentence: "My passport contains a lie." Drawing on her experience I started my talk with the same statement:

"*My passport contains a lie. All of my passports, over the years, have been scrutinised by passport officials who have been presented with a page, which says I was born in Sheffield. But that's not actually the truth. I was brought up there but I was actually born in Leicester. The discrepancy is not so huge as to amount to deception of passport officials, but nevertheless, it's a fib. It's a fib, which started as a teenager in my first application and one, which I have perpetuated in adulthood whenever a form asks me to state my place of birth. What I consider remarkable is that I was forty-two before I knew I was telling the fib. And for one who was happy in the knowledge I was a Yorkshire woman, it came as something of a disappointment.*"

Laughter. Oh. They were warming up.

"The reason why I was forty-two was that it took the death of my father before I began to make enquiries about my origins. I've always known I was adopted," I told them, looking directly around the room.

"My parents were Edward and Dorothy Kay and no matter whatever I found out about myself later in life, nothing can change that fact. At the age of five, the recommended age apparently by post-war adoption agencies, my mum cuddled me in a bath towel and told me I had been 'specially chosen' by her and my dad. I was so thrilled I went out and told my little friends expecting them to notice some difference in me because of my newly acquired 'specialness.' I have always been loved throughout my life. I was always made to feel quite special. Sometimes, that's more than children of regular families can say about themselves.

"Some years before my dad died, I was thirty-five at the time, he and my mum told me what they knew about my past. They knew my natural mother's surname, Newcombe, and a Christian name, Kathleen; they knew she had been married at the time of my birth, but not to my natural father; they thought my father had been a Polish airman; and they knew I had been called Averill by my natural mother. My birthday is in April so perhaps that influenced her.

"They also were aware of an address in Sheffield, in the Manor area, which they presumed was where my natural mother had lived at the time of my birth. They sat me down in their conservatory and spoke seriously to me. They considered I should have this information, perhaps so neither of them should

die not having told me what they knew but both found it difficult to talk about such things. Their embarrassment and awkwardness made it impossible for me to press for further information. I wrote all these things down in a small notebook but did nothing with the information until after my dad died, five years later, and although my mum was still living, she knew nothing about the day I applied for my birth certificate to St. Catherine's House."

As I spoke, I looked down on the faces, and glanced around the room trying to make eye contact with as many of my audience as I could. They all seemed to be with me. I thought fondly about my parents and smiled inwardly.

*

My parents had been married for fourteen years before they decided to adopt a baby. I have no idea whether they tried and tried to conceive a baby or just took it as it came by not using any method of prevention. They never explored whether there was something that could be done to remedy their lack of success. It wasn't done. They were engaged in 1926 and married in 1932. Both were from large families.

My dad, everyone called him Ted, the youngest of ten children, was born in the Edwardian era – in 1906 – of parents with Victorian values. His father owned a small cutlery firm in Sheffield in partnership with another man and their names can still be seen on knives in my cutlery drawer at home. Etched is 'Wall Kay and Son, est. 1879'. These were knives made by the company but I have one, a carving knife that my dad made himself which bears the same inscription. The business was handed down to his eldest brother and eventually to his brother's son. My grandfather owned property, terraced houses, which he bequeathed to each of his sons street by street.

My dad loved speed. He had a motorbike as soon as he was legally allowed to own one and photographs show my mum sitting astride a Brough Superior in their 'courting' days. Later, sometime after they were married, he graduated to sports cars and bought a three-wheeler Morgan in British Racing Green. My mum drove that, too, but without a driving licence, as there was no law that said you had to have one.

She, Dorothy, wore a cloche hat in the 1920s and was very fashion conscious wearing short skirts to show good legs sheathed in silk stockings. Born in 1909, she was her parents' seventh child of eight. She had drive and ambition and although my dad was bright academically, going to grammar school and matriculating in the late 1910s he was not so ambitious. He worked for insurance companies, collecting the premiums from door-to-door, and in the sorting office of the Post Office and when she suggested he tried to get into the civil service, after the war, he did.

They were able to buy their own house in 1935, a solid semi-detached house with three bedrooms and a long garden in Sheffield suburbia. As a child my mum hadn't enjoyed school and although intelligent enough to continue after statutory leaving age, doing well enough in exams to stay on after fourteen, chose not to tell her parents so went instead to a business college and learned to type and to write in Pitman shorthand. She still wrote her shopping lists in shorthand at the age of nearly ninety. The skills of shorthand and typing stood her in good stead all her working life and during the war she worked for a series of government ministries.

My dad joined the RAF in 1942 and had the role of talking down aircraft onto the airfield from a tender. He was posted to Holland and Belgium towards the end of the war and was present in Paris when the city was liberated. I remember his stories about handing out oranges to French children during the liberation and their amazement, as they had never seen such fruit before.

When he came home my mum talked to him about wanting a baby. A friend of hers had adopted a baby girl in 1945 and although the process was rigorous with many home visits and a careful vetting process, it had all worked out well and proved worthwhile. I guess she persuaded my dad that this was the way to go but at 36 and 39 respectively it was never going to be entirely straightforward.

People from the adoption agency called regularly unannounced and my mother, always house proud, spent her days sweeping carpets, mopping lino and polishing the heavy wooden furniture. They would look into cupboards uninvited and ask questions out of the blue about any propensity for strong drink, which of course, never touched their lips. A sniff of gin and orange at Christmas brought colour to my mum's cheeks and, although my dad liked a half of beer once in a while, he never drank in a pub. They smoked, however, my mum socially, my dad out of habit. My mum occasionally held hers in a long black and gold holder, blowing sideways smoke that had never been anywhere near her lungs. My dad smoked John Players without filter tips. He had yellow fingers, for as long as I can remember. But smoking was not seen as anything untoward in the adoption process. And all went ahead without a hitch and home I came to the semi in Sheffield in May 1946.

*

Still smiling, I continued:

"When the certificate arrived, I was aware of what was in the official looking envelope, but I opened it with a great nervousness. What was I going to discover about myself? The certificate told me my mother's full name, Kathleen Mary Newcombe, where she had been living at the time of my birth being registered and the hospital where I had been born. These latter two pieces of information were the Leicester connection and were the most surprising, and disappointing. Even more disappointing though was that under father's name and occupation, there was just a line.

"It made my heart beat when I read the information about myself, which bore no resemblance to the information I knew from my Certificate of Adoption, which had served as my birth certificate for forty-two years, signed by the courts in Sheffield in December 1946. Accepting that I had been named Averill, I now found I had been Maureen Averill. But I was Margaret, not this stranger who happened to share my date of birth. I did nothing with the information and I definitely didn't tell my mum. I

18

always felt she would have been hurt by my need to know.

"When our children were born I was in my twenties and it was easy for Brian, my husband of thirty-seven years, and me to look at them and detect elements of ourselves in them. To my delight, both boys have my brown eyes. The younger, Robert looks quite strongly a Clarke, whereas the elder, Nick, is more like me. Robert resembles Brian's brother and Brian's maternal grandfather a little. Nick doesn't have the same resemblances. Curiously, though, he has ears that don't look like either of ours. And these we refer to as his 'Polish ears'. On the day his son, our first grandson, was born six years ago, he rang to say the usual things: we have a boy, he weighs eight pounds eleven ounces and has a shock of black hair – mother and baby doing fine – and oh, by the way, he has the Polish ears.

"There is a strong need in all of us to know where we come from and have a sense of identity."

They laughed at the mention of the Polish ears and I felt I was warming to my theme and they were along with me.

*

It never occurred to me when I was pregnant with my first child, Nick, that my mum would be ignorant about this process or about giving birth. When I left work in January 1970 I drove across the city to the maternity hospital for weekly check-ups and afterwards I would call at my mum's, who had now retired from her work as secretary to an estate agent. Her shorthand and typing had taken her from one decent job to another. We would have lunch and she was always interested in the procedures I had undergone at the hospital. Both she and my dad wanted us to have a little girl, just as lovely as I had been, he said. The visits were on Fridays and during this time I felt very close to my mum.

I was two weeks overdue on my final Friday visit and the hospital asked me to come in the following morning so this reluctant baby could be induced. I was given a rigorous internal examination at this last visit and, of no surprise to the midwives, baby stirred himself and I went into labour. We phoned the hospital at four am and they said, 'bring her in'. Brian drove me to the hospital, as I groaned in the front seat. He was very good trying to avoid any bumps in the road and we arrived at the atrium that was the front entrance surrounded by the noise of birdsong, as the dawn chorus rose to full crescendo on a bright May morning. Nick, delivered by forceps, was born after a difficult labour of twenty-three hours. But we had our joyous new arrival, and he was well worth the wait.

In the early hours of Sunday morning, Brian went to tell the new grandparents. It was too early to wake them so he slept in his car on the drive until six am. Dad answered his ring and went into the kitchen to put on the kettle for a cup of tea. My mum arrived and all was hugs and congratulations until they smelled burning rubber. It was the little rubber feet of the electric kettle. My dad, having filled the kettle, had placed it on the gas stove to boil. They hadn't had an ordinary kettle for many years but his excitement had got the better of him.

My mum came to visit when I arrived home. I was sitting up in bed breast-feeding Nick. My stomach and the brown line, which appears on new mothers' contracting skin, were visible. 'Is that where he was born?' Mum asked. I was surprised by her question. She could have been asking me if he had been born by caesarean section, but that's not what she said. More likely the question was asked out of ignorance as who would there have been to talk to her about the process of birth? Her own mother had died in 1957 and her closest sister in age had been childless. Her eldest sister had given birth to both her children before my mum was married and I can't imagine any cosy sisterly chats about how her nephew and niece had come into the world. Far too embarrassing.

I became pregnant with Robert fifteen months after Nick's birth. When the pregnancy was confirmed, when Nick was eighteen months old, I phoned my mum to tell her she was going to be a grandmother again. 'Not again!' she declared as if I was some sort of loose woman. I'm not sure why she was so surprised but she soon became used to the idea and I would drop Nick off on the morning of my prenatal visits for my parents to delight in whilst I was away. Again, I think my dad wanted a little girl to enjoy but they were so pleased to have Nick, a boy would have been just as lovable. Just as well really. Two lovely boys and, of course, proud grandparents. But there was nothing of their looks in the little boys. No blue eyes, which they both had, or smile or likeness at the turn of a jaw or cheek. Did they ever think about that? I'll never know.

But looks aren't the be all and end all of a person, are they? The nurture theory is not an empty one. I didn't do very well at school. I failed more O levels than I passed but the ones I did achieve were in history and English, my dad's passions. He was interested in war, knew all the names and dates of English monarchs and much about what they did during their reigns; he read books on natural history, especially dinosaurs borrowing books from the library, going each week to change them. He introduced me to the library at an early age and I would visit with him, looking at picture books at first. I have a memory of standing beside a tall bookcase tugging on his trouser leg to get him to look at a particular book I had been engrossed in for a while. I spoke to him and looked up to smile in a complete stranger's face as my dad had already moved along. Hot embarrassment stained my young cheeks. When I eventually was able to go to university I studied English. My parents were enormously proud.

When the boys were young, my dad would sit with them and tell them stories. He had been in the RAF during the War and many of these were about this time when he was sharing his billet or Nissan hut with his pal Dougie Bowman, or rolling over the beds fighting with Harry Fellows, who had stolen his socks. His war sounded relatively safe although he spent some time dodging armed Germans in occupied Belgium. Robert went into the armed services, the Royal Navy, at nineteen, after his granddad had died, but who knows what influence he had had from his stories. They both speak with enormous fondness of both their grandparents, about the times when they went to stay with them as they were growing up, buying their ration of sweeties from Laddie's. As they were older they knew about the circumstances of my birth but it would not have occurred to them to look on their maternal grandparents any differently from their paternal grandparents nor love them any less.

*

These thoughts overtook me only briefly. I continued my story, glancing from time to time at Brian as I did so, testing how things were going. OK, his face said.

"I decided to start digging more deeply a year or two after my mum died in 1999. The information my dad had given me wasn't a lot and in the climate that prevailed after the war, adoptive parents were given the fewest of facts about the background of the child they were getting. At the end of the war illegitimacy peaked at 9% of all births. There were plenty of healthy babies available for adoption but the subject tended to be hush-hush. Adoption agencies were rigorous in their reticence and conveyed only the barest facts to prospective clients about their charges. What they learned about the circumstances of the birth, they withheld from the families. So I don't know how my dad knew what he knew and he's not there for me to ask anymore. However, one day in 2003, Brian and I went to look for the address my dad had given me five years before his death, the one I had studiously written in my little notebook. It wasn't in the most salubrious district in Sheffield and we had talked about how there might be a social gulf between my natural mother and me, if we were ever to meet. But when we got there, there was no house. It had been pulled down. Our next search was through the

23

Electoral Role for that address in the 1940s but no one of my natural mother's name had ever been registered there during the 1940s or during the 1950s. So we had drawn a blank."

*

Perhaps reticence to release any information about children available for adoption fuelled a prejudice about the whole notion of adoption. Before the Second World War, there were many ways of adopting, some legal and registered, some not. It was not unusual for mothers to visit their local GP with a tale of woe about their daughters being in the 'family way.' Such was the disgrace that to speak of it to other family members wasn't entertained. Quite often, in such cases the GP was aware of a couple desperately trying to have a baby and local doctors with greatest knowledge of their community were in the best position to speak to such couples and offer them the chance of adopting. Girls found themselves pregnant but unable to keep their babies. Perhaps they'd had under-aged sex and were little more than girls themselves. They had their babies and their mothers brought them up. The children thought their grandmothers were their mothers and their real mothers were their sisters.

In other circumstances, mothers died unexpectedly and their offspring were given to other members of the family to bring up. The children were never officially adopted but merely absorbed into the family, just another mouth to feed. Such an event occurred in Brian's father's family. A family friend of Brian's paternal grandmother died leaving a small girl motherless.   Although already a widow, his grandmother thought little of bringing up this little girl as one of her own children. She became the third daughter and Brian's father never thought of her as anything other than one of his sisters although she kept her mother's surname until she married.

Brian's maternal grandfather, a fiercely proud man, a veteran of the Somme where he was near-fatally wounded, had a very different view of adoption. I had already told Brian's mother about being adopted and was spending the day with her after I had finished work whilst I was pregnant with Nick. We went to Grandma and Granddad's house for lunch. Sitting at the table as the meal was being served, Granddad began expounding his views. I've no idea now what set him on the train of thought but he was adamant it shouldn't be done because: 'You don't know where they've come from. You don't know whose they are.' He firmly believed the sins of the father would be visited on the son. Or in this case, the sins of the mother.

Ironically, his youngest daughter became pregnant before she was married and he had threatened to take his life by jumping off the Five Arches in Sheffield because of the shame. He left the house in high dudgeon but walked up the road sufficiently slowly for Brian's father to catch him up and persuade him against such drastic measures and to come home and face the problem. He accepted his daughter's fall from grace and she was duly married. The talk at the lunch table fell quiet as my mother in law glanced sideways at me. 'Take no notice, love.' And I didn't. It wasn't important. I was very fond of this old gentleman and he thought I was something special, especially when he stood by my side from time to time and I tucked him under my arm because I was so much taller. But his views weren't unusual. It was all right taking on a friend or relative's child as you were aware of his or her origins but some stranger's child was a different matter. I was pleased that my parents didn't have that view.

*

I continued with my story to the Patong Rotary Club members, who were surprised to be listening to such a personal story.

"A year later, after talking to a friend in similar circumstances, who told me about an official procedure for people like us, I decided to go through official channels and get some help. Children who were adopted before 1975 must seek the support of a social worker to receive counselling to prepare for a search and an eventual meeting with their natural parents. This, too, is in order to protect the natural parent from unwelcome surprises. I wrote to the Adoptions Section of the General Register Office in Southport and told them when I was born and when I was adopted. I knew that there may not be any records still in existence but hoped there would be. I asked to receive counselling from someone within my own local authority, Nottingham, where we had been living since 1973, or if not the local authority in Sheffield, where I had been adopted and where I hoped my records were still held. Taking a lead from the leaflet 'Access to Birth Records: Information for people adopted in England or Wales', I said that it

may be appropriate to conduct the interview through the original adoption agency, assuming this was still in existence. It seemed all very tenuous, but it was a start.

"The result of this was a form from the General Register Office asking me to complete it and contact the local offices of the Central Adoption and Fostering Unit in Nottingham for an appointment for an interview. I contacted them, and so began a relationship with Stuart, a social worker in Children's Services. He came to the house and sat with us in our conservatory, encouraging me to talk about my circumstances and myself and about why I wanted to make this journey of discovery, because that really is what it becomes. After a short time it became obvious to me that he, too, had made a similar journey and discovery in his own life, which made him, so it seemed, more empathetic to and understanding of my needs.

"It was important that my motivation was not one of revenge or resentment and he was assured that I was sufficiently 'together' about myself to undertake the search. Significantly, one of his questions was if he was to turn up the fact that I had been the product of a rape, would I want to know? Yes, I would. However appalling, this would not have been my fault or responsibility, even if it were a violent way in which to be given life. He also said that in his experience, he thought I was unlikely to be of Polish extraction. I didn't look Polish, he thought, despite my dark hair and eyes. My dad had been at pains to tell me that the Polish airman had been Roman Catholic, rather than Jewish. Why he made that

distinction, I'm not sure, possibly because of the extent of the persecutions across Europe during the Nazi reign of terror, but he had thought it was significant and his intentions would have been good. So I hung onto the thought that my natural father had been Polish. I had fantasised in the past about a dark haired, dashing airman escaping from occupied Poland, battered by the Nazi invasion, at the start of the war and coming to England to do his bit for the war effort, as so many Poles had done in the early 1940s. I wasn't going to give that fantasy up so easily.

"Stuart wrote to the Sheffield City Family Placement Services to ask if it was possible for me to have access to the records of the circumstances of my adoption. Records are kept of conversations between adoption agencies and the mothers giving up their children and between the agencies and the prospective adopting parents. But none remained of mine. The reply to Stuart's letter said that on checking the records of the Sheffield and District Adoption Society, they believed that they had found a reference to my adoption in their first ledger, which stated that baby went to live with her adopting parents on the 20th May 1946. Beside the entry were the letters 'M', 'B', and 'S', which indicated that the birthmother was married, came from a broken home and had been in the armed services.

"Unfortunately, the papers relating to such an early adoption had not survived so no further details were available. The date of my parents' application to the agency was given as the 20th November 1945 and it was possible that the birthmother had gone to *stay with friends or relatives for the time surrounding her confinement, which would account for a different address. Sue, a social worker in the Family Placement services, had signed the letter. She had found a further address of where my natural mother had been living – in Middlewood, Sheffield, and an area across the other side of the city from the original address.*

"We drove up to Sheffield from Nottingham and sat outside the new address for a while.

"The next day we contacted the Electoral Role offices to learn that in 1945 my natural mother had been living there with others. These were Elsie James, Audrey Taylor, Sidney Taylor Jnr. and Gladys Beal. On my birth certificate, my natural mother's former name had been given as James. It looked as if Elsie was her mother. Another piece of the jigsaw was emerging but we were still far from the whole picture. Stuart said that, as there were so many other people living in the house, it might have been a lodging house and suggested we go there again and knock on the door and ask about these people who had once lived there. But my courage wasn't up to that. What would I discover?

"Then Brian met Alan.

"Alan was the husband of a friend and colleague of mine and was an expert on genealogy. Whilst Pam and I were working in Lancaster delivering training to teachers by way of a conference in a hotel, our husbands passed the time walking around the city and Alan began talking about tracing his and Pam's family members. Brian explained what I had been trying to do so Alan suggested that once we

were home we e-mail him with the information we already had and he would see if he could help. After one or two false starts he traced my natural mother's name through public census records available to access on the Internet."

*

One of the false starts proved somewhat disconcerting. In September 2005 I was preparing to deliver training to a group of teachers in Telford, Shropshire, and was enjoying eating a sandwich lunch with them before the start of the event when my mobile phone rang. It was Pam. Are you sitting down, she asked? Alan has traced a Kathleen Mary Newcombe who died aged 63 in 1986. She looks a likely match, given the information. I felt bereft. So close but still so far. If only I'd started the search earlier but 1986 had been the year in which my father had died. And what was worse, this person had died at such an early age. What hope longevity, now? The problem for all adopted children is the lack of any medical history. When a doctor asks you if there is any history of heart failure in the family? Strokes? Diabetes? And so on. All you can ever say is, I don't know. A parent dying prematurely can be a bit of a blow, especially if it means that at fifty-nine you can think you only have four years left, if heredity is anything to go by. However, I drove home after the event feeling disconsolate, but on arriving home, my spirits were lifted by reading an e-mail from Pam saying, false alarm, the dates don't tally. A short time later Alan traced a far better match.

*

"A Kathleen Mary James had married a Joseph William Newcombe in Sheffield in 1942. This lady had been married aged nineteen and her husband aged twenty-one. She would have had to get permission to marry, wrote Alan, and as she had been born sometime in 1923, she would be eighty-two now. When I had first had my interview with Stuart, the social worker from Nottingham, he had told us about some remarkable successes he had had recently in reuniting daughters with their natural mothers who were aged eighty-six and ninety. Eighty-two was nothing. For a few moments I felt hopeful. Alan advised that I send off for this marriage certificate. He gave me the website address to apply through and I did this sending my credit card details for the fee of £11.

"A copy of the certificate arrived after a few weeks. It confirmed the ages of Kathleen and Joseph when they were married and their addresses at the time; it told us the church they were married in, the church of the Sacred Heart in Hillsborough in Sheffield; a Roman Catholic couple, then; it told us the date of the marriage in 1942; and really interesting, the signature of one of the witnesses to the marriage was one S Taylor, one of the residents at the house in Middlewood in 1945.

"We also learned that Joseph William had been a gunner and engineers' fitter with the Royal Artillery. So he had joined up during or before 1942. Perhaps they were getting married before he was posted abroad. Kathleen was a cutlery warehouse woman, a coincidence of sorts as my father's family had owned a cutlery firm in Sheffield. However, as

31

Sheffield is famous for its cutlery making, perhaps it wasn't all that unusual. Their fathers' employment was given, too. Mr Newcombe, Joseph, had been a check weigh man but, although William Henry James had been an engineer, he was deceased. Could this be the source of the letter B for broken home given in the notes in the adoption agency? And could Joseph William being in the services be the S referred to? Or indeed, was this actually some reference to the Polish airman?

"I supplied Alan with all the important information from this marriage certificate. And the next day Pam phoned with the address in Sheffield where my natural mother and her husband were living. At least, an address where they were living, according to the Electoral Role information available in the public domain up to the year 2000.

"This was 2005. Was she still alive?"

*

In 2005 I was working for myself. I had decided that teaching was for younger people. I was never happy with less than my best but given some classes where children were patently not interested in learning, some weeks were very tiring. 'Make me redundant! I'm nearly fifty' I used to ask my head teacher, putting my head around his office door. 'Get out of here!' he'd say. Until at last, I told him that 1999 was going to be my last year. I was head of a cross curricular faculty with responsibility for an area of the curriculum known as work related learning. It had been an area of interest for some years and was developing fast because of the government's desire to increase the skills for work that had been sadly neglected through the slavish desire to deliver the National Curriculum. I had been engaged to teach English at this, my second school, back in 1985. Shortly after my arrival the head of sixth form asked in the staff room if anyone was interested in becoming part of a team to develop work related learning in the sixth form. I went to the meeting and told him I had a background in work other than teaching – I was thirty eight when I started to teach and had worked in the civil service almost from school until I gave up to have Nick in 1970, so felt I had some experience to offer young people. I joined the team and after the head of sixth form left started to lead it.

Our success as a school with our sixth-form students led to the examination awarding body offering us the opportunity to be a pilot school to develop similar courses for fourteen to sixteen year olds. And so began a successful time in my teaching career developing courses for this age range, travelling about the country training teachers in other schools to develop and implement these courses and going off to London to talk at conferences run by the Qualifications and Curriculum Authority. I still taught English mostly to exam classes at GCSE level and A Level and communication skills to the increasing numbers of young people who were opting for the work related learning courses. Life was becoming very hectic. 'Make me redundant?'

'No. We're a successful school. How can I justify it? Go away!''

In 1998, during the Christmas holidays, I was reading the job advertisements in the local paper and there it was. The perfect job. I showed the advertisement to Brian. 'Did you write this?' he asked. I could have done, as it sought so much of what I could offer. I applied the next day and the following February was in post as an adviser to Nottingham City schools on work related learning for 14-16 year olds. It was a secondment so I never really resigned my teaching post but they gave me a good send off. I loved the new job.

However, after three years my boss left and things started to go adrift for a while. I became less satisfied with how the post was being managed. So I resigned. I resigned from my school at this time, too, taking my teachers' pension early. But the importance of the curriculum development was also being recognised by other local authorities and I was asked to be involved in training teachers further afield. I became self-employed in order to do this work with other local authorities. I advised on the curriculum for Nottinghamshire schools and schools in Lincolnshire. Whilst I had been working with Nottingham City schools I had become involved in a national project funded by what was then Department for Education and Employment. I continued to do this work, as the purpose was to produce a resource and to offer training to help schools develop work related learning. I worked with two advisers, Mary and Pam, who later became my friends, from Hampshire local authority and together we ran conferences for teachers, all over the country. This is what I was doing when Pam and I were working in Lancaster and Brian and Alan went walking. There are times when things are just meant to be.

*

I continued my story for the Patong audience:

"*As I was working, the following day, Brian rang the Electoral Role offices in Sheffield. But they weren't allowed to give the current information. 'Oh,' said Brian and explained how disappointing that was given the searching he and his wife had been involved in to trace these people and he explained the reason for the enquiry. 'If I was to give you a couple of names, would you at least be able to say yes or no?' 'Try me,' she said. He told her. The lady from the Electoral Role said yes! To both names. So we knew that up to December 2004 at least, she was still alive. When I was making a note of the address it suddenly became familiar and I remembered that a year or so earlier, whilst visiting my mum in law in Sheffield, I had borrowed her telephone directory and made a note of all the Newcombes listed, their addresses and telephone numbers; there were only thirteen. I had also listed the James and there were only twenty-one of those. I snatched up the list from my papers and there they were. JW. Same address and of, course, a telephone number.*

"*Well, that was it then. All I had to do was pick up the phone and tell her who I was!*

"*But of course not. What I did was to phone Stuart to tell him of our amazing discovery and to ask him what to do next. Would he help? Would he write to her? But he was off work and his office thought his sick leave would be long term. No one was handling his caseload of these kinds of cases – non-urgent – and no one could help. We'd drawn another blank.*

"*What to do next?*

"We drove up to Sheffield and went to sit outside the house at this new address for a while. But this time my natural mother was inside.

"We went a time or two after that, sat for a while, and then drove away. One time a young man was cutting the privet hedge. He looked about nineteen. He could be a grandson, we thought. Should we get out of the car and ask him? No fear. We had the name and phone number of the social worker, Sue, who had supplied Stuart with the information from the adoption agency in Sheffield, the three code letters and the new address. As we sat watching the hedge being cut, I rang her and left a message. On the following day she phoned as Brian and I were travelling back along the M6 from a conference Pam and I had been running in Wigan. I explained who I was; she remembered the case and was sympathetic to hear Stuart was off sick. Would you act on my behalf, instead of Stuart, I asked? Yes, she would. Would I write to her with all the information I had and she would see what she could do to act as an intermediary. On the 26h May 2005 I wrote to her giving her the information she had asked for."

*

I wrote that in her letter to Stuart she had supplied an address in Middlewood, Sheffield, and it was through this that we had been able to trace my birthmother's marriage certificate. I enclosed a copy of it for her to see. I said that through friends who were familiar with the open records that are held on the Internet, we had been able to learn of an address where we thought she was living. A phone call to the

Records Office in Sheffield Library Service and another to the Electoral Records Office showed that a K M Newcombe and Joseph William Newcombe were still living at this address in December 2004. I told her the address and that the Sheffield phone directory also showed that J W Newcombe lived at this address. I went on that, as I had been explaining on the phone, Stuart was off work at the moment and was likely to be so for a time. I asked her if she would act as an intermediary to approach my birthmother on my behalf in whatever way was appropriate, and then let me know how best to proceed. I emphasised the point that Brian and I were not aware whether Kathleen's husband, who was married to her at the time of my birth, but who was not my father, had knowledge of my existence. Protecting her was very important to us.

I asked her to ring me if there was anything else she wanted to know.

*

"Sue wrote to Kathleen telling her someone was trying to trace someone who had lived at the Middlewood address in 1946. Her letter was non-threatening and benign. Anyone picking up the letter, with no prior knowledge of the circumstances, would not be suspicious, but to Kathleen it would have meant something. The choice was with her. Whether to ring the number on the letter. Or not.

"After a month Kathleen rang Sue.

"Following the phone call Sue rang me and told me she had talked to her. Kathleen was hesitant when she talked, obviously wary. The issue of the

baby, in 1946, hadn't been talked about in the marriage. Her husband hadn't talked about it with her. The reason she was ringing then was that she had the house to herself as her husband was in hospital as he had mobility problems. She had had the task of caring for him but it was proving problematic. She visited him every afternoon. She said she knew that I would have been well cared for and loved and that she was making the best choice.

"She had two sons and there was a grandson who lived close by. (The hedge cutter?) One of these sons was in France at the moment as he and his wife had a house there and he'd gone to tile the bathroom. Neither of her sons knew about her former indiscretion but, strangely, one of them had said years ago how nice it would have been to have had a sister. That could have been a moment to tell all, but she hadn't.

"She was one of three sisters, one of whom had died many years ago and another was in a nursing home. She considered herself in 'good nick' and was an impulsive sort of person: do first, think later. She said she had had a good life together with her husband, who, she said, was a good chap. From time to time, she had wondered how I was getting on.

"She asked a question: does she want to meet me? Sue said she would need to ask me but in the meantime she would get me to write to her with a picture of myself and some of my family. Kathleen said she would ring again in two weeks' time but Sue's and our collective thought was that we didn't want to frighten her.

"Good grief, I had half-brothers! An only child for fifty-nine years, and I had two half-brothers. Does her husband know about me or was it that they just hadn't talked about things since I had been given up for adoption? If her husband had known all about me did he want his feelings of the time raking over again after all these years? On learning that his wife was pregnant when he came home from the war he could have said: never darken my doors again and left her, but then again, he was Roman Catholic, so divorce wouldn't have been an option back in 1946. And what about her? She is impulsive, like me. But what does she look like? Am I like her? Does she have brown eyes, like me? Is she tall, like me? Do her feet turn out, like mine?

"Straight away, I wrote to Sue. I looked out some photos: one of me at five weeks old
in the garden being held by my mum on the day I arrived home with them, wearing a knitted suit with leggings one of which dangled down, empty; another of me at five years old in the same garden; my passport photo at 20, one I've always liked; a wedding photo of Brian and me standing outside the Victoria Hall in Norfolk Street in 1969; and two more photos. I chose one of my sons, Nick and Rob, looking smart and laughing, shaking hands on the morning of Robert's wedding and the picture the same photographer took of Brian and me at the wedding. Both those photographs showed us all in profile. I chose these because if it were me looking at us for the first time, I'd be curious to see more."

*

On 21st June 2005, the letter I wrote to Sue said:

Dear Sue

It was wonderful to hear from you yesterday with news of your conversation with Kathleen; it made me feel both excited and anxious. I am writing, as you suggested, with some information about myself and I have included some photographs as well.

It's hard to know where to start but the most important information is that I have been a happy, confident, well-rounded individual since childhood and that is due mainly to parents who loved me and were proud of me. Always curious about my background, I never wanted to find out more until after the death of my mother, although I sent off for my birth certificate in1987. My father, some years before he died, told me a little about my natural mother but as he died in 1986, the opportunity to know more is lost.

I went to Abbeydale Grammar School and worked in the Civil Service where I met Brian. We married in 1969. It is a good and happy marriage and we have two sons, Nick (35) and Robert (33). Each son has a son of his own. Our grandsons are Joseph aged 5 and Jack aged 2 and we dote on them both.

I left the Inland Revenue in 1970, to have Nick, and stayed at home until in 1980. We moved from Sheffield to Nottingham in 1973. At school, I always thought I wasn't very bright but circumstances changed and I went to Nottingham University to study English. After I graduated, I trained to teach juniors but ended up teaching secondary pupils. I became a head of department for Work Related Learning. I loved the teaching and the responsibility but as the teaching grew increasingly demanding, I decided to leave. At the same time, I saw a job advertised and went to work as a curriculum advisor (for Work Related Learning) to secondary schools with the education department in Nottingham City Council. I worked there for three years and left to work for myself as an education consultant, which I have been doing for the last three years. I work with teachers from schools all over the country and travel quite a lot running conferences for them.

I am tall; 5'8", which is quite tall for my generation, I think; I am fairly slim and like to stay fit. I have dark hair, which has some grey in it now. My eyes, and those of my boys, are brown. When I'm not working, which is increasingly more now, Brian and I go on holiday. We have a property in France, near La Rochefoucauld, in the Charente, which we have had renovated and we spend the summer there and other times in holiday periods such as Easter. We took Joseph there last half term. We are planning a visit to friends in Thailand and Australia at the start of next year. I like to keep fit at aerobics classes several times a week, when I can. Brian plays golf; and we both read a lot. We have a good social life and friends and family come to eat.

There are many unanswered questions for adopted children. I've been reading recently an autobiography by Nicky Campbell, the radio and television presenter, about his search for his natural parents, and he asked loads. Mine are questions such as where do get my height from, why are my eyes brown, why does my left foot turn out more than my right, who do I look like? Why am I often impulsive; do first, think after? I might know a bit of the answer to that, now.

Brian and I have talked long and hard about what I am doing and the implications. As I explained on the phone, the last thing on my mind is to cause upset to Kathleen or to her family. We will only proceed with whatever she feels comfortable with and what she can cope with.

Yours sincerely'

I found a brown envelope with a cardboard protector, put in the letter and the six photographs and posted it off to Sue. All we could do now was wait to see if Kathleen phoned again.

*

My Patong audience was waiting.

"Kathleen phoned again. She wanted to see the photos but coming into the offices in Sheffield city centre might cause a problem if someone saw her. She spoke about herself: she wasn't tall, and she wasn't dark, had been fair, in fact, mousier, and now she was grey. She had blue eyes, not brown. She had often thought she might like to be a teacher, if there had been the chance and, in fact, she had a friend in Nottingham who was a teacher. A lady from Bulwell called Cooper. Did I know her? No. She was interested in the aspects of coincidence in our lives: two sons, the house in France. I had noticed a caravan parked in the drive at her house on one occasion we had been sitting there and we had always caravanned, which was what had led to our buying a house in France, after years and years of caravan

42

holidays there. Perhaps she and her husband had taken such holidays and her son had decided he wanted a house in France as a consequence. She said she had some connections with Nottingham in her past. Little did I know at this stage how significant they were to be.

"Her husband had now left hospital and was in a nursing home close to her house so she could walk each day to see him. And he was still a consideration for us, as we didn't want to cause disruption to their lives. She was still curious about me but wondered if we were ever to meet how it could be managed. Sue asked her to keep in touch and think about how she could get to see the photos. She said she would and rang off.

"Twice more she rang and left a message on Sue's answering machine. Sue only works in the afternoons and the last two calls had been made in the morning although a recorded message tells callers that Sue is only available in the afternoon after 1.00pm. The messages she left indicated to Sue that Kathleen was feeling guilty about not contacting her directly but things were difficult at home, presumably with arrangements for her husband's care. When Kathleen had received Sue's first letter she had concealed it in a book, getting it out to note Sue's phone number, and returning it there. What struck us all was the fact that there she was, aged eighty-two, all on her own, handling a difficult situation. No one to talk to about her feelings or to ask for advice about what she should do.

"Then everything went quiet."

When my mum died Brian and I used her legacy to buy a house in France. It was a coincidence that of one of Kathleen's sons had a house in France. In the letter to Sue Tomlinson I had given details of where in France ours was in case Kathleen was able to say where her son's was. What if they were in the same department? Or in neighbouring ones? The fact that her son was tiling his bathroom was an indication to us that he and his wife could have bought a property that they were renovating.

*

I continued the story of my 'Long Search' with the multi-national group in Patong Beach.

"*In October of 2005, Brian and I moved home. We left Nottingham and went to live in a village near Burton upon Trent. Walking around the nearby market town of Ashbourne one afternoon I rang Sue and told her our new contact details. Nothing more had been heard from Kathleen and Sue advised that it was just a waiting game. Kathleen would get in touch again when she was ready.*

"*We were spending the evening with our friend in similar circumstances with whom we had shared details of the search. Paul was fascinated that we had managed to make contact with Kathleen, albeit through the social worker and he suggested that as Christmas was approaching, how about just sending a card with our new address and telephone number included. I did just that. At first I wrote 'from Margaret' and put the contact details on the opposite page. But what if someone else should look at that* page? So I tore up the card, wrote the same thing but put the address and telephone number onto a yellow 'post-it', so she could conceal it if she wished. It sat on the hall table long after I had posted off all our other Christmas cards. Then a week before Christmas, I thought, don't just keep looking at this – post it!

"On the 2nd January 2006, in the early evening, I was looking at the television. The phone at my side rang. The caller said she didn't know exactly whom she was phoning but she had received a card with this phone number on. Her name was Kathleen Newcombe. My heart hammered in my chest and I struggled to steady my breathing. Oh Crickey!

"She had rung to ask, she said, who sent the card and in what way we were connected. I told her the connection was 10th April 1946. The phone went quiet as she pondered that for a while but then she went on talking. A moment later she said: 'Are you Averill?'

" 'Yes, I'm Averill.'

"And there we were: I was talking to my mother. We talked about things – her husband had known about me. He wasn't known as Joseph William because she had called him Bill. He wasn't well; and when we talked further she said she couldn't talk about such things on the phone. I told her we had moved from Nottingham and that we lived near Burton upon Tent. She knew Burton quite well as she had a niece living in Branston, a suburb on the east side. She'd shopped with her in Burton town centre. More coincidences. We should meet, she said. "

"And meet we did. On the following

45

Saturday, the 7ᵗʰ January 2006. "

*

But this wasn't straightforward. At the end of the phone call we left it that she would ring me again in a day or two when both of us had had time to consider where and how we could meet. When I came off the phone, after about twenty minutes, I felt flushed with the adrenalin rush. Brian felt, hearing my side of the conversation, that I could have been talking to a friend I hadn't seen for a while and was just catching up. It was so easy. There was a lot of laughter. As I was so shocked to receive the call, I can't remember everything about the conversation; I wish I could. Bits of it still keep coming into my mind even now. What I do remember is I was talking to a woman I had never met in my adult life at least but who sounded warm and funny. Her voice was warm and sort of comforting. I felt I knew her. We agreed that she should phone when she felt safe. Not safe she said, she had no intention of deceiving anyone. All right then, comfortable. Yes, comfortable, she said.

So wrapped up in my own experience I hadn't given enough thought to what she must have been thinking. There she was making this phone call not really knowing whom she would find at the end of the phone and suddenly she finds she is talking to her daughter; the daughter she gave up almost sixty years before. All on her own in the house, there was no one to tell when she put down the receiver.

She didn't phone the following day or the one after that. She hadn't phoned by the Thursday. We

46

were due to go on a month's holiday to Thailand, and I told her we would be there and in Australia and New Zealand from the 11th January. What if she phoned after we'd left? You phone her, said Brian. What if someone else is in the house, I asked? I didn't do it on the Thursday. I tried on the Friday evening after a few wines for Dutch courage. No one picked up the phone. But the following day was different. I managed to phone and she invited us to come straight away.

We were due to visit Brian's cousins for a meal on this Saturday evening. Ann and David live in Sheffield about twenty minutes from where Kathleen lives.

Coincidently, when Ann was a girl her parents had lived quite close to where Kathleen lived now. I was all ready to go out waiting downstairs for Brian to come down. Ten minutes to spare before we were due to leave. I'll ring now. I'll ring now. Go on, I'll ring now. I dialed. If she picks up and I lose my courage I can hang up. If she picks up and there is someone there I can say it's a wrong number. Heart beating too rapidly, hands cold, cheeks pink, a need to breathe more deeply to keep control. Terminal cowardice.

'Hello,'

'It's Margaret.'

'Oh, yes.'

'We talked last Monday. We were thinking about where we might meet and I wanted to ask you if you had had any thoughts about where that might be.' Rushing on, 'We're going on holiday in a few days' time and I didn't want you to be ringing when we weren't there. Can you talk to me?'

    'Oh, yes. No one's here. I'm on my own.'

*

"In a phone call to her we learned that she was on her own as her husband was still in the nursing home, her sons weren't likely to call as the one with the house in France had just arrived home and had phoned to say so and the other and the grandchildren didn't call on a Saturday evening and her friend who sometimes does had called earlier in the afternoon instead. So would we like to come round now? And will your hubby come?"

*

The short answer, in very different circumstances, would have been: well, no actually, we're just off out! But I said yes we could come but it would take us about an hour. Oh, you're not local, she asked? No, Burton upon Trent. Oh, yes. Well, in an hour, then. She gets a little confused, I was learning. She's eighty-two, it's allowed.

We jumped in the car and sped up the A38. Phone Ann, said Brian. I did, to let her know we weren't sticking to plan and could she hold the meal until a bit later. I explained why it was and she understood straight away as she had been privy to some of the details of my search and knew it was a moment that couldn't be missed. Our intention was that Brian would come into the house to meet her and after a short while leave us to it. It was always in his plan as he thought there would be things better said between the two of us.

48

He was right. Butterflies set up home in my stomach for the hour and a quarter of the journey. I talked all the way there but I can't remember what about. I just had a need to talk; make inane small talk with Brian as a way of covering up the nervousness I was feeling. I couldn't concentrate on anything. My hands were cold. I felt quite chilled despite the car heater. I also did what I usually do when I am faced with something difficult. Put how I am going to cope with it to the back of my mind. I couldn't rehearse what I was going to say; I was just going to let it happen. I never once thought, what am I doing, what am I getting myself into here? I never gave a thought to Kathleen waiting at home for a child she had not seen for nearly sixty years but her nerves must have been like mine. Stretched taught.

*

"*I had said on the phone that as soon as we got there, I would call her to say so as if her circumstance had changed and she was no longer on her own, it would be quite easy to say so. I did this. 'It's me. We're sitting outside. Is it still OK?' She came out to the gate as I crossed the pavement to meet her. There stood the woman who had given birth to me nearly sixty years ago. And there was I seeing her for the very first time.*

"*She looked a bit like me. Square about the lower jaw. And the hair. It was my hair. Grey all over now, as mine would be, if I were to live as long. Someone who looked like me.*"

*

People who know who they are and where they come from never have to give a second thought about where they get their looks as they can see it every day. And if they can't always see it, there's generally someone to say oh you're like your dad/mum/granny. When Brian goes shopping in Hillsborough with his mum, who is 93 now, relatives and old neighbours are just amazed at how like his father Brian has become. They regularly remark to his mum: 'Oh, he's your Reg to a tee!' It's so obvious to all. No one has ever been able to say that to me. There was one exception, however, when I was a little girl, about four years old. My grandma, my mum's mother, used to take me to her local shop and the lady behind the counter once told her, 'Oh, yes, she's like you, you can tell she's your Dorothy's daughter.' But that seems to me to be more a matter of pleasing the customer. My grandma might have felt a kind of pleasure although she used to smile enigmatically and say nothing.

*

"My natural mother and I hugged over the gate, pulled apart, and looked hard at one another and hugged again. We followed her down the path and I introduced Brian to her. She told us: 'My name's Kathleen. It means sweet and pure. They got that wrong, didn't they?'"

*

She had had a slight fall a short time ago and her crutches were resting behind the back door. She put the kettle on and while she was in the kitchen we looked at pictures on the wall in the living room. A

50

son with cap and gown from the Open University; photos of grandchildren; a photo of her and Bill on a holiday abroad. There were two Joe Scarborough prints on the wall; one of Hillsborough Corner in the days of the trams – the first lot – and a picture of Sheffield town centre. They had been given to her and Bill by their sons, both of whom had been fire officers at some point in their lives.

*

"We sat together on the sofa with Brian across from us. We drank a cup of tea and smiled a lot. It felt quite exciting; as if I was in some sort of adventure. But it was as if I were a spectator looking at the scenario from a distance. After a time, Brian left so we could be alone. He felt she could say things more freely if he wasn't there.

"I suppose you'd like to know things, she said? 'You bet!' I thought.

"And what did I discover first? That I had been conceived in Nottingham. Would you believe that?"

*

Bill had come to Nottingham to do his training before being posted abroad and had palled-up with another soldier. They were in a cinema queue and the chap behind them had got talking to them. It turned out his family had a lodging house in Bulwell and if Bill's wife wanted to come to Nottingham to stay before he was posted, then she could stay there. So Kathleen came to Nottingham by train or bus. The family had two daughters a similar age to Kathleen and they became friendly. Eventually, Bill was posted

51

to the Middle East but Kathleen continued to come to Nottingham and stay with the sisters. They liked to go dancing and so Kathleen went, too. She wasn't much of a ballroom dancer preferring instead rhythmic dancing. At school, her teacher used to say: 'Look every one; look at how Kathleen James is doing this. That's how it should be done!' but she had never been taught to ballroom dance. So she sat out the dances and continued to do so when a young Polish airman came to sit with her. He asked her to dance but when she said she couldn't, he continued to sit with her and talk.

*

"Kathleen talked to me about her time in Nottingham and so I learned the most intimate details of her life which by some strange quirk of fate happened to contain the circumstances of the beginning of my life.

"My father had been a Polish airman she told me.

" 'Was it a love affair?' I asked her.

" 'I suppose it must have been', she said. 'I ended up having a baby.' She paused and said, 'He was a pilot.'

" 'Did he know about me?'

" 'No. He had gone home before I knew. Then Bill came home and the hardest thing I had to do was to tell him I was having a baby. I said, 'I'm pregnant.''

" 'What did he say?'

" 'He said, "Don't expect me to bring up another man's child."

" 'And his father, a staunch Catholic, told him to make sure he didn't. He stuck by her, though. He went with her to Leicester to stay with her mother's sister for her confinement."

*

There was so much more to my conversation with Kathleen but insufficient time to speak about it all to the Patong audience.

I asked Kathleen, 'What did your mother say when you told her?'

'What could she say? It was done. What she advised me was that I should go to Leicester to stay with Auntie Jesse. No one would know although my sisters knew. We went and she told me she wasn't going to keep me and I needed to find work. I found a job with the Post Office in Leicester. Not posting letters, though.'

'In the sorting office, perhaps?' My father had worked in the sorting office in Sheffield before the war.

'I remember I did a lot of stamping.' She hit one hand into another in imitation of a stamping machine. I could see by her far away gaze that she was drawing a long way back into her memory. 'Then I went into a nursing home, a maternity home to have you. Bill came, too. He was at the hospital when I had you.' A Catholic, he hadn't wanted to bring up another man's baby, but he was there for his wife in her time of need.

'I called you Averill.'

'Yes, I know.'

'Do you? It was my favourite name. A

lovely name don't you think?'

'Yes. You also called me Maureen.'

'Maureen? No, I don't think so.'

'It says Maureen Averill on my birth certificate.'

'Just Averill, I thought. I don't remember where Maureen came from. No just Averill.'

I let it go. Averill is fine. Her brow furrowed trying to remember.

'I knitted a legging suit in yellow. I didn't know if you'd be a girl or a boy so chose lemon.'

'Was this the suit, do you think?' I asked, showing her the photo of me in my mother's arms at five weeks; the one with the empty legging hanging down.

'It could have been,' she said.

'I'm sorry it's not in colour. It's hard to tell.'

'Yes. Make sure it's in colour next time,' she smiled. 'Bill held you. You were breast fed, you know,'

'Oh, really. Good.' It's always best to get a good start in life.

'When it was time to go back, Bill took you home.'

'To Sheffield?'

'Yes. Although I can't remember how we got there. And he handed you over to the adoption agency. To save me, I think. I gave you to him and he gave you to the woman there.'

I was so eager for these details that I gulped them down and savoured each one but at the time I wasn't considering what it was costing Kathleen to recall them and speak of them for the first time in sixty years.

*

"They returned to Sheffield and Bill handed me to the woman at the adoption agency so Kathleen wouldn't have to and saved her some of the pain. They got on with their lives, then and in eleven months they had a baby of their own. A son, John. Three years later they had another son, planned so there were three years between them. They called him Paul."

*

Kathleen told me more about Paul and then went on to share some very personal things about herself that I wasn't prepared to share with my Patong audience. Paul lives across the road with his two children who were aged sixteen and twenty-one. Their mother left home a while ago and Paul has brought them up. He gave up his full time work as a fireman and works for a bakery as the hours suit him better with the children. He had gone to grammar school, coincidently the same one as Brian. When they were younger, he was the clever one but John was the one who had gained a degree by working through the Open University. John has one son. "The hedge cutter," we'd decided.

I had brought a photograph album of myself from babyhood to adulthood, intending to show Kathleen. She looked at the first page or two briefly, then put the book behind a cushion and there it remained until Brian came to collect me.

'I'm a Jehovah's Witness,' she told me, with a somewhat challenging look. 'What do you think of that?' All my prejudices about peddling religion on

55

the doorstep rose up. Heavens, what do I think of that? Somewhat taken aback I merely asked her, 'What made you become a Jehovah's Witness?'

'I always let people into the house when they call and two ladies came to talk to me about it. I liked what they had to say so they came again and I said I would go with them to their meetings. I like it there and I believe what it says in the Bible but I don't think you have to go anywhere to pray. I think you can pray anywhere.'

'Yes, so do I.'

'What are you? Do you believe?'

'Well,' tricky this one, I thought, and deep, too, for a first meeting, 'if I was to be asked what my religion was if I went into hospital, I'd tell them I was Church of England. I do believe, and we go to a C of E church at Christmas: the late service on Christmas Eve. I take the Eucharist, even though I've never been confirmed.'

I told her of the belief held by a friend of mine that God wouldn't mind whether I'd been confirmed or not. If I wanted to reaffirm my faith God would be pleased and the vicar who married Nick last September, in the same village as the one where we are now living, led the service at Christmas and positively encouraged us all to come and take communion, if we wished to. If people didn't they could just come forward for a blessing instead. That's my kind of approach. She agreed that offering a little prayer whenever you felt the need was a good thing.

'I don't get down on my knees,' she said. 'I can just sit here.' Bill hadn't minded that she had joined the Jehovah's Witnesses but said it wasn't for him. He'd let Kathleen get on with it and didn't mind when she went off to her meetings.

The furthest she had got onto her knees that evening was to try to light the gas fire once or twice. I had tried and failed but Brian managed it when he came back. 'You need a special knack,' she said. It was always the same with my mother's gas fire. You needed a strong wrist to push and turn the switch. She felt I was cold because my hands remained cold all the time. She knew this as she took hold of them from time to time as we talked. I looked down. They were my hands. Her hands and my hands were the same.

'I'm fine,' I said. And I was. It was nervousness that kept them cold. The rest of me was warm and the redness of my cheeks was an indication of this.

'I always have red cheeks,' she offered. 'If I'm nervous, my cheeks glow red. These aren't my teeth, you know,' she said tapping her top set.

'These aren't mine, either,' I said tapping mine in the same way. I'd had mine taken out when my dentist advised it when I was twenty as he knew he couldn't go on filling them anymore. They were crossed at the front and had more fillings than a range of M&S sandwiches. It was the thing to do in 1966. Other dentists since have told me it was wrong to have them removed as there were other ways to save them. However, had he left it until I was twenty-one, I would, into the bargain, have had to pay for the indignity of losing them.

We laughed at this shared misfortune. I'd always thought my poor teeth would have been caused by a lack of milk during the war years, but I'd been breast fed for the first five weeks of my life. Hereditary, then. Nick has poor teeth. I'm passing it on; a lineage of 'sweet tooth.'

'It was the sweeties,' she said by way of explanation. 'I'd be given a penny on the way to school each day and spend it on sweeties. I was never without a sweetie.'

'I lost mine at twenty,' I told her.

'Seventeen, mine,' she said.

I'd rather have inherited Kathleen's eyes than her teeth, if there'd been the choice.

I told Kathleen that I had sent for her marriage certificate while I was trying to trace her, and because I had found out there were five people living at Middlewood, wasn't surprised to find the name of one of them on her marriage certificate as witness.

Sidney Taylor. He turned out to be her brother in law, had been Bill's best man, and was still alive. Elsie James had indeed been her mother and the other women at the address were her sisters. Audrey had married Sidney and had been in a nursing home when she had had her first conversation with social worker, Sue, but unfortunately had recently died. She had been helping Sidney find a new place to live and had helped him move into a flat. Gladys Beal was her eldest sister but she had died in her twenties. She talked about her sisters for a while. They were late additions to her parents' lives. Gladys had been born when her mother was thirty-eight and she and her sister had quickly followed. They had been good pals and seldom fallen out. She seemed to have had a happy childhood but I'm uncertain why she hadn't chosen to confide in her middle sister when she found she was pregnant, even though they were living in the same house.

*

"Kathleen told me she had two older sisters

" 'I'd have liked sisters,' I said.

" 'Couldn't your mother have children?' she asked. 'Perhaps they didn't want them.'

Mmm. A little confusion here.

" 'Erm....I wouldn't be sitting here with you, if my mother could have had children, would I?'

"A perplexed look. 'Oh, no, I suppose not.

"I tried to tell her a little about my search for her but the details were too confusing. I had the impression she thought that sometimes, when she had been speaking on the phone to Sue, that Sue was me. So I told her: 'I've spent some time sitting outside your house, you know, when I knew where you lived.'

"Surprising me and making us both hoot with laughing, she said, 'Yes, I know. I've thought once or twice about bringing you out a cup of tea.'

" 'I came to look for you once, you know.'

"No I didn't know. 'When was that?'

" 'Darklands Road wasn't it?'

" 'Yes.' How had she known? Mothers giving up their children weren't supposed to know information about the adoptive parents, any more than they were supposed to know about them.

" 'A relative of Bill's was buried in the cemetery at the end of your road and we'd come to visit the grave. There were three little girls playing in the cemetery and I asked them if they knew where Margaret Kay lived.' She'd known my name, even

59

then! 'You'd be about four. And one of them said she did and started to run off saying, it's just there, and shall I get her mother for you? I said, no, no, it's all right. But I went and stood outside your house just to see if you'd come out.'

"'Did I?'
"'Yes. After a while.'
"'And then you went away?'
"'Yes.'

*

Such a poignant moment. Kathleen would have had both her sons by the time I was four but it was an indication that heartbreak and longing and a sense of loss are enduring emotions. Feeling again the sadness, I paused.

The silence of the audience brought a tension to the room.

I picked up my story.

*

"Bill and Kathleen got on with their lives, as so many had to at the end of the war. I think they were both very brave. For myself, I feel a sense of completeness at having found an identity. There is still a lot to learn and we will meet again and, hopefully, Kathleen will be able to remember some of what I want to know. Of the three letters beside my adoption entry, 'M' was for married and Kathleen has now been married for almost 64 years. 'B' was for broken home and perhaps neither of us will be able to interpret that, as her pregnancy didn't break her marriage. Her father's death could have indicated a broken home but this is an odd explanation. And the

60

'S' for services doesn't, as far as I know, refer to Kathleen herself.

"I haven't undertaken this journey lightly, out of idle curiosity, but for a fundamental understanding of who I am and I feel that at this point in my life, I'm well on my way to finding out.

"And the fib in the passport? Well, it's too late to change that, isn't it?"

*

I laid down the final page of my notes and looked up.

Chapter 2

What happens now?

The applause was surprising and very gratifying. I started to leave the podium but Godfrey asked if there were any questions and to my amazement, there were several. The most heart wrenching was from an American gentleman at the back of the room. He stood up:

"I have two boys who my wife and I have adopted. We said we would help them meet their birth mothers if they wanted to. So far they haven't expressed that need but do you think they would want that later?"

I thought about this for a moment and told him:

"My adoptive parents loved me very much and I would never have done anything to hurt them. It took the death of both of them for me to even consider this search. It wasn't until I was well into adulthood before I felt a need to look. The need to make the search has come, as I am older. I shall be sixty later this year. Perhaps it could be the same with your children but if your children love you in the same way it will be all right."

He smiled, said thank you and sat down. Later in the evening Godfrey asked the members and any assembled guests to come forward and contribute to the 'Happy Box'. People were asked to come forward, put money into the box and say: 'I'm happy because…' After several people had done this, their light hearted contributions eliciting laughter, the

American came forward and putting his folded Thai bharts into Godfrey's box said: 'I'm happy because I have been able to be here this evening to hear this lady speak which has meant so much to me as it has deepened my understanding.'

I felt a little tear swim into the corner of my eye and rapidly blinked it away. I was very touched by his gratitude. I shook his hand and before we left, as the Belgian President was thanking me profusely, the Norwegian lady grasped me to her and hugged me. 'I couldn't follow every word you said but it was so beautiful. You have been so brave to come here to tell us.' Wow! I had no idea the effect of my story would have on this audience. I had been anxious they might not be interested or that I had made the story too 'English' but instead they were a really appreciative audience. My friends were amazed that I had told the story in the way I had. It was the same story they heard by the pool the previous evening but I knew there would be a need to tell it in a different way from that said in an intimate chat among friends.

We went out from the hotel into the still warm Thailand evening to see Patong. The street noises were loud and exciting and people pressed alongside us as we crossed the road and walked up the Bangla road. It was the centre of entertainment on the island with all manner of bars selling beer, nightclubs and go-go bars. The music emanating from these was vibrant and infectious. Linking elbows, we chasséed up the road in a line of six. Hustlers tried to entice us into the review bars to see the shows but the most persuasive were the katoi or 'ladyboys'.

How glamorous they were in glittering evening dresses slit to the thigh and low décolleté, wearing feather fascinators with feminine aplomb. They attracted more attention than anyone as they posed to the click of digital cameras of European tourists. We heard people say, 'They're not! They can't be!' but if you looked hard enough at Adam's apples or listened to responses to requests for photographs the depth of the voices gave the game away for many, although not all. We weren't tempted into the cabarets, though. Instead, we stopped at a bar and ordered cold beers to quench our thirsts. As we nursed our drinks, we chilled out and people-watched.

Pat, Maxine and I teased the men that if we ladies weren't there they would be ripe for the picking of the Thai girls who postured on high bar stools smiling mechanically showing straight white teeth but empty eyes. Giggling was the common language and many of the unaccompanied 'forangs', foreigners, communicated their needs through overt caresses and sly smiles. Thailand seems to be the place for older European men to come in search of young girls to marry, to employ for sex or to entertain for massages and companionship, or for all of these. Ill-matched, the girls pout and pose whilst the men stroke and caress enticing with promises of regular meals and a more secure life-style. We were expert people watchers by the time we walked back into the underground car park at the Aloha Villa Hotel.

A few days later Brian and I flew off to Perth for a week's holiday staying with other friends in the suburb of Duncraig and leaving behind our four friends in Phuket. We had another week away in New

Zealand then flew back to Phuket. Godfrey picked us up at the airport and we chatted about our experiences in the southern hemisphere as we drove back to his house. Sipping chilled sauvignon blanc, sitting around the pool once more, we told the other three friends about what we had been doing and the sights we had seen. They exchanged with us stories about their experiences and told us how much they had enjoyed their continuing holiday, although they had missed us while we had been away. The Rotary Club met each week so Godfrey had attended again. He had listened to another member tell them about her recent holiday. Interesting though that talk may have been, he told us, the speaker didn't hold her audience.

'They were still talking about your talk. The best some had heard since they joined the Club, they were saying.' How gratifying was that? And mega-brownie points for Godfrey into the bargain.

One thing people who set about tracing their natural parents need to be is prepared for any eventuality. Stuart, the Nottingham social worker, had been quite clear about that. What if you find you have been the product of a rape for instance, he'd asked? Oh, it would be all right, I said. And of course I still think it would be but I had always harboured the romantic ideal that I had been born as a product of a loving union. A service man in wartime far from home seeks the comfort of a lovely girl and all that. Well the truth didn't look as if it were too far away from that. There'd be some lust in there for good measure, I suppose, but although I think I have mentally prepared myself for what I might learn, I don't think I have given a second thought to any consequences of my search either for myself or more particularly for Kathleen.

'What are you going to do next?' asked Godfrey.

'About what?'

'Well, you've made that first contact, had the first meeting. Will there be other meetings?'

Just at that point I couldn't give them an answer. I would have to think carefully about what I did next.

Part 2

Family Histories

Chapter 3

Horns of a dilemma

<u>*1st March 2006 – diary entry*</u>

I have been giving some thought to Godfrey's question. Why have I taken all this effort to discover Kathleen? Why have I contacted her? My own childhood has been very happy. I've had a good upbringing by parents who loved me. I've missed out on nothing regarding parental nurturing: their love for me or their pride in what I have become has always been evident.

I think it's that I wanted Kathleen to know about my happy upbringing and to realise that she need not feel guilty about having me adopted. Now I've met her I have to decide how much further I want the relationship to go.

When Brian and I had first gone into Kathleen's living room, standing on a teak shelving unit, was the Christmas card, which I had sent in the hope of tempting her to make contact. I looked at my signature. Margaret. No 'love', or 'from'. Just my name. She truly hadn't known who Margaret was. Curiosity had led her to make the phone call on the 2nd of January, but now the yellow 'post it' was missing. When we were preparing to leave, Kathleen and I wondered aloud whether we should meet again. Not prepared to make a definite date, I suggested that after we came back from our holiday, she telephoned me again and we would arrange a further meeting. She said she would and I asked her if she still had the

69

'post it' with the phone number on it. Not sure. So I wrote the number on the card and added that we would be home from holiday on the 10th February.

We left the house after hugging once more by the back door. We drove off to Ann and David's for our belated meal and during the short journey I told Brian the more intimate details I had learned about my life. My father **was** Polish, I told him excitedly, not only an airman but also a pilot. He didn't know about me. He'd gone home. She said it had been a love affair as she had had a child. She's got my hands, my hair, my jaw. I'm like her. But her eyes are blue. And she's not very tall. He could see all these things for himself, of course.

We arrived at Ann and David's and they overwhelmed me with hugs. They wanted to know all about the meeting and so the meal was delayed even further. They had put champagne on ice while Brian had been to fetch me and they cracked it then and offered a toast to finding Kathleen.

The series of coincidences that connected Kathleen and Ann's lives were uncanny. As a girl Ann had lived in Handsworth, in Sheffield, with her parents in a house, which was opposite a close where six prefabs had been erected. She remembered them going up. Kathleen and Bill had been offered one of these prefabs after the war, sometime after 1946. It was their first home together as they had been living with her mother after their return from Leicester. Kathleen's older son, John, could have been a playmate of Ann's younger brother, Charles.

Ann has a sister called Margaret. Until her death in late 2005 her mother-in-law had been living

70

in Handsworth. Handsworth is a large district but the old lady's house had been further down Kathleen's road. Kathleen hadn't remembered the lady but had seen the 'for sale' sign go up recently when walking down to visit her friend.

Other coincidences concerned Brian as his family had lived quite close to the house in Middlewood. He knew the church in Hillsborough where Kathleen and Bill were married. The details in the Joe Scarborough print of Hillsborough Corner on Kathleen's wall were as familiar to him as the back of his hand. Paul, Kathleen's younger son, had attended the same grammar school as Brian, although Brian would have left long before Paul had gone there.

There are many districts and suburbs, in Sheffield, and numerous secondary schools; we have a large circle of friends, which also includes relatives whom we see for meals on a regular basis but a curiously tight circle joined together all the lives of the people involved in this evening. While food cooled we talked long into the night at Anne and David's. It was fascinating to all of us so we were late home.

As we drove home other curious snippets of conversation with Kathleen came back to me. She hadn't always lived in Middlewood. She had been brought up in Crookes, in Springfield Road and gone to school there. I told her I had gone to Lydgate Lane County Primary School in Crosspool and she looked briefly surprised. The house she had stood outside of all those years ago when I was four was in Crosspool and the school had been five minutes' walk away. She had told me her cousin, Helen Dawson, had gone to the same school.

'I remember Helen Dawson,' I exclaimed, 'we were in the same year.'

'Yes, you would be,' she said.

'Do you mean your cousin, or was her mother your cousin?'

'No. Her mother was my Auntie Phyllis. Helen was my cousin.'

I don't suppose it was so surprising to be a generation apart from a cousin. I am from my closest cousin; Margery is an age where she could be my mother. It was only when we were driving home that I remembered that in my red photograph album, which we had thought to rescue from behind the cushion, contained a photograph of the very same Helen Dawson. If only there had been an appropriate moment I could have shown it to Kathleen.

*

The year I first went to school, 1951, had been a bulge year. Nineteen forty-five and the year I was born, 1946, were referred to as the bulge years because of the high numbers of children born after the war. Fascinating to statisticians, these children still arouse demographic interest as we will all be sixty around the same time, and as far as the women are concerned, will be drawing our state pensions together.

My year group throughout school, from age 11 to 16 was large. There were fifty-two children in my class at junior school. We were streamed and mine was the A group. There were a similar number in the B class and about twenty-five in each of two other groups: C and D. When I passed the 11+ and went to grammar school in 1957, the school, based on a four-house system of Darling, Cavell, Marvell and Nightingale, all famously heroic women, had to create another house: Fry, to accommodate a maximum group size of thirty. Helen Dawson was in the B stream in junior school, if I remember rightly and the reason I have her photograph is because we were both in the end of year school leavers' play. Heaven knows what it was called but Ian Hague was the king and we were all his courtiers. Helen and I, and other girls, arranged around the king on either side of his throne wore long courtly dresses. And the boys wore knee breeches and lace ruffs. For some reason, as I haven't done this with other group photos, many years ago when I was first sticking photos in my album, I had written down the names of every child I could remember on the page beneath the picture. It was this that enabled me to identify, Kathleen's cousin.

*

I loved junior school and went willingly every day. I played goal defence in the netball team against other schools when I was in my last year and was asked one time to collect the visiting team and their teacher as they came across the boy's yard rom the car park. Overcome with shyness, I could only gesture with my arm for them to follow me through the small green gate into the girl's yard. Miss Clements was the teacher who made the greatest impression on me. Everyone has a teacher to remember and she is mine. She was the class teacher for J3 and then into J4. Her main task was to get all fifty-two of us through the 11+ exams. And so she did. She never had problems with discipline and heaped praise when it was justly deserved and administered the cane sparingly for serious crimes such as the occasional fights in the playground between boys and girls alike. We were seated according to ability. Fifty-two desks and chairs, however small, took up quite a lot of room, especially as we had to make room for a nature table as well, and they were arranged in five rows across the classroom. Back right was top of the class and, in front of her – it was usually Carole Barker who went on to pass for the Girls High School – was number twenty, in front of whom sat number twenty-one and so on snaking through to number fifty-two on the front row, nearest Miss Clements.

Spelling Bees were the best but conducted in the cramped spaces at two sides of the room. Two teams were picked and Miss Clements asked a person in turn from each team to spell the words we had been asked to learn. If you got it wrong, you sat down, until there was a winner and thus a winning team. I was mostly on the winning team and often one of the last to sit down. We got class points for doing well. Miss Clements was fond of team games and we responded well to them as a rule.

A number of the class would be asked to come to stand at the front and each would be given a word from a proverb or saying. We would have to stand in a line in order of our word and another team would ask questions the reply to which must contain the word. Cunning pupils would give great long answers to their questions in order to conceal their word but this made it boring as no one was able to guess the proverb. I stood in line for 'Great oaks from little acorns grow.'

'Where did you go for your holidays?' I was asked.

Quick as a flash with no thought for concealment, I blurted, 'Great Yarmouth!' I hadn't been to Great Yarmouth, as it happened, but it was a puzzling answer to the boy who asked the question and Miss Clements said it was a good answer. I went home on air.

Miss Clements taught me to make a dirndl skirt. Strange word dirndl. Girls and boys in my class were taught separately for some subjects, which were considered appropriate to each sex. Boys learned to make things in wood and to weave baskets. The girls had to choose from pieces of material the school provided and we were taught to thread our needles and sow a straight seam. When the fabric was joined, we sewed a top seam to contain the elastic and then hemmed the bottom at the desired length. Andrea Taylor had to have loads chopped off the bottom of hers, but in her favour, small in stature or not, she could turn somersaults and cartwheels without touching the ground. Over she would go tumbling round the school hall in gym lessons. My skirt was barely long enough and had only a small hem. But I could stand on my head for ages, if asked – although I was too scared to do handstands.

I couldn't sing either. We were asked one time in assembly to come out if we wanted to join the choir. My friend went up so I went up, too. It was fine whilst we all sang something together. But then we were asked to sing in pairs or threes. I sang with my friend. They asked me to sit down again. Kathleen can't sing either but neither could either of my parents. I recently learned that people who can't sing in tune are people who don't listen carefully enough to the sounds of notes. That'll be me then. I can clear a room in seconds when I start.

Kathleen loved school, too, and had a certificate at age fifteen to say how well she had done and something about her character that gave her a sense of pride. She had kept it for years then recently had kept it in her bus pass. It had disappeared, though. But I didn't know about that until the second time we met.

*

When nothing had happened for a time after our return from our long holiday, I wondered what I could do. Should I just ring Kathleen and risk someone being there or should I just wait and see. It was a genuine dilemma but I took the easy way out. I did nothing. The lack of contact also made me think seriously about what I wanted from any continuing contact. I had seen my natural mother, noted similarities in our faces and hands and learned about the circumstances of my birth. Wasn't this enough? But there were other questions, particularly about my natural father and about her life both before and after I was born. I should continue then. But not yet.

20th March 2006 – Diary entry

Going to France for a week. What, off again?
It's all right for some this retired life. And so it is.
We've had this house for six years now as a consequence of Mum's death in 1999 and her legacy

to us. She said to me many times after my dad died that all she had was mine and Brian's, meaning particularly her bungalow. We said thank you and were really grateful but the fact was we didn't really need the money. Instead, what we would like to do was to buy a house in France with the proceeds. She was delighted that we had chosen to do that. In the 1960s when the fashion was for continental holidays, my dad had taken my mum to Paris so she could see the places he saw at the end of the war. She liked Paris, but she didn't like the French because they wouldn't import our lamb. She never bought a French golden delicious apple. She would have preferred to take poison. So we started a search in the October of 1999. And found what we were looking for in April 2000. We bought an empty, semi-detached farm cottage with no sanitation, except for a defunct 'thunder box' in the field behind the barn, and only electricity and running water connected. The windows and doors needed replacing and so did the floor downstairs. The wall, which divided the two rooms downstairs needed taking out and the upstairs, so far only a grenier, *has given us two bedrooms. We needed a kitchen and a bathroom. What attracted us to the house, however, was its potential and the fact that there was half an acre of wild flower meadow with a gentle pastoral view of neighbouring fields and acres of trees. The property had a huge barn attached to which were three, now defunct piggeries, a henhouse and a pigeonnier set in an open hangar, which also contained a splendid traditional bread oven.*

We went again in the summer, lived in our caravan in the barn, and took off all the ivy from every external wall. We were as brown as berries by the end of the summer but dirty as urchins at the end of each day with dust in our hair and eyes. The water from the shower cubical outlet pipe under the caravan ran dark brown each evening.

Now, all these jobs both inside and outside the house have been done and more. I wonder if my mother looks down on us and is happy we have put her legacy to such good use. We remember her every time we take items of her cutlery from the kitchen drawers or look at one of her ornaments on a shelf. Her bedding and towels are in all the bedrooms. I hope she know as this is what makes the French house so special to us.

Booking an overnight crossing with Brittany Ferries on the Portsmouth to St. Malo run off we went on a wet March evening. We like the overnight crossing as the sailing leaves at 8.30pm and the restaurant is excellent. We fill our plates at the buffet and eat it as the boat gently cruises down the Solent. We watch out for the boat Robert sailed on, when he was in the Navy, HMS Illustrious, to see whether it's in harbour; we watch the lights of Southsea twinkling bright dots in the distance reflected in silver and red lines on the dark waves. Then comes the main course from a choice of delightful French cuisine washed down, usually, with a bottle of chilled Sancerre served from an ice bucket by the table. This is followed by a sweet from the buffet where there is always too much choice despite the fact we are already full from the two earlier courses. Replete, we wander around the *shops, no longer 'duty free' but, none the less, cheaper than at home and then fall into bed in our cabin to be gently rocked to sleep for seven hours until awakened by gentle music by Delibes or Bizet and an announcement that we will be arriving in St. Malo in forty five minutes. Time to get in the shower and present ourselves again in the restaurant for the continental breakfast given free to French property owners. The drive to the house takes us between four and five hours usually but on this particular occasion we took longer. Too preoccupied, perhaps.*

Chapter 4

The second visit

I still had to solve my dilemma. I'd been able to defer my decision whilst in France but I needed to face it now. I'd ring Kathleen, not today but soon. But I didn't ring straight away. One Friday evening, I did manage to pluck up the courage and phone but there was no response. I didn't ring again. Instead, I took the easy way out. I wrote a short note and posted it. Once again I put my letter into a card, a blank write your own message sort and posted it off on the 17th March. I told her we had met before in January and arranged to phone again after our return from holiday. Afraid to place her in an awkward situation, I asked please would she ring the number on the letter. I hoped that was enough for her to remember who I was.

Arriving home from shopping on the 20th March there was a message on the answering machine from Kathleen. She'd had the courage to phone, therefore so must I. I practiced what to say when I phoned her back that evening. But there was no need to have been worried. Once again we chatted like old friends. I said we would like to come up to Sheffield to see her for a cup of tea. When would be convenient? We agreed that Thursday afternoon would suit us both.

'I bet you'd like to come tomorrow,' she said.

In fact we were free on Tuesday but Thursday was better for Kathleen. She spoke of her eldest son, John.

'He asked me recently if he had a sister. What made him do that?'

I hadn't a clue, but knowing how vague she could be and what an unsettling thing it was meeting me after all these years, it could be possible that she had let something slip to John earlier.

'I think there is a hand greater than ours that could be playing a part in this, it's just so amazing.'

She could be right.

'I've been looking at old photos today. Clearing a whole case of them out.'

'Have you? What, all of them?'

No, not all.

Kathleen and I agreed on 2.30pm.

*

I remembered looking at old photographs of my parents after my mum died. There were loads of them. Sepia memories of my mum's and dad's lives. Later black and white ones and just a few coloured ones from the more recent years. This is where we turned up pictures of the Brough Superior and the cloche hat. Brian and I had got them from my mum's loft before her funeral and in the evening afterwards we had sat with Brian's mother and my cousin, Margery, and her husband, Fred, and reminisced on my parents' lives, fascinated by what we saw. One day we will make a montage for our study wall of the most interesting and evocative. We were pleased there were so many as they gave us pleasure to reminisce together with my cousins Margery and Fred who remembered those early years, Margery in

81

particular remembering the very early years from her childhood. Aunt Dot was a favourite aunt.

*

It was only when we were driving the last ten minutes of the journey that I began to feel butterflies in my stomach. We had the made same arrangement as before: I would ring when we were there to check all was well for her. At the bottom of the road, I phoned her.

'We're here, at the bottom of the road. Is it all right?'

'You'd better ask them at the bottom of the road,' she said.

Laughter from both of us. 'We'll be with you in a minute.'

A neighbour was washing his car on what appeared to be the access to their drive but we didn't look up when we approached on foot, having parked once more outside the little gate to the path. Brian and I walked up the path and I rang the bell. We looked at the garden, in need of some care at the moment but daffodil bulbs were about to come into flower. There were discarded plant pots under the hedge bottom, evidence of last summer's annuals. The lawn needed a trim. A job for the hedge cutter no doubt. Bill's input was being missed. I turned to the door as Kathleen opened it.

She had dressed in a belted lilac floral-print dress. Her grey hair was ruffled. I stared into her face afresh, as though we hadn't recently met, smiling in recognition. She smiled a greeting and asked us in. Gone from the back of the door were the crutches.

She walked more confidently than at our first meeting. We kissed and hugged. She kissed Brian, warmly. We went into the living room once more. There was a repeat of the gas fire ritual as it failed to light. Brian bent to put it on for her and it lit first time. She went into the kitchen to put on the kettle and returned in a short while. We looked again at the Joe Scarborough prints and marvelled at his portrayal of Hillsborough Corner, so familiar to Brian. But could only speculate at the portrayal of Sheffield city centre. We guessed at Commercial Street and the place where Victoria Station used to be.

'That's the City Centre,' Kathleen volunteered but could shed no light on where exactly it was.

'They bought those while they were in the fire service but Paul had less money.'

'They're both very good, though. This one is a representation, that's all. Less accurate.'

'Sit down. Are you warm enough?'

We were. Very warm in fact. The gas fire was doing its job. We sat down, Brian in an armchair, me on the sofa where I had sat before. Outside, the neighbour continued to wash his car.

'He wouldn't be doing that if Bill was here, you know. He used to go out to him and tell him that was the access to our drive. But the poor man doesn't have anywhere else to wash his car except out on the road so I live and let live and he just gets on with it.'

Kathleen disappeared once more into the kitchen. There was a rattling of cups. I stood up and looked at some photographs placed without frames on the unit. These must be what were left from the turn out. She came in to find me looking at them. One was of her in her wedding dress, a crinoline with ruffles of lace all around the skirt.

'I had that made,' she said. 'I had to have it dry cleaned later to preserve it.'

'It's very pretty.' More to the point, it was she who was very pretty. A good-looking woman. I looked more closely at it trying to see any family likeness. There was something about the set of the eyes. I took out the passport photo I had included in the package to Sue, the social worker in Sheffield and we looked together at the two photos.

'Mmm. Good looks in common,' one of us said.

There was another wedding photograph of Kathleen and Bill standing with two bridesmaids in blue (the photo has been coloured by hand at a later date) one of whom was Kathleen's sister Audrey, who had recently died. They were flanked by two men: the best man and Sidney Taylor, Audrey's husband. Here was a photo of one of the witnesses on the marriage certificate. I scrutinised this closely.

'That one is my sister,' said Kathleen. 'She's died now. My other sister died at twenty-six, you know. Her husband was twenty-nine. Neither of them long livers.'

'Yes, I know.'

'Did I tell you before?'

'Yes. I remember these things. Who gave you away? Your marriage certificate said that your father had died.'

'My uncle gave me away. He had to step in at the last minute because my father had died earlier that year.' How sad not to survive to give all your daughters away. 'This other photo is of my Auntie Phyllis getting married to Uncle Percy.'

We looked at a black and white photo of a woman who was probably a similar age to Kathleen. 'My cousin is Helen. This isn't Helen. This is her mother.'

'Helen Dawson?'

'Yes, do you know her?'

'I must have known her once because we went to school at Lydgate Lane together. I have a photo of her with me. I had it when we came before but for the life of me I can't understand why I didn't show it to you then. Too much to talk about then, I should think.' I reached for the red photograph album and produced the school photo of the end of year play.

'Here's Helen,' I pointed out. I placed the photo of her under the one of her mother getting married and they had very similar faces, a real family resemblance. 'And that's me, on the other side.' Kathleen looked hard at it.

'How did we meet?' she asked sitting heavily into the vacant armchair.

'We came here before, Brian and I, last January, after I sent you a Christmas card with my phone number on it.'

But what she really wanted to know was how we had managed to get in touch with her. I tried once more to explain. Brian helped out with the explanation from time to time and as we spoke we raised our voices somewhat as she had appeared a little deaf, especially when Brian spoke to her.

'When I was in my thirties my parents felt they had to tell me some information they had about me.

My dad had already had a couple heart attacks and I guess he wanted me to know what they knew before it was too late. He told me your name and where he thought you lived. And he said that you had called me Averill. I wrote it down,' I told her, pulling from my handbag the very same address book, tattered now, in which I had written things down all those years ago. Kathleen looked at the page of writing with amazement. I started to speak again.

'No, no,' she said, moving to the sofa, 'not so loud. You come and sit here,' she said to Brian, patting the seat beside her, 'so you don't have to shout. These walls are so thin. I'd hate my neighbour to hear any of this. I used to sit talking with my friend when we had the settee next to the wall. I moved it to here...' under the window...'because I thought we might be overheard.' We resettled ourselves with Kathleen between us on the sofa and I continued, this time lowering my voice.

'There was an address he gave me.' I told her where it was. 'But when Brian and I went to look for it, the house had been pulled down.'

'We never lived there, that's why. But perhaps Bill's mother and father lived there for a bit before the war. I can't remember.'

'I applied for my birth certificate after my dad died and it had your name on it, Kathleen Mary Newcombe, where you were living in Leicester, where I was born. But under father's name it didn't say anything. Just a line.'

She contemplated this for a while.

'They call me Kath, you know. Not Kathleen.' Are we to call her that? I asked her and she said yes, if we liked but then she changed her mind. 'No,' she said, 'you can call me Kathleen Mary, my full name.' Yes, miss. 'Someone wrote to me recently, calling me Kathleen, though.' That'd be me. But I didn't say anything. 'I went to Auntie Jessie's when I knew I was pregnant. My mother sent me.

'And your sisters knew nothing about it?'

'Oh yes, they did. It was getting impossible to hide. Bill was there when I had you and…''

'We think he's a remarkable man, your Bill.'

'Oh yes, he is. …And you very nearly didn't leave Leicester.'

'How was that?'

'Because Auntie Jessie had a son, John, and he took a shine to you.'

'Really?'

'He was about ten or perhaps as old as fourteen at the time and I came back to the house with you and he fell in love with you. He was an only child and had never had anything to do with babies. He thought you were remarkable. Auntie Jessie saw how he was with you and thought for a while she might keep you.'

I was astounded. I would have had a very different life. Strange how so much could have turned on these whims and fancies.

Kathleen went on, 'But my uncle wasn't sure that it was right. So you came back to Sheffield.' Good job, too. 'Yes he is a good man, my man. I see him every day. I just walk up when I want. We can't do much. We spend a lot of the time just holding hands.' She smiled fondly.

'Do you think you would like to go and see him in the nursing home when you come again?'

When we come again? This assumes she would like there to be another time, then? I looked over her head to Brian and although he was non-committal, I could tell he was thinking about this.

I continued with my explanation in answer to her original question about how we had found her.

'When I had my birth certificate I didn't do anything to find you then. But later when my mother had died...'

'Your mummy?'

'Yes, we applied to Nottingham Social Services for help in finding you. You can't just turn up on folk's doorstep saying, 'remember me?'

'Good job, too.'

'Yes. Well, a social worker from Nottingham helped us but a lady called Sue from the Family Services in Sheffield helped us more. She wrote to you to ask about someone trying to trace someone from Middlewood who had lived there in 1946.'

I looked expectantly at her but she had no recollection of the phone calls to Sue or anything about the conversations. I moved on. 'We met someone who could help us to find out where you lived.'

'How could they do that?'

I hesitated. 'On the Internet there are public records. It's not hard to find people.' I couldn't begin to explain the rigmarole of our search and expect her to understand it. 'So when Sue didn't hear from you for a while, I sent you a Christmas card.'

'Yes,' she mused. 'The Christmas card. I remember that.'

'You rang me.'

'So I did. I didn't know it was you, though. I'm your mother aren't I?'

Scrutinising me, she looked carefully at my face, my features and I smiled at her even though my beating heart had made my mouth dry.

'Yes,' I murmured feeling a stab of pleasure. 'Can I ask you a question?' She looked expectantly at me.

'What was my father's name?'

'Sigmund.'

Sigmund. Crikey. I liked the sound of that. Is that a Polish name? It must be.

You're not getting to know his last name. I'm not having you tracing him. Anyway... he'll be dead by now.'

I reassured her we wouldn't be doing that. Just think of the extent of the hornet's nest we'd be opening there. Unthinkable. Although we had managed to find *her* without too much fuss once Alan had been on the case...

'Do I look like him?' Kathleen looked hard at me for a moment.

'No.' This was a bit disappointing. I didn't get my height, hair, and eye colouring from her. 'But since you were here last I have tried to remember what he looked like. I lie in bed remembering. He was a pilot, you know'

'Yes.' She chuckled whether at secret memories or not we weren't to know. 'You could write a book about all this, you know. Or someone could.' I didn't say a word.

'Bill met these people in a cinema queue, two sisters in Nottingham. Where were they from?'

89

'Bulwell.'

'Have I told you this before?'

'Yes. But tell me again.' This was a slightly different version of the story. Perhaps there would be more. And there was.

'They were sisters, about my age. When Bill was sent overseas I continued to go and see them. I stayed at their house and we had bicycles. We used to ride up to…er…that place near Bulwell.'

'Hucknall,' I prompted.

'Yes, Hucknall. Where the dance hall was. I didn't dance, you know, except for rhythmic dancing at school and he used to come and sit by me. He sat by me a lot. Perhaps if I had been able to dance things would have been different because I would have had lots of different partners. But I continued to go to the dance hall because to tell you the truth, it had become quite exciting. I looked forward to seeing him there.' She smiled ruefully, perhaps expecting criticism but who were we to criticise?

'I took him home once or twice.'

'To Sheffield?'

'Oh, yes.'

'So this is how your sisters knew about everything?'

'Yes. They were a bit jealous, you know?' He must have been handsome, I thought, but didn't say this.

'He met my mother. They all liked him. You must think this is awful but things were different in the war.' I felt sure this was so. Moral values changed when people were faced daily with the prospect of death. 'Things were so exciting.'

*

I remember my dad telling me about his experience of the Sheffield blitz in 1942. The Germans bombed Fitzallen Square, a bomb falling directly on the Marple Hotel, a public house where a lot of people had gone for shelter when the raid had started, killing dozens. The bombers decimated The Moor, a main shopping thoroughfare, leaving great craters in the road. My dad was working the night shift in the Post Office sorting office in Fitzallen Square but the building had been spared. He came out after the all clear and picked his way up The Moor amongst the craters desperate to get home and my mother frantic for his safety. This wasn't the era of the mobile phone. Transport was brought to a halt and the phone lines were damaged so he couldn't get her on the phone at home.

*

'It wasn't *so* exciting all the time. People at home were in danger, too, from the bombs.'

'Oh, yes. But we weren't affected directly by that.'

I don't know what was happening in Nottingham at the time or whether the city was affected by bombing raids but the excitement seemed to be happening in Hucknall for Kathleen. She returned to the kitchen to make this seemingly elusive cup of tea. I took the opportunity to ask Brian what he thought about going to see Bill. He wasn't keen.

'What if he asks who you are? What will Kathleen tell him?'

'Mmm. Tricky. And too risky.' I smiled for a moment.

Well?'

'Sigmund, eh?'

'So now you know.' We smiled together. Sigmund.

We looked at other photographs in the room. There was a new one of Bill in his forties. A find from the sort-out, perhaps? And there was a photograph of both boys shaking hands as one of them was about to get married. This was taken some time ago. They both looked so like their father, just the younger one a little like his mother. Neither looked anything like me. Kathleen returned to the room to find us still looking.

'Bill's been a good father.' Her eyes misted briefly. 'My father was a good father, too. He never smacked us, my sisters and me, not that we really needed it, you know. We didn't go out clarted up in make-up. Although he'd tell us off if we needed it. But we didn't need it much.'

*

Neither had I. I recalled my dad's discipline when I was a child. He was a kind man and I loved to please him. He rarely told me off and he never got cross except for one time when I must have been so naughty, probably rude or cheeky, that he became angry and smacked me on the leg so hard that the imprint of his hand was left there. I howled at the hurt he had inflicted but my anguish was no less than his own when he saw the wheal his hand had left on my leg. He never smacked me again.

We turned to the subject of her children. She said she had no favourites but the young one seemed to her to be more sympathetic to her plight of being alone, even though she couldn't recall Paul's children's names or ages. Then she did remember Linsey who must be older than sixteen as she had left school and was working.

'Although she doesn't hold a job for long, that one.'

Paul had given up his job after his wife had gone, to look after the children. They should be grateful for that, she thought.

'I asked him not long ago whether his marriage had broken up because his wife had found somebody else. And he said that yes she had. It's a shame. And to leave the children, too. You can't help but feel sorry. They don't help him though. They don't help with the house and that. They let him do it all.'

'That's a shame,' I volunteered sympathetically.

'Yes, but he's to blame. He should make them do jobs around the house rather than running about after them. But I don't tell him that. I don't interfere.' A very honest assessment, no doubt. 'But he's a good boy. He took me shopping this morning to Aldi. Do you have an Aldi? He just comes round and calls up the stairs: are we going then? And I put my coat on and off we go. He asked me whether anyone else was coming to tea today as I had already asked someone, he thought. I told him I couldn't remember who I'd asked in the first place, so if anyone else turns up all of a sudden I shall just tell them you are my friends, just come to call.'

What if Paul just turned up out of the blue right now? Then what would we say? But I secretly wanted this to happen.

'That'll be fine. We are your friends.'

'John's very good, too. I go to tea every Sunday since Bill's been in the nursing home. They come and fetch me.'

'Where do they live?' asked Brian. She pondered, brow furrowing. She couldn't remember but it was on the other side of Handsworth, near Darnall, she thought.

She recalled a previous conversation where John had asked her if he had a sister. I couldn't bring myself to ask her what her reply had been but it did occur to me that, as she was prone to confusion, she could have started a conversation with John after our previous meeting saying a little too much and then when challenged, backtracking and changing the subject. She said again that she thought another greater power was playing a hand in our meeting like this.

'I am guided by Jehovah. I'm a Jehovah's Witness, you know.'

'Yes, we know.'

'I like to get it out in the open. People can be so judgemental. It's better to be honest. I'm nothing if not honest.' The phone rang in the kitchen and she jumped up to answer it. We could hear her tell someone called Roy that she wouldn't need a lift tonight, thanks, because she had visitors and wouldn't want to rush off. She explained this when she returned to the living room.

'That was Roy. He gives me a lift on a Thursday evening.'

'To Kingdom Hall?' asked Brian. 'Where is it in Handsworth?'

'No, not Kingdom Hall. It's up the road where we meet. Kingdom Hall is in the Manor, not near here. He's one of my converts, he and his wife. She didn't want to know at all at first but she comes with us now.'

She made coverts to Jehovah?

She stood up and knocked on the glass door between the living room and the hall beyond. 'I go on the doors, preaching.'

'Do you?' We must have looked amazed. She was elderly. Was it safe to do that sort of thing? And all the door slamming in faces that was typical of the stereotype of Jehovah's Witnesses. Was this a good thing for an elderly lady? But she was capable of charming her way into people's living rooms, I was sure.

'Yes, I do that. And I go to the meetings once a week. We pray there and talk about the Bible.'

She looked challenging but we didn't want to challenge her. Brian said, 'I would never condemn what I didn't fully understand. Everyone is entitled to what they believe in. Don't knock what you don't know about.' His oft quoted maxim.

Brian asked her whether she had worked after she got married but she hadn't. Bill hadn't wanted her to. Brian's own mother was typical of her time and hadn't worked after she'd married his father. Brian told Kathleen about this and she asked what his mother had done before she had married.

'Do you know where the Basset's factory was in Owlerton?' Yes, she knew it well.

'Well, she made the liquorice All Sorts there.'

'Oh what a lovely job. I'd just be eating them all day, if it was me.' And, recalling our earlier conversation about teeth, I could well believe it. 'Linsey worked there for a while, but she gave it up fairly soon.' She didn't say whether her granddaughter had been employed making the sweets or in the offices. Machines will make sweets these days so it would probably have been in the offices.

We told her that her marriage certificate had shown she had been a cutlery worker at the time of her marriage to Bill. No longer surprised by what we knew, she agreed.

'For Walker and Hall.' Walker and Hall are a very well-known cutlery manufacturer in Sheffield. 'I polished the silver cutlery and packed them into boxes for display or export.' No connection with Wall Kay and Sons, then. 'I went there straight from school.' The mention of school brought something to mind.

'I had a certificate from school, a report written by my last teacher. I kept it tucked into my bus pass for years. And this year it's disappeared. I told John about it but he couldn't understand what I was so upset about. 'It was only some old thing, he said, but I would have liked to show you what it said about my character. Reliable, clever, enjoyed school, things like that.'

'John has an Open University degree, doesn't he? Did he do that as an adult?'

'Oh no. He'd only be about nineteen on this photograph.' She stood up to remove it from the wall.

We peered at it together but he looked older than nineteen to us, more like in his early thirties. 'You might be right,' she agreed. 'But I'd have liked to show you my report. John thinks I lose things sometimes. I know I forget things. He's had to remind me it's my birthday. I can't remember how old I'll be.' We knew. She'd be eighty-three, but we were too polite to remind her.

'When would that be?'

'It's tomorrow, actually. The 24th March.' An Aries like myself. The Aries maxim is 'I want it. And I want it now!'

'Happy birthday for tomorrow. Will you get flowers?'

'Thanks. No, I don't expect so. You can't eat flowers.'

Perhaps chocolates would arrive.

Putting the photo down on one of the armchairs, she moved into the kitchen and in a few moments brought in a cup of tea for us. Did Brian mind a mug? He'd love a mug. No problem. We had been there for over two hours now and the tea we had come to take with her had at last appeared. She didn't drink tea with us but returned to the kitchen.

We looked once more around her living room. It was tidy and well kept. There was a picture of two dogs, Jack Russells, on the wall. The fireplace containing the temperamental gas fire was of beige tiles with a low mantle large enough to hold ornaments. There were porcelain flower baskets. My mother used to like those. And pottery teddy bears. My house is full of teddies, mostly of the soft and cuddly variety, some of which growl when tipped and others who live in a basket and on the bookshelves in what is now a room for the grandchildren to stay in. But Kathleen was no stranger to cuddly things. There was a soft fluffy dog on one of the armchairs, which she had fondly moved to allow Brian to sit down much earlier.

After a while we could hear the clattering of crockery. What was she up to? I got up to see what she was doing. The kitchen table was laid for tea.

Chapter 5

Staying for Tea

'I only meant a cup of tea when we spoke on the phone,' I tried to explain. 'We didn't come to be a nuisance.'

'Nobody comes here for just a cup of tea. Can you open this box?' It was foccacia bread with a tomato topping which needed eight minutes in the oven. She had lit the oven and was struggling to remove pans and dishes from the shelves. It proved too much so she said we wouldn't have this and proceeded to put them all back. She turned away to open a packet of boiled ham and, smelling a sudden whiff of gas, I noticed she had turned on the gas tap for the oven but not lit it. I hastily turned it off.

'Would you open this, please?' she asked handing me a tin of corned beef. I struggled to discover which way to turn the key and went into the living room to seek Brian's help.

'What's happening?'

'It looks like we're stopping for tea.'

'Right oh.' He opened the tin and handed it back to me.

'It's becoming a little chaotic in there.' Saying this I was reminded of a chaotic moment I'd had in my own kitchen three Christmases ago.

*

For many years we had visited Brian's parents before Christmas, usually in the first week in December as they had taken the sensible route, once we both living in different parts of the country, of visiting Brian's brother, Norman, and his family in one year and us in the next for Christmas Day and Boxing Day but they thought it would be a good idea if we all met together for a pre-Christmas lunch and so the pattern was set. We used to go to their house in Sheffield and a long table would be set for ten of us. Brian's father always peeled the sprouts and the potatoes while his mother busied herself with the turkey and Christmas pudding to be served later with rum sauce, and her pièce de resistance – the Yorkshire pudding. No Christmas lunch is complete without Yorkshires. This is true to this day with both our sons and ourselves. We would pull crackers, wear the paper hats and read out inane mottos and riddles. In later years each grandchild either married or had a partner and so the table had to be longer to accommodate a further four. It was then that it all got too much for Brian's mother so we started to go out to restaurants and pubs instead. We still took our Christmas crackers and kept up all the traditions. Except, that is, for the Yorkshire puddings.

Later still, after Brian's father had died, Sue and I took it upon ourselves to host in turn the pre-Christmas affairs so Brian's mother could stay for a while at the house of the son she wasn't going to be spending Christmas Day with. Three years ago it was my turn. I was busy cooking lunch for all the family. The numbers had risen to fifteen by that year with Brian's mum, Sue and Norm, their daughter, Emma, and her husband Marc, Andy, Emma's brother and his partner of the time, Nick and Debbie with their two children, Rob and Lisa and us. So, fifteen for a full

Christmas lunch, turkey cooked, glowing and golden on the work surface and just as I was putting back the second shelf in preparation for the roast potatoes and Yorkshire puddings, the oven blew up.

Not literally, you understand, not like a bomb, but with blue sparks and flames in the back of the oven rendering it totally useless. In true Dunkerque spirit, we panicked. I rang Robert for advice about what to do about the Yorkshire puddings. I hoped he might say, because at that time he and Lisa lived quite close: don't worry mother, I'll do them and dash over with them. Instead he volunteered, 'Just don't do them!' At this point, suddenly inspired, Brian lit the caravan oven. Outside through the pouring rain and a north easterly gale, I did a test case and the pudding swelled. I cooked the roast potatoes and all looked well. Then the gas ran out. By this time the kitchen was filled with relatives all with a glass in their hands talking loudly. I heard Sue saying to someone – Lisa, I guess, as they had just been introduced – how we always congregated in the kitchen at these dos, and thinking, 'Just everyone move out of my way,' as I was having to dash from caravan to kitchen and back in my rescue mission.

All was well in the end. Robert cooked the Yorkshire pudding batter on the top of the hob, pancake style, and Sue took care of the microwave where all the vegetables were to be cooked anyway. We managed to sit down altogether and drink a toast and Brian's mother said her traditional few words about how happy she was that we were altogether again shedding a tear as she did so. I don't remember clearly how the rest of the day went. I think this was because the wine flowed in my direction, often of its own volition because I don't remember filling my glass. When everyone but ours had gone home Debbie, Lisa and I collapsed and we have a photo of us sprawled on the sofa, looking exhausted. Brian's mother slept blissfully on in the armchair.

I never want to relive that nightmare. I'd cornered the market on chaotic kitchen capers.

*

On my return to Kathleen's kitchen, she had placed several slices of boiled ham on a plate, sufficient to feed a large family, far too much for the three of us. At her request I sliced the corned beef, though only half of the tin. There were six hard-boiled eggs which she'd sliced in half, a whole box of tomatoes, a whole cucumber sliced with an apology it wasn't presented in vinegar with sliced onion (something my mother had loved to do) – where is that vinegar? – it was on the window ledge actually so I put it on the table – lettuce in a colander and celery chopped into pieces. There might just as well have been others coming for tea. How would we eat all this between us?

Did we like salad cream or mayonnaise? I saw the mayonnaise already out so put that on the table.

I found plates and cutlery and laid the rest of the table. She was concerned we weren't going to be warm enough eating in the kitchen but, of course, we were as the table was placed beside the central heating radiator.

'We'll be fine in here,' we said. She showed us a box of meatballs.

'Will these be nice?'

'Yes, but there is plenty here. Pease don't open anything else.' She had bought a packet of waffles, too, and we managed to persuade her not to open these.

'Bread and butter?'

'Yes, right.' But it didn't appear.

'Do you like cheese?'

'Yes,' said Brian, 'but there's plenty here.' A large piece of Cheddar appeared.

'Do you like red cheese?' she asked with an unopened packet of red Leicester in her hand.

'Yes, but this will be plenty, thank you,' said Brian as he cut himself a piece of the Cheddar.

At last she made the tea, in a large yellow pot. It sat on the table to mash for a while but as soon as I started to pour three cups, she appeared with a blue teapot. We had two now. She poured from the second pot, which contained much stronger tea.

What had Paul thought she was going to do buying all this food? Feed the five thousand, I suppose.

We talked about caravanning holidays for a while. She and Bill had started camping, just as we had and then progressed to a caravan when they had the family. They hadn't had a lot of money and their courting days had consisted of walking, going on long walks. Bill had loved the outdoor life. And going to the cinema once or twice a week. They had bought a nice smart caravan but then decided to sell it after a few years, as the boys hadn't wanted it. But then they regretted it and bought the little Monza that now stood in the drive. It was full of junk at the moment as she used it to store garden furniture and the like.

'Bill always organised our holidays. I wouldn't have gone anywhere if it hadn't have been for him. All that walking. It's where I got these strong legs.' She held a shapely leg out for us to admire.

'Did you have a dog?' I asked remembering the two Jack Russells on the living room wall.

'Bill did. He'd always had dogs.' And she turned to a photograph of two little dogs sitting with a much younger Bill that was hanging on the kitchen wall. She took it down to show us. 'There's a little Jack Russell and a wirehaired terrier. Lovely dogs. Both dead now. We used to walk miles with them.' She replaced the photo.

I told her of our decision to buy a caravan. We had spent years, every holiday, camping with the boys. Then one Whitsuntide half term we drove to Snettisham in Norfolk. While we were struggling to put up our frame tent in a howling gale, a small caravan drew up beside us. The legs went down in a jiffy and before long we could hear the noise of a whistling kettle. There and then we decided that was for us. Even though we have a house in France, and even though we haven't used it in ages, we still have our caravan. It's hard to part with.

Kathleen and Bill had taken their original caravan to France and it was probably this experience that had tempted John to have a French house, too, although Kathleen couldn't be sure whether it was his or a friend's where they visited every year. She still enjoyed walking. She had taken a long walk around

Handsworth on Tuesday, when she knew that we would be coming to tea in a couple of days. 'I do most of my thinking when I'm walking. I was out ages. One of the boys said, 'where have you been, mother?' I told him I had been to see his father and then just fancied a walk.'

We munched our way through as much of the food as we could manage but surprisingly, Kathleen didn't join us. She just drank tea. Brian asked her about the past. When Bill had joined up, what had she done? Had she worked, as so many women in that time of war had, doing the work of men? She told us she had worked on the city transport as a conductress on the trams.

'I was on the transport,' she said, 'on the trams. I wore a uniform.'

'A hat?'

'No not a hat, you didn't have to in those days. I wore a skirt and jacket with a tie. I loved it as you got to meet so many people. Our route was from Middlewood to Ecclesall and from Malin Bridge to Fulwood.' Brian felt it was strange to be talking about places he had known so well as a boy. Images of Middlewood and Malin Bridge brought back childhood memories for him.

I knew Fulwood well as my dad had lived there as a boy and his sister, my Auntie Alice, had continued to live in the family house on Crimecar Lane for some years after the war and in another house nearby until her death in the 1970s. She could even have been a passenger on one of Kathleen's trams.

'I enjoyed running up and down the stairs and getting to know people as the same people would be on each of the routes.'

'Did you have to change the seats at each terminus?'

'Yes. I just swung the back of the seats over one after the other as I went up the aisle. We had a mate who was the driver and you worked in a team. It was fun. This is fun. I haven't talked about this in years.'

'On the days when I missed my bus home from school, I used to catch a tram into town,' I told her.

'Where did you go to school?' she asked. I told her Abbeydale.

'My sister, Audrey, went to Abbeydale Grange. Did you know her? Of course not,' she corrected herself, 'far too old.'

'It was just Abbeydale when I went there. Grange was a different school, in the same grounds but a different school with a different uniform.'

'Where did you go?' she asked Brian.

He told her, 'Firth Park, the same school as your son.'

'Oh yes.' She remembered from an earlier conversation. 'But you would have left a long time before he went, wouldn't you?' He nodded. 'Paul hated it, you know. He hated the fact that he had to catch two buses and it meant that he couldn't play football or anything after school. It was all school, travel and homework and not much else. Yes, he didn't like that. Two buses were just too much'

Returning to the subject of the trams, Brian asked her if she had continued to work on the transport after the war.

'Oh, no. Bill wouldn't have liked that. Women didn't usually work.' Then suddenly, 'Will you come and see him in the nursing home?'

We had already decided this wouldn't be a good thing for any of us. Although we thought that it would be a marvellous experience to meet this amazing man who had held me in his arms when I was a tiny baby, we couldn't take the chance of making problems for Kathleen.

'What would you say if one of your boys arrived unexpectedly? And what would you say to Bill if he asked you who we were and where we had met? You would have to make up a story.' She pondered on this for a moment and agreed the risk would be too high. She didn't mention the matter again.

The kitchen looked like the wreck of the Hesperus as nothing had been put away. We stood up to go first offering to clear the table, tidy for her, and wash the pots. She declined all offers saying that it would give her something to do that evening. 'I've nothing better to do. It'll keep me busy.' This was from a woman who had turned down the opportunity of an evening out. It would take hours to clear up but she wouldn't hear of our helping. We were leaving to see Brian's mother, as it was Mothering Sunday in three days' time. In the car were two bunches of tiger tulips.

Should I go and get one of them? Perhaps not. You can't eat flowers. But it was more than that.

Giving the flowers said: 'These are for Mother's day. You're my mother. I'm accepting you as my mother.' Now, if ever, was not an appropriate time. And, once again, who had brought them for her either for that day or for her birthday?

As we were all standing, she pulled us both close to her and said, 'Do you want to come again?' Her face was very serious. She looked at both our faces closely. I couldn't answer straight away.

'It doesn't matter if you don't.' She was giving me a get-out, if I couldn't commit myself. I couldn't bear it.

'Yes, we'll come again.' I've got to own up to myself what it is that I need to get from this. I'm still not sure what I want.

'Well,' she said, squeezing Brian's arm tightly against her chest, 'I could run off with your husband.' He put his other arm round her and gave her a hug, pulling her into his chest. She is a very tactile person, but so are we. My own mother hadn't been quite the same, always seeming to hold something in reserve.

We laughed, which broke the tension somewhat.

'You could just ring, you know. I've worked out what to say if someone is here. I'd say, 'Oh hello, Margaret, it's nice to hear from you. I haven't heard from you for such a long time. How are you?' So you see, I've thought about it.'

'I'll ring you. I won't be afraid. But you mustn't go to so much trouble for us. It's too much for you.'

Oh, it was all right, she said. She liked people to come for tea. People came to tea from the Witnesses.

*

One last hug and we left. We didn't say a lot in the car going to Brian's mother's house. I felt a profound sense of sadness at leaving Kathleen. She had tried so hard and then there was the worry of the gas tap. But I couldn't just ring one of her boys and point this out to him. Would I ever be allowed to meet them? I could hope. And another thing. Were we to call her Kath? Difficult. We had become used to calling her Kathleen now.

*

When I had written to Sue, the Sheffield social worker, I had mentioned some things about myself that I would like to know more about. One of these was about my feet. Sue might have thought that asking whether Kathleen had feet that turned out, one more than the other, was a frivolity. But it wasn't. My left foot has always turned out.

When I was a little girl, about four years old, my mum took me to see Doctor Dowson, the family physician, to ask what could be done about this. 'Send her to ballet classes,' was his response. So she did. I joined a class for little ones in Crosspool and learned to *entrechat* and *plié* with the best of them. I loved it. I enjoyed moving gracefully to the music, waving my arms in time to the rhythms. I enjoyed the little red shoes. I enjoyed wearing the little satin dress, keeping warm in a crossover mohair hand-knitted bolero. I went to tap-dancing classes as well, shuffle-ball-changing my way round the church hall in red tap shoes held with a huge white ribbon bow.

Eventually, as I grew older my parents paid for private lessons at my teachers' house: John and Josie Whaley, a brother and sister dance duo, were the experts. They had a board they placed on the dining room floor to facilitate the tap-dancing but I danced on the carpet for the ballet. The fact that my feet turned out naturally was such a bonus. Far from being a cure, my ballet lessons were enhanced by these feet. First position: heels together – feet wide apart. Second: step to the side – feet wide apart. Third: bring that right foot in again and place it across in front of the left – feet placed wide apart. And fourth? Stepping forward from third. And, yes, you've guessed it. And so on into fifth. *Entrechats* were a doddle. From one feet-turned out position to the next with a jump in the air. Tap dancing was no different. Who has ever seen a tap dancer with straight feet? Those pre-war Clark brothers in the black and white films had nothing on me.

At the yearly concerts I was allowed to do solo performances as I was tutored privately. And so I became a gypsy, in a white rustic blouse and a wide completely circular red skirt edged with white rick-rack braid that my mother had to make for me; a soldier – white shirt and black braided trousers, an icicle in pure white satin bodice with the skirt ripped upwards in tails to resemble icicles, and an anemone in a rich purple tu-tu with shoes dyed to match. I know this was a purple outfit as the original black and white photograph had been coloured by hand afterwards, much like Kathleen's wedding photo had.

110

I felt like a star whether on the stage at the local church hall or performing at the Montgomery Hall in the centre of Sheffield.

The performance as a soldier was at the Montgomery Hall. This wasn't as a part of the dancing class, but as a result of it. I performed it with a group of classmates from grammar school. I was a tall eleven by this time. There were twelve of us: six soldiers and six maids in cotton gingham skirts and white ruched peasant blouses. We performed to 'Soldier, soldier, will you marry me?' The maids sang: Soldier, soldier, will you marry me with your musket, fife and drum? whilst tripping across the stage towards and away from my group of soldiers, who stood sternly with our thumbs placed firmly in our cummerbunds. The soldiers sang (I probably mimed, in the interest of not clearing the hall or it could have been that we performed to a record.) Oh no, sweet maid, I cannot marry you as I have no shirt to put on. This whilst marching strongly towards and away from the maids. Then up went the maids to their grandfather's chest and found the soldiers each item of clothing, of the very, very best to put on. And on we went tripping and marching until all the clothes were provided and the soldiers were forced to confess to the pretty maids that they were a deceitful group of no accounts because they all had wives of their own already. Naïve at eleven, I had no idea about the wrong intentions of the soldiers and just thought it was loads of fun. And so did our audiences. We performed the same dance three nights in a row and exhaustedly returned to our classes the morning after each one, pretending we had missed that bit of grease

111

paint in our hasty washes in the morning and complaining bitterly how all the lipstick refused to come off.

I kept up my dancing until I was a year or two older. Then I gave it up. I'd discovered boys. But none the less it left me with a good legacy, including the turned out feet.

*

However odd, my feet have drawn the attention of a few admirers in their long and oft-maligned lives. One time, when I had been teaching for some years, I crossed the almost empty staff room floor to use the telephone. I stood making the call for a while, probably to an irate parent, and when I turned round one of the art teachers was looking at me. Bill worked part-time at the school to supplement his work as an artist. 'Have you ever been a dancer?' he asked.

'Well, I haven't danced since I was a girl, but I used to go to ballet classes. Why?' 'You walk like a dancer,' he said. That'll be the feet, then.

Much more recently, whilst standing on the escalator rising from the Victoria underground line to the turnstiles at King's Cross, I felt someone rise closely behind me. Turning at his touch, somewhat alarmed, I looked into the face of a man in his fifties with a tan and a dashing moustache. 'Are you English?' he asked.

'Of course.' This curtly, so as not to be encouraging strangers to speak to me in this dangerous world we now live in.

'Do you know you have a beautiful walk?'

'Well,' beaming now, all fear forgotten under the glow of flattery, 'thank you. You're not English, though are you?'

'No. I am Sicilian. I used to teach dancers.' We arrived at the top of the escalator and I slipped off ahead of him. We smiled our goodbyes. I glided off to St Pancras for the train home.

*

By the time I was nineteen and already seeing Brian on a regular basis, we would visit some friends of his, one of whom had two small children and the other three little ones. Both mothers wanted to get back into shape after their recent pregnancies and they joined the Women's League of Health and Beauty in Sheffield. Did I want to come, too? So off I would go with them on a Thursday evening and in our black leotards and tights we would perform movements to music that weren't a million miles away from the ballet I had loved as a girl. We had bare feet and occasionally pirouetted and leaped about the room like dervishes. Very good for fitness and all made easier by feet that turned out. I only stopped going when I became pregnant for the first time myself.

Not long after Brian and I moved to Nottingham, I joined a ladies' keep fit class. I went with a group of young mothers to the local village hall on a Wednesday afternoon. This was very convenient as we could take our children and they would play together behind a line of upturned chairs as we exercised. As soon as I heard the music start up I was ready to perform. Stretches, bends, leaps, lifts, turns. I was straining at the leash. The Keep Fit Association

113

was short of teachers at the time so my Wednesday afternoon teacher recommended me for the training. It took three years of Monday nights at Arnold and Carlton Further Education College to become competent enough to teach others.

I eventually got my first class. This is a long time before the trend of high impact aerobics that is so popular now where heavy beats of popular music keep people motivated to step and jog and calls of 'crunch those abs!' ring out to choruses of grunts and oohs. I still go to aerobics on a regular basis to keep myself fit, and I intend to be still doing it in my sixties, if I can. No, in the early days we had pianists. Gladys was mine. In her sixties, she was a lot more experienced than I was and although she played the pieces as we had discussed before the lesson, she drew me on one side after my first efforts and asked me if I realised why my class was leaning exhaustedly against the walls of the community hall. I didn't. I was going way too quickly for them. The ladies didn't have time to learn anything or even to draw breath before I was rushing on to the next movement. Poor things. It was the nerves. I was the same with my first teaching in a school.

To teach adults, it wasn't enough to be qualified in your own subject. You had to have an adult education teaching certificate, too. So I took Thursday afternoon classes at South Notts. College for a year and learned the theory of how adults learned. I learned about Piaget for the first time and read articles our tutor gave us on motivation and sustaining interest of the learner. I had my first experience of micro-teaching and hooted with laughing at myself

114

performing on the video tape. But I passed the course and the tutor mentioned to me on the last afternoon at college whether I had ever considered taking up teaching as a career.

Me a teacher! Ha! I couldn't think of anything more unlikely. If there was any profession my dad scorned the most, it was teaching. All those holidays and short days. But he had a different view on it when, persuaded I might be good at it, I studied hard and became a 'proper' teacher. His little girl had gone to college to get three A-levels to start with and an O-level in Maths, a subject I had failed so badly at sixteen, I had been ashamed to own up to the marks. Then off to the University of Nottingham for three years to study English, his favourite subject, graduating with a creditable upper second, and finally a year at Trent Polytechnic to get a post-graduate certificate in education.

When I was ready to teach, there were no jobs in junior schools until Christmas of 1984. I was raring to go in July. I couldn't wait for Christmas; I'd been working for this for the last five years. I wanted it; and I wanted it now! So I answered a job advertisement placed on the last day of the school summer term, in the Nottingham Evening Post for a teacher of English in an upper school in Newark where the youngest pupil was fourteen, a far cry from the pleasing, well-behaved children of nine, ten and eleven that I had tried my skills on in teaching practice. I turned up for the interview, the only candidate, to be interviewed by the retiring head teacher. No one else was there but the caretaker as it was by now the summer holidays. What do you think will be the difference teaching this age range as opposed to the one you have trained to teach, she asked me? Piaget sprung to mind and I told her what I knew about concrete and abstract thinking and how this affected learning and crossed my fingers. She offered me the job there and then. No waiting about. But what did she care? She'd be away into retirement by the time I took up my post.

I don't regret becoming a teacher one bit. Brian supported me all the way in my journey to qualify. Five years where we had two small children, at the beginning aged eight and six, who had such needs as being picked up from school and taken to swimming, football, gymnastics, cricket, cubs, parties and all the events young children attend as they are growing up. He looked after the house with the boys helping out for increased pocket money, as they grew older; they became very competent ironers during this time. Brian supported me emotionally when I occasionally fell into despair struggling to complete assignments, weeping about why I had ever started this education malarkey in the first place. But, with his help I struggled on and became a 'proper' teacher.

I really want to be able to tell Kathleen this story but the chance has not arisen yet. But she might be amused to know how it all began with feet that turned out. We haven't known her long enough to watch her walk any distance which could give us a clue as to whether her feet turn out, too. Perhaps my feet, like the ears, are of Polish origin.

Chapter 6

Becoming sixty

Kathleen and her beloved Bill had achieved their diamond wedding in 2002. This year they will have clocked up sixty-four years. We are no strangers to long marriages in our families either. Brian's mother and father were also able to celebrate a diamond wedding and my parents managed fifty-four years together before my father died. We went to my cousins, Margery and Fred's, golden wedding celebration in 2000. In these days of marriages on and off as quick as fast-food fads those made in heaven, built to last are rare.

Brian and I can lay claim to thirty-seven years together although we have known each other for over forty. We met when I joined the Inland Revenue in 1966 as a tax officer. I had been promoted from clerical assistant in the Telephone Manager's Office based at the lower end of West Street in Sheffield and settled into the offices of the tax district, Sheffield Seven, situated further up West Street. Sitting down ploughing through repetitive clerical duties, I was interrupted by a hip sliding onto my new desk. My eyes followed the line of the leg and up the body, to rest on a strong face and a slightly crooked smile. He smiled more widely and said, 'How would you like to join the union?' He's a bit of all right, I thought. First impressions – good looking, one slightly chipped tooth, clear grey eyes, large ears, curly brown hair, and that wonderful smile.

I joined the civil service union; signed up at once. After I had completed my initial training in Leeds I went to work on Brian's section and he continued to train me. I had a boyfriend but once he knew I would be away in Leeds doing more of my training he disapproved, not trusting me, I suppose. My mum didn't help the time the boyfriend and I were just leaving the house to go out: when speaking about my work she referred to Brian as 'your Brian'. He wasn't my Brian; he was my boss. But my mum was no fool. Anyway, the boyfriend and I split up after a while. Brian was getting over a painful divorce and we found we could sit and talk after work. As ever with the Revenue there was always a lot of overtime after budget day and Brian and I worked on until eight at night.

One of Brian's union jobs was to order wine for the members before Christmas. He gave out the lists, people ordered their Leibfraumilch and Blue Nun and he collated them into one large order then handled the collection of the money once the wine had been delivered. He needed an assistant. Would I help? You bet. I began to like him a lot. I knew he spent certain evenings at a local dance hall with friends and I asked him if he would be there one particular evening. My parents were entertaining at home the parents of an old flame of mine, a boy I had been engaged to years earlier and the last thing I wanted was to be there. No, he wouldn't be at the dance hall but if I were to work overtime as he was doing, he might take me out for a rink afterwards. This sounded promising.

We stepped out of the building in West Street and walked round to the car park to where Brian's yellow Mini was parked. We got in and Brian drove into Derbyshire to the Strines Inn. 'What will you have?' he asked me.

'Half a bitter, please.' He couldn't believe his luck. A good-looking girl who drank beer! Later he drove back into town and parked a short distance from a Chinese restaurant on The Moor. The Zing Vaa was a favourite and we talked as we ate our way through chop suey and chow mien using chopsticks, washing it down with lager. We did that in those days. We got back into the yellow Mini and he took me home. A familiar car was parked in the driveway and I realised my parents' guests were still there, probably waiting for me to return. I didn't want to go in just yet so Brian drove off again up the Manchester road we had driven up earlier in the evening. I chatted on in my usual way and Brian reached over and took hold of my hand as he was driving. That shut me up. No good night kiss, though. This was 1966. The 8th March.

I was in trouble for staying out late but it had been worth it. We went out regularly after that and celebrated the date by getting engaged two years later. On the 8th March 1969 we were married in the Victoria Hall Methodist Church. A cold bright sunny day with a touch of snow on the ground, I was twenty minutes late as is every bride's prerogative but Brian knew I would be there. My parents' next-door neighbour told him the wedding car had arrived at the house before he and his wife had left for the church. We have had a strong marriage, strong enough to weather occasional rough patches, and no regrets.

119

Love is as strong as ever and we support each other because we have it. The phrase today is that we have always been 'there' for each other and the older we grow, I can't see that changing: here, there and everywhere, wherever...

*

Some sad news today. Fred has died. My cousin's husband of fifty-six years. Margery phoned to tell us and we felt the raw shock of unexpected bad news. We drove up to Sheffield to see her and spoke to her brother in Canada on the phone. He was feeling helpless as catching the next plane and coming over from Toronto was what he would have liked to be doing but being eighty-four and not in the best of health, this wasn't an option. With Margery we reminisced about good times with Fred. I had always called him Torment because as a child he had teased me so I nicknamed him my Torment Fred. I had been one of their three bridesmaids at four years old dressed in a pink crinoline and bonnet when they married in 1950. He was a special person in my life and Brian and our boys felt this, too. Margery was concerned that she would not manage to come to my birthday party, which Brian had been planning with Nick and Debbie's help for quite some time. We told her not to worry about this but after a long chat on the phone with Brian's mum, with whom she has always had a good relationship, she decided she would manage it. I appreciated how strong she was as it would be difficult to attend her first social event without Fred. But she would do this for me. Fred died on a Monday and the funeral was planned for a week the following

Wednesday. Sandwiched in the middle, on Palm Sunday, was my sixtieth birthday party.

This was memorable for me. I had planned a surprise party for Brian when he was fifty and we had had a lunch for friends and family at home when he was sixty but I had never wanted a celebration before for myself. But as my sixtieth approached I felt the urge to make a fuss. Brian attempted a surprise party getting in cahoots with Nick and Debbie to organise the invitations and a caterer but after three days had bottled out, as Nick told me later, as dad was never one able to keep a secret or run the risk of having to tell lies. So I knew about the party before we went to Thailand. Nick wrote all the invitations and handled the replies and some secret phone calls as most people who were invited thought it was a surprise do. Later I chose the menu from a selection the caterer had given to Debbie.

On the morning of the party it dawned fine but very cool. We hoped to let the children, grandchildren and neighbours' children, have a little party of their own in the garden and set up a gazebo, borrowed patio heater, ground sheet, and chairs and table on which to serve crust-less sandwiches, grapes, raisins, cheesy wotsits, crisps, fairy cakes and pink wafer biscuits, all brought by the caterer who knew the kinds of things little ones prefer at a grown-up do. But an hour into the party it started to snow. They came in and played pass the parcel and musical bumps in the lounge supervised by our eldest grandchild, Debbie's daughter, Aimee. I had been lying in bed at five that morning, awakened unusually by the dawn chorus, thinking about how things might go and about how lucky I was to have such an amazing family to help me celebrate and I had had to close my eyes against the brightness as the sunlight penetrated the curtains. Such is the English weather.

The caterer arrived at eleven with trays and trays of vol au vents, ham, beef, three sorts of quiche, sausages in honey and mustard and fresh salmon with prawns. There were soft rolls and butter pats. The puddings of cheesecakes, coffee roulade, lemon and lime torte, fresh fruit salad and individual trifles looked delicious. She brought a good selection of cheeses and a box of Jacobs's biscuits for cheese. She said there would be too much and she was right. My close friend Libby made the cake, moist and delicious iced fruitcake, and decorated it with fresh flowers in blue and white. It made a striking centrepiece.

People started to arrive at noon. Rob and Lisa and Jack had driven down from Sanquhar in Scotland setting off at about eight o'clock and making good time to arrive at half past eleven and Brian's mum was already here as she was staying for a few days. We had invited many really long-standing friends. Friends who we have known since early-married days in Sheffield came together and brought Margery. One of their husbands phoned half an hour into the party to wish me happy birthday, which was good of him as he lives and works in Gaborone in Botswana. Friends who we had known for over forty years came, too. We had invited newer friends and neighbours who we are only just getting to know in our new neighbourhood and community as well. Many people travelled a long way to join in. Family were there, of course; my niece and nephew and their other halves, the grandchildren, Joseph, Jack and Aimee.

I eventually served the food at 1.45pm. I had to move people out of the kitchen for a while so I could get to the oven to warm the quiches and sausages. And people ate and drank with gusto and talked loudly and excitedly, or so it seemed to me, when I took a moment to stand back and listen to the volume of noise in the kitchen rising as people introduced themselves to others who they had never met before or spoke to those they hadn't seen for some time. I tried to speak to everyone and introduce people but often they said, oh we've already met, until eventually the time came for speeches and the toast.

Brian said a few words telling people about my legs. He told his own story about how we met in the offices of the Inland Revenue and mentioned that it was my long legs that had attracted him to me and later how he couldn't believe his luck that he had chosen someone who was not only good looking, had these long legs (no mention of the feet here) but who also drank halves of bitter and took orders from him. What more could a man want in a woman?

'The first time I came into contact with Margaret,' he said when people were quiet, 'was when I looked up from my desk in an office in Sheffield and saw these legs walking towards me. Enough to make your trousers tremble. On looking up, I saw that the rest wasn't too bad either. As time went on she came to work for me so I was then her boss.' Hoots of laughter here. 'We quickly found we got on well together and had things in common. She realised what a good catch I was so much so that *she* actually asked

123

me out. Unfortunately work was frantic at that time and there was a need to put in extra hours. So I suggested that if she cared to work overtime...' huge guffaws '...we could go for a drink afterwards. To my delight she accepted and when I asked her what she would like to drink she said a half of bitter. I couldn't believe my luck. An attractive girl who did what I told her and was cheap to entertain.' More laughter. 'Even though I only got one out of these three right I took on the job.'

Looking around the room at every one he went on:

'It's great to have so many friends here today and they range from old friends to very new friends and the reason that there are so many people here is entirely due to Margaret. She's enthusiastic about maintaining contacts; she works hard at keeping people around us. Because it's the school holidays, there are some friends from her teaching days who can't be with us but she's had cards from Canada, America and France, flowers from Suffolk and greetings from Botswana so they haven't forgotten even if they can't be here. There are too many things to tell you about Margaret and I could go on forever but I'll always be grateful for the day those legs walked into my life.' Rapturous applause, tears to the eyes, fond smiles and murmured assent.

Then it was the turn of the boys. Brian had greeted Rob in the hall as they arrived with, have you got your speech prepared? Speech? Er, no, actually. I'll speak to Nick. Did Nick have something ready to say? Apparently not. At least, that was what Robert told the gathering. But I suspect they had had a few words together before the day as Robert spoke lovingly and gratefully that they had a mum like me. I could hear the sniffling behind me and watched through my own misty eyes as others shed a tear. It was lovely.

The boys and their girls gave me an exquisite white gold chain with a diamond-studded pendant – diamonds for a diamond occasion. Part of me wishes we had had a video camera to record the occasion for posterity; the other part is glad we didn't as my red hot cheeks would have set tissues on fire if I had stopped to dab my eyes. Declining the offer of tissues and wiping my nose with the back of my hand, I said a few words of my own in thanks to my wonderful boys – all three of them – and to my lovely girls and boys, as I refer to my daughters in law and my grandchildren. I thanked people for their presents, too, and for sharing in my super day.

I had some amazing presents but none so fantastic or surprising as Brian's. Whilst we were in Thailand he bought me a beautiful torque in 18ct white gold, which should be enough for any lucky girl but during the speeches and toast he presented me with an envelope with two tickets for a balloon ride, something he knew I'd wanted to do for years. We're looking forward to that now. Up, up and away in a ladybird balloon over Derbyshire. I have read many times that mothers who give up their children for adoption remember their lost children with sadness and longing, if, on no other day, then on the anniversary of their birth which is etched in their hearts. On other 10ths of April I would be forever the five-week old baby in her mind or perhaps that little girl of four years old who pushed a dolls pram outside twenty Darklands Road. Until earlier this year she could have no concept of me as an adult but now she had met me, for the first time in her life she would be able to picture me as an adult. As I woke in the early light of Monday April 10th 2006 to begin my sixtieth year, one of my first thoughts was to wonder whether Kathleen was thinking of me.

Part 3

The Extended Family

Chapter 7

The Balloon goes up

Three months have passed since I last saw Kathleen. I feel I want to make contact once more. If I leave it much longer I will be on holiday during the summer and will have to leave it until September. I could pick up the telephone but with her tendency to become confused I think it would be better to write her a little note saying I would come on Tuesday of the following week and ring the day before to see if this was all right. I included two photographs taken at my sixtieth birthday party: one of me and another of Brian, Nick, Robert and me as the boys handed me their present. I'm peering into the bag but the boys can be seen clearly. I wondered as I posted the envelope whether she would see Sigmund in either of the boys.

Since my sixtieth birthday party Brian and I have enjoyed our balloon flight. We chose what turned out to be a perfect, calm, balmy June evening. The deflated balloon, lying on a grassy field in Ambergate, in Derbyshire, was prepared for launch as two huge fans began filling it with cold air. As this was happening some of us were asked to get into the basket, which was lying on its side connected to the balloon. Four of us lay on our backs in the basket and clutched rope handles listening to the roar of the fans and finally the intense roar of the gas jets, which heated the air.

It felt hot behind my head. Slowly, slowly the basket righted itself and the rest of the would-be balloonists climbed in. There were eleven of us in all. A small crowd of people had gathered to watch the launch and several strong men were asked to clutch the outside of the basket to avoid a premature launch. Eventually all passengers were standing feet astride in the basket, holding a rope handle in each hand assuming a sort of brace position with knees bent. Still more strong men held the basket down on the ground whilst the balloon, fully inflated now, strained to take off.

At last everyone outside stood aside and we rose into the air. Drifting gently, listening to the roar of the gas jets, we cleared the hedge around the field and it slowly dawned on us we were airborne. Stillness descended. We looked with wonder at the roofs of houses in Ambergate. No one came out to wave. They were probably used to such events and had grown blasé. The river Amber weaved below us. A canal cut a diagonal line. Parallel train lines scored the land. A patchwork of fields unfolded below us, of pale-greens and corn-yellows. In contrast were dark green broccoli heads, which were the tops of deciduous trees. Houses growing smaller and smaller clustered as hamlets. Farmyards drifted into view surrounded by fields studded with sheep, like clouds from the top down. Cows, motionless, mooed, heads down, undisturbed by the sudden sound of the gas jets, as if a child had just placed them in a farmyard set. Dogs barked noisily unhappy at the strange but unexplained sound from out of the sky. We drifted over Derbyshire countryside as pilot Dave, pointed out the landmarks. *Cameras clicked. Video cameras, hand-held over passengers' heads whirred gently. Binoculars peered to gain a closer view of the ground. It was said it was possible to see into people's living rooms from the air. Not from four and a half thousand feet, it wasn't. At this height, I was pleased I had put on my sweater, although for the rest of the flight I was warm. It is very warm in the basket as the gas jets give off a lot of heat and the evening air was far from cold. Silence again.*

The sun was getting lower in the sky and the shadows on the ground lay long. In fields where the harvest was complete single bales of hay were encased in black plastic. The shadow of each trailed like a black comma. As we rose higher they were tadpoles caught by colourless pondweed. Even higher, shiny balls in a bagatelle set. We approached Chesterfield. Familiar with this town we strained to catch a glimpse of the Crooked Spire. There it was unfurling its leaden limb upwards into the evening light. And more mundane, we saw the dual carriageway from the M1 forge its way into the town bobbling with toy cars and die-cast trucks, which paused at a traffic island before careering along the ring road.

We were coming into land, descending swiftly on Chesterfield. Housing estates sprung into view. We could see who had above-ground swimming pools, conservatories, patios, landscaped planting. We surprised some people who were enjoying the privacy of their gardens lying on sun beds. No privacy here. We could have reached out and touched them Lilliputians to our Gulliver. On Tapton golf course

131

golfers lined up careful putts only to be disturbed by our noisy descent. In a field a mare and her foal, spooked, galloped wildly by a fence. Oddly to me, the gas jets seem to be employed more frequently to control the landing. We missed the roofs of a smart housing estate, just. We missed the golf course. We hit a farmer's field of newly cut grass carefully selected by Dave to limit any damage. The landing was perfect and we rolled over in the basket clutching our rope handles laughing hysterically as we were dragged along the field. Back to reality, the minibus arrived to pick us up.

Dave disconnected the balloon from the basket and everyone helped to roll it up and stuff it back into a huge fabric bag watched by a gaggle of small children who had rushed over the field on seeing the descent. They were wide-eyed with wonder that so many of us had emerged from the sky in such a small basket. We drank champagne poured by Sophie and John, employed as ground staff but who regularly have the joy of ballooning high across Europe with Dave. Over the French Alps at ten thousand feet, breath freezes, they told us; whilst high above the snow-capped mountains the view is breath-taking. We roared off back to Ambergate clutching certificates of success in balloon ascent.

21ˢᵗ June 2006 – Diary entry

I am going away for the weekend to the hen party of my nephew's fiancée and, instead of waiting until Monday I rang Kathleen's number before I left to drive up the A1 to Knaresborough with Debbie, Nick's wife. There was no answer. Brian went off to watch World Cup football in the pub with Nick. Later, I rang Brian to let him know of our safe arrival to be told that whilst he had been out there had been a message for me from Kathleen saying that she had received my letter and had shown it to her sons. She had also said that she would be looking forward to seeing me on Tuesday, eleven o'clock would be all right, and 'I'll send fondest love and say good bye for now.'

I was pleased to hear this news but a little alarmed she had said she had shown my letter to her sons. What had she done with the photographs? Had they seen those, too? Well, hello, boys, this is the sister I know you always wanted! Instant sister. What were they going to think?

There was nothing I could do about it and went off to York in a minibus with the girls. We ate a splendid meal in an Italian restaurant. Before we went in we were all given a red satin sash to wear, which said 'Hen' and lit up in tiny fairy lights, a headband with little devil's horns and a badge. Mine bore the legend 'wild'. The bride-to-be chose 'sexy' and wore a red veil on her headband to mark her out from the rest of us, although my sister in law, Sue, and I were sure no one was going to mistake us for the bride.

We walked on to Toff's nightclub after the meal and entered an alien world. The noise was loud. Decibels off the scale. When we sat down with our first drinks I could feel the music through the seat and the back of the banquette. We got up to jig on the miniscule dance floor from time to time inspired by

133

pop music we knew. As the evening grew older the sights grew funnier. Girls who should have known better wearing low-slung jeans and crop tops, midriffs bulging in folds, which I have since heard referred to as 'muffin tops', queued for the ladies, leaning against the wall, holding bottles of Moet. Chaps, out on a stag night, dressing the groom-to-be in a wig and tight dress, attempted to queue for the ladies. Breasts appeared everywhere. Bulging over skimpy tops, décolletage bordering on something a Regency lady of the court would have been proud of.

The smoke was the worst, far worse than the volume of the music. We just got on and enjoyed the music, joined in and sang the lyrics we knew at the tops of our voices, jigged around on the dance floor and tried to breathe elsewhere. By far more young women smoked than didn't smoke. Some men smoked, of course, but not so many. The atmosphere was thick. Sue and I went for a look round the nightclub, into other rooms, partly to get away from the smoky atmosphere. We went upstairs and sat in a room where a young man was murdering a guitar. He must have had a death wish as his voice missed every key he couldn't play. We had our photograph taken and for £3 a misty Polaroid appeared of Sue, myself and a stranger. His name we learned was Simon and he just turned up head thrusting between us, hand clutching his glass of beer. 'We've pulled!' we shrieked.

We arrived back in Knaresborough at 3.00am and woke late. I phone Brian after breakfast. I told him of the fun we had had the night before and how late we had stayed up. We had some small talk and then he said:

'There's been a development.'

'A development?'

'Yes,' he said. 'I had a phone call yesterday evening. The phone rang and a chap asked for you. I said you weren't in and asked him who he was. John, he said.'

'Oh, my lord.' I knew straight away who this would be. My half-brother. 'What did he say?'

'He said he'd ring back later and rang off but I realised if he did that you'd still be out. So I rang 1471 and rang him back. He has a Sheffield accent.'

'What did you say?'

'I said I was Brian, Margaret's husband and asked him why he had rung. He said you had written to his mother.'

'Oh dear.' I recalled the voice message.

'Both boys are going to be there on Tuesday.'

Chapter 8

The Brothers

Both John and Paul? I felt a sudden surge of excitement. This is what I wanted to happen but what did they want to happen? Would they prefer I hadn't just emerged from the woodwork? They would be fine without me. They had been so for over fifty years. Brian learned John was nearly sixty, too. Next March. So he had been born just eleven months after me. Just over nine months after Kathleen and John's father had handed me to the adoption agency. She and Bill had picked up the pieces of their lives and made their own child, their own family.

At pains to put John at his ease and to reassure him that we had only good intentions and did not mean to disrupt their lives or bring any harm to his parents, Brian made small talk. He mentioned he knew John had a house in France. Where was it? Normandy, apparently. They talked about caravanning. This made John aware we had had conversations with his mother before. He was surprised. Brian asked him to understand that I had needed to find his mother and had made contact. John explained that his father was in a home and that, not only was losing the strength in his legs, as Kathleen had pointed out, but was, sadly, 'away with the fairies.'

'Margaret is about eighteen months too late, in actual fact. Up till then my mother's been sprightly and sharp but she is getting quite confused now.' Of course, we had come to realise this. He asked Brian if I had been the Margaret who had sent the Christmas card. And another thing. Paul had tried to make sense of who had been coming to tea on the day in March Brian and I had gone. His mother couldn't remember. There were people coming for tea on two occasions; one was an old family friend who the boys knew but she said she couldn't remember the names of the others who were coming on a different day. Perhaps she was having selective amnesia: a diversionary tactic to avoid saying too much. Reluctant to put the phone down, Brian asked John if he remembered living in a prefab in Handsworth. Sure he did, he said, he grew up there. My aunt and uncle and three cousins lived at the end of your road. Learning what their name was he exploded – the police inspector! He had played with Charles and his sister Margaret as a boy and so had his brother Paul. He didn't remember Ann as well as she was older. Kathleen hadn't been able to remember her neighbours but John would be realising that for Brian to know about where he spent his childhood we would have been talking to his mother quite a lot.

It occurred to Brian from some things John was saying that he didn't have all the facts. In fact, he knew very little of what had happened already. Perhaps Tuesday would reveal more.

*

As we left home on Tuesday morning of 27th June 2006 setting off up the A38 I wondered if I should buy flowers. We hadn't taken them before as I thought it might be difficult to explain where they had come from but today to turn up with them wouldn't be a problem. But I didn't. I drove by the florist. Why did I do that? We always take flowers to friends or to Brian's mum when we go to visit. Perhaps walking in with flowers made things look too much of a commitment.

When we arrived there were no cars parked outside the house. We went to the front door and rang the bell. No answer. We rang again. We looked at the front garden admiring the peonies. We waited. No one was coming. I felt a sudden feeling of loss, of disappointment. Then a car pulled up. We looked to see who was getting out and saw a man who resembled the photographs in the house of Bill. Surely he was the father's son. He opened the gate and walked up the path. Brian held out his hand.

'Are you John? I'm Brian.'

'And I'm Margaret.'

We shook hands. I looked at him hard and he looked at me. He was about 5' 6" tall and dressed casually. He was losing his hair a little and had a round face and a pleasant smile. He looked nothing like me.

'Isn't she answering?' He strode over to the door and rang the bell that we had tried.

'Sometimes she's upstairs. She's going deaf. We've got her a hearing aid.' Getting no success either, he went round to the front door and rapped firmly on the knocker. Still no reply.

'I'll see where she is,' he said reaching for his mobile phone. He phoned his brother but his mobile phone was turned off. He phoned the nursing home where his father was and asked if his mother was there. Yes, she was. He asked if they would ask his brother to ring him.

'Her memory's going,' he said, smiling ruefully, 'but our Paul's no better.'

'Has he forgotten we're coming?' I asked.

Probably, even though he rang me yesterday to make sure he had the right day.'

We waited. 'This is a rum thing, then,' John said.

'Yes.' What else could we say? Brian had been quite clear about why we were coming when he and John had spoken on Saturday. There was an awkward silence, which Brian filled with further reassurances that I hadn't undertaken the search for my mother lightly and that our intention was not to cause upset for any of their family, especially for his father.

'How is your father?' I asked him.

'Not good,' he said ruefully. 'He sleeps most of the time and when he's awake he's not really with it.'

'It's sad.'

'Yes, and for my mother, too.' He looked closely at us for a moment then looked away at the garden. 'Were you born after the war was over?'

'Yes, in April 1946.'

'I was born in March 1947. My dad would have been in the Middle East until then. I'm not sure when he came home.'

He was trying to work out if I had any connection to his father. I wanted to tell him what I already knew but I realised he knew much less than we had thought. Kathleen hadn't told him anything except that he had a sister, older than himself.

'How did you find her?'

There was so much to tell. How could I condense the story of my search into a few minutes or my reasons for needing to? Which bits should I leave out because they were sensitive to speak about? This was Kathleen's story as well.

'When you are an adopted child,' I began 'you aren't allowed to trace your birth other without the intervention of a social worker. You can't turn up on someone's door after sixty years and say, 'remember me?' I have had the help of someone in Sheffield Family Services, who wrote to your mother.'

'She never mentioned it.'

'Well, no. I sent off for her marriage certificate before that so we knew we had the right person.'

'I sent off for it, too,' he said, when they'd been married for sixty years. You have to send it off to get a telegram from the Queen.'

'We did that for my mum and dad,' Brian told him.

'You'd probably be sending off for my mother's at the same time as us,' John mused.

'Well, mmm, probably a bit later, last year in fact. Your mother rang the social worker a couple of times after she got the letter and that's how I got to know some information about myself. But then nothing happened so I sent the Christmas card.'

'It was funny about that card. She'd no idea who'd sent it. She asked us about it but the only thing we could think of was that it had something to do with caravanning.' I looked puzzled. 'You see, because it

140

said 'farm' and 'barn' in the address we wondered whether it were from someone they'd stayed with. Some farm. One of those small sites.'

'A CL?' I said.

'Yes. It was the only thing we could think of.'

'Does she get Christmas cards?'

'Er, a few. She's given most of that up, you know. We're Catholics, Paul and me. We don't have anything to do with the other stuff. We just let my mother get on with it.' He was referring to her beliefs in the teachings of Jehovah's Witnesses. I was, too, but neither of us actually voiced this and just at that moment another car pulled up at the roadside.

'It's our Paul,' John said. 'His memory's as bad as my mother's. He forgets things all the time. I rang him yesterday to remind him and my mother rang me three times asking who was coming today, whether they were coming to tea or what have you.'

'Just like *my* mother,' I murmured to Brian as John moved forward to open the gate for his mother. She was dressed in a smart navy and white pleated skirt, and a thin off-white knitted jumper under a navy blazer. Her grey and brown, salt and pepper hair was tidy as she carelessly brushed her hand through it. She beamed as she came through and immediately took my hand and kissed me. She patted Brian. 'Did I forget? I knew someone was coming,' she said, 'I was looking forward to it but when Paul came to fetch me to go and see Bill, I thought it must have been that!' she laughed. She turned to John. 'Look, I'm wearing it,' she said fingering the hearing aid behind her right ear. 'I remembered to put it on.' He looked approvingly at her.

'That's good.'

'But I don't always do it.'   She smiled impishly, like a naughty girl, over her shoulder at him and as she turned he raised his eyebrows, knowingly, at me.

Paul followed her down the path and, while his mother busied herself with unlocking the door we introduced ourselves to him. He shook hands firmly. He was tall, over six feet, much taller than John although there was a strong family likeness. There was no doubt they were brothers and resembled their father and I remarked on it.

'Yes, he's my brother. The long and the short of it,' John smiled looking up at Paul.

We went into the house and Kathleen left the boys to put on the kettle in the kitchen as we went through into the lounge. We sat on the brown sofa and Kathleen chatted on about Bill. He wasn't too well but she thought she was lucky to have a husband at all as there were plenty who didn't have her good fortune. She picked up a photograph from the mantel piece. 'That's my daddy,' she said kissing the photograph. 'My lovely daddy.' It was black and white and had been scanned into a computer and reprinted. A man faced the camera unsmiling. He wore a trilby and a suit with a shirt and tie. The original had had a crease across the bottom, which was evident from the new print but did not spoil the image. I mentioned this and Kathleen said, 'John did that for me. He's very clever at that sort of thing. He'd do it for you if you ever wanted him to.' I felt a sudden pang of sadness.

'I found him at the top of the stairs, didn't I?' she went on as John came into the room. 'It was face down. I don't know how I missed it,' she told him. He told me how he had scanned it and I nodded and said I had scanned the photos I had sent Kathleen, but there was no evidence of those in the lounge.

'This is William Henry James,' I said. He gave me an old fashioned look but he wasn't prompted to ask me how I knew.

'He fought in the Boer War, you know. A sergeant major,' said Kathleen.

'My grandfather fought in the Boer war, too,' I told her. My mother's father, a warrant officer, had received the DSM. Kathleen's father wore a buttonhole. 'He always wore that. And a hat. He was proud of the way he looked, always smart.'

There was a further family photo. Kathleen reeled off the names: my daddy, my mother, my sister Gladys holding Brenda (a little girl of about five) and my other sister Audrey. 'Gladys had red hair, you know, not ginger but golden. She died young, at twenty-six. He husband died young as well.' There was a coloured photo on the coffee table of a woman in a turquoise suit, in her fifties or sixties standing beside a man. That's Brenda and her husband. They were at someone's wedding.

While we had been in the lounge I had heard voices in the kitchen and presumed Brian was trying to answer Paul's questions about who we were and what we were doing here. Kathleen went out to join them as they came in with a tray of teacups.

She continued through to the kitchen.

'Where are you going mother? It's all here.'

'I'm getting some cakey. Do you want cakey?'

Silly word 'cakey' but it's a word I use with Brian.

She brought in chocolate cake cut into slices and a plate of iced fancies.

We ate our cake and drank our tea making small talk like the strangers we were.

Paul asked us if we were watching the World Cup and we discussed the relative merits of the games between Switzerland and Ecuador, rubbish, and Portugal and Holland, a disgrace.

We spoke of holidays. The subject of French houses came up again and we talked about the French, taking mother to France in the seventies, staying in a Eurocamp in Royan then buying the house in Normandy, and the relative merits of travelling by ferry and by air.

Paul told Brian about trying to learn to play golf but being unsatisfied by his lack of progress, he had given it up. Brian talked to him about going to Firth Park grammar school and he realised Brian knew this about his past because his mother had told him. He was learning we had been a time or two before. I guess he wondered why he hadn't known about it. The two buses there and back and always having to wear your red cap were what he had hated.

John went to the local secondary modern and left school as soon as he could to go and work in the steel works. I mentioned they had both been firemen. 'Fire officers,' corrected mother.

Paul had joined the fire service a few years after leaving school, as he didn't enjoy his work in a laboratory and John had joined him shortly afterwards. Paul had loved the life and stayed on after retirement age to train others. John reached retirement age and then had an accident. 'I got blown up,' he announced and explained there had been an explosion at a fire. He indicated his right leg and said it was mostly titanium.

When he left school he decided he wasn't very bright as he had few qualifications and, just as I had, had come to higher education in his thirties. He undertook an Open University degree, which took him six years, and he gained a degree in chemistry.

'That was the end of it. I'd had enough after six years,' he said, 'although saying that, I'm doing another course.'

What in? French, of course, so he can speak to his French neighbours.

The subject of the photographs came up again. John had found the photo of his grandfather at the top of the stairs and chastised his mother for losing it.

'You're always tearing them up,' he chided. 'Whenever I come she's ripping them in half; there'll be none left soon.'

'Oh there's plenty. I only rip up the rubbish ones. I'm saving the best.'

She mentioned again the fact that her sister Gladys had died so young and that her husband had, too.

'Did he die of an illness?' I asked. She couldn't remember. John knew.

'His ship was torpedoed off Iceland in the war and although he survived and came home, he never recovered. His health was affected.'

'Oh yes, I'd forgotten,' said Kathleen looking puzzled. Looking again at the group photo on the mantel piece she named everyone again except Brenda. Who's that?

'It's Brenda, I said. 'Oh, yes. Such a shame to lose both your parents at such a young age. My mother brought Brenda up. She was hard work. We weren't allowed to smack her and my mother used to say, 'Somebody has to love her!' 'She laughed. 'She lives near Burton on Trent, you know.' I remembered.

'I can't remember where.'

'I don't know,' said John.

'Branston?' I offered.

'That's right,' she said.

When Kathleen identified her mother on the photo, Brian chimed in, 'That's Elsie James!' Both Brian and I must have seemed to know so much about the family of these brothers, retaining snippets of information that wouldn't be of any real importance to them, but were really significant to me and had been a piece of the jigsaw that was my search.

Kathleen spoke about names. Gladys was Gladys Mable and Audrey was Elsie and I'm Mary, you know.' We knew. 'Do you have another name?' Brian and I told her we didn't but we had given our boys second names. I told her what they were. 'You've got boys, too, have you? I've just the two boys. No girls.' Except me, I thought. 'Paul spoiled it by having a girl.' Paul smiled. 'Not spoiled it, he broke the mould. He named her Linsey. My father's mother was called Linsey.' Brian's grandmother was Lindsey Elizabeth. If we'd had a girl we'd have named her for her.

'My boys are just John and Paul. My rock. Paul's my rock.' Paul looked suitably embarrassed. 'And John for steadfastness and loyalty.' John looked away, eyebrows up.

'I had a favourite name for a girl,' she suddenly said, 'but I can't remember what it was.' Kathleen looked puzzled.

Could it have been Averill?' I asked.

'Yes, that'd right!' she exclaimed, amazed I should have known. It seemed inappropriate to tell her in front of her sons but alone I would have reminded her that I was Averill.

John and Paul spoke about their families. John has a son, Hugh who is twenty-three and Paul has two children, a son, Stephen, who is in his early twenties and a daughter, Linsey who is nineteen. She came into the house while we were talking, was introduced, said, 'Hello, Grandma', smiled hello at us and left. No one spoke up to say who we were. It would have been a mistake to do so. So I have two nephews and a niece who will never know I exist. How do you tell your children grandma transgressed as a young woman and had an illegitimate child? Oh, and by the way, here she is. Mmm, not good.

Paul regrets his marriage but agreed that without it he would not have his children.

We finished our tea, refused more chocolate cake and, when Kathleen offered more tea, John stood up to leave. Paul took his lead and got up, too. We have to go,' they said. John shook hands and went into the kitchen. Paul took hold of my hand, shook it and leaned down to kiss my cheek. He looked fondly at

147

me as I whispered that I didn't think his mother could remember who I was, but offered no comment.

When they had left, Brian and I said we must be on our way. 'You weren't coming for lunch, were you? Or tea? No? Oh, that's good, I haven't got anything ready.'

'We came for tea before and didn't want to put you to so much trouble.'

'It's never any trouble. Everyone who comes here gets the same treatment.' She grasped my hands as we stood in the kitchen and leant her body against mine. She looked up into my face and said, 'How do I know you? Where did we meet?' I put my arms around her and held her to me.

'I am your child,' I said slowly. 'I sent you a Christmas card and you phoned me.' Doubt peeled from her eyes. 'The card. You sent the Christmas card?' She kept hold of me.

Yes. And there was almost a year's search that to begin again to explain would be folly. She was forgetting.

'Do the boys know? Have you told them what happened?'

'No. It wasn't for us to tell them anything.'

'Why were they here just now?'

'You must have mentioned it,' I ventured.

'But how?'

'I sent you a little note. There were some photos in it. You showed them to your boys.'

'Where are they now? I hope I haven't lost them.'

'They'll be in here, probably. They have seen the photos and you told them they had a sister. The letter said I was coming today'

'At eleven o'clock!' she remembered. 'And I forgot, didn't I? I'd been looking forward to you coming but when Paul arrived we went off to see Bill.' She pondered for a moment. 'What shall I tell them? They'll ask who you are.'

'You can tell them I am their sister, if you like and what happened to you...'

'Yes, I'm ready to tell them now. They won't judge me...'

'They love you, they'll not criticise you. But you could wait and see what they ask you.'

I could see this idea appealed. 'If they want to know more, they'll ask you questions.'

'What shall I say about how I've got to know you?'

'Tell them about the Christmas card. Tell them you got the card and rang me and we came to see you in January.'

'Yes, that would be good. You see they know what a nosy person I am. It wouldn't be unusual for me to ring you.'

'Tell them about the card and that you rang me,' I repeated, holding her. 'Show them the photos, so they'll know. It'll be fine.'

Brian then told her that John had already spoken to him on the phone, the previous Saturday as he was curious who we were and Brian had told him a little of our search for her. He told her about the connection between where they had lived years ago and his own family and what a bizarre coincidence that had been as John remembered his cousins. The doorbell suddenly rang. Kathleen went to the door to be confronted by a lady with a clipboard conducting a survey about milk. Kathleen said she bought her milk from the supermarket when her sons took her shopping and wouldn't want to be tied to a pint a day. The lady asked her the name of the street. Kathleen told her the name of the street from her past that we had just been talking about. We corrected her and the lady went on her way.

'We must go,' we said, 'as we're going to Stannington to see Brian's mother for lunch.

'Yes you must go. I mustn't keep you.'

We gave her one last hug and she touched Brian's face briefly. 'Such a lovely face,' she said. We stepped out of the door and walked to the car. When I turned she had gone inside and the door was closed.

*

Would this be the last visit? I was eager to learn what had been said in the kitchen between the boys and Brian.

'We talked about football,' he said, 'small talk. This and that.'

'Is that all?' I was amazed. 'Didn't they ask you anything?'

'No. What you have to remember is that until last Saturday they hadn't got any idea who you were. John said he thought it was one of his mother's tales. He had never asked if he had a sister, it all came from her. I suppose she has been dropping hints for the last few months, ever since she got to know about you.

150

They are going to take some time to adjust to the facts. And their mother has become confused. She has deteriorated considerably since we first met her, hasn't she?'

I wondered whether our going to find her and meeting with her from out of the blue hadn't helped. It had certainly caused her a lot of anxiety. Did her boys resent that? And John had said we were about eighteen months too late as far as meeting with the sparky, lucid person his mother had been then.

I felt unhappy she had received the original letter from Sue, the social worker in Sheffield, all alone with no one to support her. Yet if she hadn't been alone the time wouldn't have been right for her. If she hadn't been alone she might have ignored the letter afraid of what it might do to their relationship if she had to talk to Bill about it.

She had been brave to pick up the phone to talk to Sue on two occasions and through that I had learned so much of my past. She had been brave enough to phone me, with no support from anyone else, when she received the Christmas card and on the two occasions I wrote asking her if it would be all right to visit.

Each time I have learned more about myself. But, perhaps, each time, this has taken its toll on her health and made her more confused. It's a lot for an elderly lady to take on by herself. I hope I haven't interfered too much in her family. Her sons are good boys and look after her very well. I can only wonder what they will ask her, if anything, about her former life in the war. They may not be curious. They may think asking questions gives them information they would prefer not to have. She is their mother. They may not need a sister in their lives. They may not wish to be burdened with an extra person who is interfering in their mother's life. Kathleen and Sigmund are a closed chapter in their mother's life. Kathleen and Bill are their only concern.

*

There may not be a fourth meeting for me. I will have to be satisfied with what I have learned. But nevertheless, I have met Kathleen. I have got to know her a little and something of her life. I know things about my conception, and my very early life in Kathleen's care, things which were only a fantasy until a year ago. I know I look something like her.

People who are secure in their family likenesses and who understand their lineage often take those things for granted. Those who are not so fortunate seek to discover these things about themselves. My journey, although it has taken me quite some time has been positive and rewarding even though it is tinged with sadness. We all have this basic need to know about ourselves, to achieve an identity and in this I feel that so far I have achieved some success and satisfaction.

Part 4

Family Matters

Chapter 9

Cousin Brenda

Today, some weeks after my meeting with half brothers, John and Paul, I received a letter in an envelope addressed to 'Margaret'. No surname but the correct address. The handwriting was in neat, carefully formed letters. The writer said that Kathleen Newcombe, her aunt, had given her my name and address and that she was the daughter of Kathleen's late sister. She'd just signed it Brenda.

'I hope you don't mind me writing to you,' she writes. Mind? I was thrilled.

'If you would like to get in touch with me my phone number is above.' I began to wonder:

Supposing she doesn't know about what happened in the war. Supposing she hasn't been in contact with the brothers. I waited twenty-four hours and then I phoned the number on the letter. I introduced myself then waited.

'We're cousins,' said Brenda, 'we share a grandmother.'

'Elsie James,' I said. She said she had been to her uncle's funeral and there had met up with Paul and John who had drawn her on one side to tell her that it appeared their mother had had 'a bit of a fling' in the war and there was another child who had recently turned up.

As she told, I recalled Kathleen's sister Gladys had died when she was only twenty-six and

155

two years earlier her father had died, so at seven Brenda had become an orphan. Brenda was the woman in the turquoise suit in the photograph of someone's wedding. I told her I had seen her photograph. She told me it had been taken at her daughter's wedding. 'I hated that turquoise suit,' she said.

She went on to tell me Kathleen had phoned her recently and spoken to her about me saying enough to make Brenda wonder about the truth of having another cousin but as her aunt was becoming more confused these days she dismissed it as one of her tales.

And then came the funeral. As she talked I began to wonder. Was the funeral her Uncle Sidney's? Audrey, Kathleen's recently deceased sister, had a husband who was still alive. I asked Brenda whose funeral she was talking about.

'Uncle Bill's,' she said.

I felt a physical wave of shock wash over me as if I'd been hit. Bill had died only three weeks previously. Kathleen had lost her courageous husband of sixty-four years. I felt bereft for a man I had never met. Well, at least not within my memory.

I commiserated with Brenda. She was very sad, as he had meant a lot to her, as has her Auntie Kathleen. At the funeral John had confirmed that the story his mother had told her was far from a tale but the truth and indeed I existed and lived near Burton only seven miles from her home. His mother, he told her, had had 'a bit of a fling' in the war, had a baby and then had it adopted. He told her both he and his brother had met me.

156

When she came home from the funeral, she and her husband came to see where I lived and then she decided to write to me. She was overjoyed to know she had a female cousin. She is the eldest offspring of the three James sisters: John, my half-brother followed, then another cousin, Christopher, son of Audrey and Sidney, and finally, Paul. Suddenly, now, after sixty years, here is another girl.

I arranged to see her the following afternoon and went for a cup of tea. She lives, with her husband Al, in a Victorian villa with an imposing hallway.

*

We don't look alike. She is shorter than I am and at sixty-five a bit greyer although her hair is dark. We looked each other over in her hallway as I shook her hand. Shelves and furniture in the hall contained numerous photographs in antique frames of the James family. And there on their various wedding days, were all the James sisters. Brenda was eager to talk about her childhood and I learned she had lived in the house at Middlewood with the rest of the family until the early 1950s when she went with her grandmother (our grandmother, she insisted) to live in Totley. Later, when Kathleen and Bill had moved to the prefab in Handsworth, the prefab next door had become vacant and Brenda and her grandmother moved in there. She did not recall Brian's cousin or the police inspector who had Been Brian's Uncle Jack but felt assured her cousins would have.

'What did John say to you about how he had received the news from his mother about what had happened to her?' I asked Brenda.

157

'Tut, tut!'

'Tut, tut?'

'Yes. Tut, tut, mother, he said apparently.'

'It doesn't sound as if he took it too badly, does it?' I smiled.

There were several albums of family photos many of which were of Brenda on family holidays with Kathleen's family and grandmother (your grandmother, too!) Elsie James. Some of the photos were replicated and I was delighted when she gave me a small photo of Elsie James dressed magnificently in a gown and hat of the 1920s and a posed one of Kathleen holding baby John on her knee which would have been taken in 1947. The wedding photographs fascinated me and I borrowed all three to scan and copy and I later took them, with Brenda's encouragement to a photographer in Burton to have them copied professionally. I also borrowed a colour photo of Kathleen, Audrey and Sidney, who I learned was known as Uncle Sid, taken presumably by Bill in a park in Derbyshire. Both sisters are wearing fuchsia jackets and look strikingly similar. Kathleen looks very much as she does now although the photo is probably ten years old. While we were looking at the photographs I told her the story of how I found Kathleen. She was very interested and realised she was the first person in her family who knew the full story of my search and my need to do it. I felt she understood me.

I shared the photographs of my family I had taken to show Brenda and she saw Brian and me at Robert's wedding in Scotland, and he and Nick there too. These photos were in profile and I explained how

I had included these when I sent photos to the social worker in Sheffield in the hope Kathleen would see them and want to see more. I showed her my passport photo at twenty and she scrutinised it to see family likenesses. She concluded I looked like Kathleen as a younger woman. She could discern a family resemblance.

20th September 2006 – Diary entry

Brenda and Al came to visit us. She brought some more photographs for us to look at and as we talked about these she produced a political leaflet with Kathleen's photograph on it. She looked dependable, attractive and eager as her face shone out above the text of the leaflet. She would have been forty. In 1963 she and Bill had decided to stand as candidates in the local municipal elections for the Liberal party in Sheffield's staunchly Labour Attercliffe ward, which has been the domain of David Blunkett for many years. She put herself forward as a Liberal candidate urging voters to vote for her if they wanted to make Sheffield, especially Attercliffe a better place to live. She describes herself as housewife and mother supporting the Liberal party's 'wonderful policy' of 'PEOPLE COUNT' and the party as a classless party where everyone was considered. Her main interest, she says, lies in the social welfare of the Attercliffe people. The address given is that of the prefab in Handsworth. In the middle pages of the leaflet are set out the policies of the Liberal party with ideas for improvements in transport, redevelopment of the city and education. Neither she nor Bill was successful, Brenda said, which wasn't surprising given the years of socialist tradition of the city and the ward.

Brenda spoke again about her Uncle Bill's funeral and the conversation she'd had with John and Paul. It hadn't been the right moment to talk to her Auntie Kathleen about her wartime escapades, her 'bit of a fling' but her intention was to go to Sheffield and bring it into the conversation. She didn't intend to mention to Kathleen that we had met. What she wanted to do was to gently get her to talk about her past life and as part of the conversation ask her if she could remember Sigmund's surname.

Having that information could be the start of another adventure. But more likely not. The chance of her remembering the name was very limited, in my view.

Brenda went on to tell us about Paul. When she had been at the funeral John had mentioned that Paul was not well. I recalled he had described to us, when we met him at Kathleen's, that he was becoming forgetful. Unable to tell her fully under the circumstances, John had telephoned Brenda later to explain Paul had been diagnosed with a progressive type of dementia in which sufferers experience frequent lapses in attention and drowsiness. They can become lethargic and stare into space for long periods. They can also have hallucinations and experience the motor problems that sufferers of Parkinson's disease have. Immediately it was diagnosed, doctors advised Paul that he should give up driving his car. This diagnosis has come as a huge shock to his family. Kathleen is as yet unaware of the

160

seriousness of it. The prognosis is poor as there is no
cure.

Adopted children, when asked by doctors
about their family medical history cannot answer any
questions. There is always a risk in tracing birth
parents that they could have died of some dreadful
disease. I suddenly find there is a worrying trend of
dementia in my background.

*

I discussed this trend with my cousin, Margery. She came to stay a short while after my meeting with Brenda and has been interested in my search. I have never attempted to conceal this from her, not in the way I kept things from my mother and haven't felt she would feel threatened by what I wanted to do. In fact she has never been anything other than supportive. Her strong belief is that we are who we are not by an accident of birth but through our upbringing and she knows that mine was good and happy, creating a confident and enthusiastic adult. She has known for several months what I have been doing and was eager to know the latest events. I told her of my meeting with the half-brothers and mentioned my contact with Brenda. Then, I needed to ask her what she thought about Paul's diagnosis of dementia.

I wanted to ask how, Margery, a cousin through adoption of sixty years views my discovery of another cousin who is a blood relative. This is what was in my mind but I didn't need to ask it directly as she and I know that the strength of our relationship means that I won't suddenly drop the relations I have had all my life in favour of a new set, newly discovered. She speaks with her brother, Les, every Saturday on the telephone when he rings from Canada and they said only recently, after the death of Fred, that they never see me as an adopted relative. Happily, I'm just one of them.

On the issue of dementia, I asked Margery whether she was ever worried by the fact that her mother, my auntie Daisy, died of Parkinson's disease. She looked surprised and told me that she wasn't. She doesn't think about it. She is more concerned that she has high blood pressure that her doctor is struggling to regulate and that Les, too, suffers with the same thing. Their father had the same problem. Blood pressure is one of those things that can run in families. She thinks there is no evidence that Parkinson's disease is the same, so what's the point in worrying about that. The dementia in Kathleen's family seems to run through the male line considering the circumstances of Bill's death. Kathleen is becoming confused, as many older people do and reminds me of how my mother became in old age but her forgetfulness doesn't seem to me to be an illness. I hope I'm right.

*

My memories of my aunt's Parkinson's disease are about mistakes. She came with Margery and Fred to lunch once sometime after we moved to Nottingham. I served peas. I couldn't imagine at the time I planned the meal how difficult this would be to someone whose hands trembled and whose motor skills were impeded. I watched with horror as she tried to negotiate the peas on to her fork. Margery doesn't remember this. What she does remember is

162

how kind four-year-old Nick had been to his great aunt when she had wanted to go to the toilet, which was down two steps off the hall, and he had held her arm to make sure she was safe.

*

On our next visit to Brenda's house we learned that she had found out some information about Sigmund. She had spoken to Kathleen on the phone and, as she had intimated when last we met, she didn't mention that we were acquainted. However, after only a few moments conversation steering Kathleen onto the topic of her 'bit of a fling', she not only mentioned the name Sigmund but his last name, too. Roseac. Or something similar. The problem with foreign names is either one of spelling or pronunciation. Brian has been reading *Poland* by James Michener and feels that the spelling of Sigmund will be Zygmunt and then Roseac could be Rosiac or Rosiak. I tried rolling the names around in my mouth and they sounded very romantic but that's just the fantasy. I now need to consider what I want to do with the information. Possibly for now, nothing, but, I wrote things down in my little notebook. From information gleaned by Brenda from Kathleen I also wrote that he was of average height and not too dark. Could this be my father she's remembering? Am I their child? Where am I getting my height and my dark eyes from then? It's still a mystery.

As well as speaking to Kathleen, Brenda had recently been speaking to John. She casually speculated to me about whether or not he would maintain a relationship with me. Was she expecting me to be upset by this? I didn't feel it. I wouldn't necessarily want to be associated with me if I were him: a new sister out of the blue, unannounced, uninvited, interrupting my relationship with my mother. Instant sisters could be troublesome.

Finally, Kathleen had told Brenda that Zygmunt had been about three years older than her. This would make his birth date 1920. I wondered if this would be enough to trace him if I wrote to the Polish Club in Nottingham.

We arranged to make contact again when I had managed to get the photographs copied or if Brenda talked again to Kathleen and there was more to tell. I am grateful to Brenda for her 'detective work' because she has found more about Zygmunt for me and acted as a spur for me to make a decision.

Chapter 10

A Merry Christmas

Before setting off for France once more in November, Brian and I arranged to call on my friend, Mary, who lives in Alresford, in Hampshire, a short stop off the M3, to have an evening meal on our way to the late night ferry from Portsmouth. We were also looking forward to seeing Pam and Alan, the friends who had done so much to help us trace Kathleen through their interest in genealogy. Both Pam and Mary were now retired. Pam's birthday was in December 2005 and Mary's in August 2006. Pam retired shortly before my sixtieth birthday and Mary in the July before hers. All our work together on the national educational project for work related learning for fourteen to nineteen-year-olds was behind us and all three of us were finding no difficulty in filling our time in retirement enjoyably without a backward glance or regret.

Over dinner we discussed the possibility of Sigmund's name being more likely Zygmunt as I told them that Brenda had given me his last name. Pam asked me what it was and said she would find out from her mother's carers what a likely spelling could be. Her mother, who has had a stroke, is being looked after by carers who are Polish. She asked me to e-mail her with the details when we got to France and this I did.

Pam also included some interesting website addresses where information on Polish fighter pilots can be found and we spent some time looking at these.

No Zygmunt Roseac was listed. One particular site gave us some information how the Poles escaped Poland at the start of the World War II and joined the RAF.

*

Life for the Poles was grim in 1939 since the defeat of Poland and its occupation by the Nazis. Records show that, following defeat, significant numbers of Polish airmen, managed to escape by various routes to continue the fight in exile. The Underground Movement moved small groups during the first few months of the war and was instrumental in assisting individuals. From October to December 1939 there was a mass movement of volunteers and an evacuation of military personnel for re-enlistment from countries such as Romania and Hungary who were allied with Poland at the start of the war.

The decision to evacuate was based on the notion that both France and Britain would need help. The evacuation was meticulously planned. Whilst Germany was putting pressure on Hungary and Romania to keep the Poles interned in camps nearly all those held in the camps managed to escape thanks to the people of those countries who provided civilian clothing, visas and passports. Ninety thousand personnel were moved from Rumania under the noses of the Gestapo.

The Poles wanted to re-establish their air force in Britain, as RAF equipment was superior to that of the French and they had been given some training on British-made equipment. France suggested they should be divided and then incorporated into their armed services for a quicker reinforcement. Britain took three hundred pilots and 2000 technical support staff whilst the remainder would be moved to front-line defence positions in France.

Most escapees were directed to Constanza, Balic or Efori on the Black Sea then via Syria or Malta and then on to France. Others escaped via Split in Yugoslavia and then by ship to France. Some were directed to Piraeus in Greece. Others came on foot via Yugoslavia through northern Italy and then on to France. The programme of evacuation was reasonably orderly despite the frustrations of the internees and anger at the collapse of Poland. The Yugoslavs, Greeks and Italians in particular assisted in the evacuation and the crossing of borders. There were many other escape routes across Europe some more successful than others but if or until I learn more about Zygmunt then I shall never know how he came to be in Hucknall in Nottingham in 1945.

Further news from Pam: she emailed again with details of a footballer who plays football for Southampton. His name: Grzegorz Raziak. Could this be a grandson, she asks? What did she want me to do: write to this young man and ask him if he had a grandfather, Zygmunt who was in Nottingham during the Second World War and had a relationship with an English woman? No fear. I need to do some searching of my own. But where to start? Pam would help if she had some more information but only Kathleen could supply this and that would mean revealing my hand. I'm back at the 'let's do nothing stage.'

*

167

<u>23rd December 2006 – Diary entry</u>

Brian's mum and my cousin Margery are our Christmas guests. We will be seeing Joseph, who is seven now, on Christmas morning to see what Santa Clause has brought. Nick will already be there having arrived at some unearthly hour in the hope of watching his son open his presents from under the Christmas tree. We will have coffee or a drink and mince pies, see Joe's presents, give him ours and exchange gifts with Diane and her husband. Nick will go home later and we will see him and Debbie and Aimee on Boxing Day when Rob, Lisa and Jack will drive down to us from Scotland, their hotel having been open for Christmas Day lunch: forty-one expected this year.

*

I was at home on Christmas Eve. Earlier in the day I had glazed and baked a piece of gammon, having boiled it on Saturday, according to a Nigella Lawson recipe I'd watched being demonstrated on BBC 2 a couple of weeks ago. It went well for lunch, despite the fact that Brian said it looked more like pork loin although I told him that would be because I'd boiled it, in part, in red wine. I later found the ham joint in the cool box when I went looking for the pork loin on Boxing Day. We'd had Joseph to stay overnight and when his mum came to collect him we'd invited her and Joe to stay and eat this with us. Not too easy. Diane is a vegetarian. But she enjoyed the vegetables I had prepared and substituted cheese for the glazed ham. Tea would be a small meal as we had filled up at lunch. Mum, Margery, Brian and I

168

were in the kitchen contemplating how little we all needed to eat when the phone rang. I picked it up.

'Hello?'

'Margaret?'

'Yes,' cautiously, as I almost recognised the voice.

'It's John.'

'Hi, how are you!' loudly, jolly, welcoming. Amazed. Needing time to gather myself.

He was well. He was looking forward to Christmas. He was ringing because he had been thinking he should ring for some time now and had picked up the phone on several occasions and just not been able to make the call. Wuss. Exactly like me. Sometimes no one had been in – shopping in Burton, holidaying in France, visiting in Scotland? And he had put down the phone.

'But here you are now.'

'Yes.'

He said he had been asking his mother if she had heard from me again. At first she hadn't remembered who I was but then with prompting from him had been able to say, no, she hadn't heard. So that was one reason he was ringing. He was making it sound as if he was doing it for his mother's sake but I felt he wanted to make contact for himself.

'When we met, Brian told me that you didn't want to be overwhelmed by a new set of relatives so I have held off making any further contact. But at this time of year it just seems the right thing to do.'

I thought about this for a moment and was fairly non-committal. I think there has been a slight misunderstanding as Brian's motive was to protect

Kathleen and to reassure the brothers that we weren't a threat to them and their existence.

'But I'm very pleased you have.'

'Are you?'

'Yes.'

'Why?'

'Well, I thought because you had just gone away on that day we met, that you didn't want anything to do with me again.' No mention here about the fact that Brenda had said as much.

He told me his father had died.

'Yes, I know,' I said.

'How do you know?' he asked. Oops. Now I would have to mention Brenda.

'Your cousin Brenda wrote to me and told me.' Not quite accurate but I didn't want to go into details about this contact at this point. He laughed, snorting down his nose.

'We were really sorry to hear about your father, though. I hope it hasn't been too difficult.'

It hadn't but he had had to deal with everything, as Paul hadn't been too well. I said nothing about his illness. Too much information on my part. I mentioned that I remembered he had been forgetting things, as that is what John had told me himself. It was proving difficult, as John had to take responsibility for both his mother and his brother.

We turned to small talk. John was going to France for the New Year again. He had told us when we met that he had been there last year in the really cold weather.

'We're looking forward to it as we've a wood burner and we light it and batten down the hatches.'

170

'Sounds like fun.' I meant this, as it's what we do.

*

A year last February we had experienced six inches of snow on a day when we were expecting six friends to dinner. They won't come, they'll not get through this, we said, but continued to stoke up the wood burner, light the gas fires and prepare the food for the evening. Banging their shoes on the front door step as they stumbled into the room, bringing in the cold air and snow on the shoulders of their coats, everyone arrived on time. One couple had a 4X4 so wondered why we should even doubt their arrival, another told us the snow was worse at our house than theirs and the last swaddled in waterproofs and scarves and wearing hiking boots had walked down the road. What was our problem? We had an entertaining evening but wondered whether we would be able to set off for the ferry home in the morning. We drove away from the house with trepidation and after fifteen minutes driving, all downhill into the nearest town there was hardly any snow left. It had all been at our front door.

*

'Our son Hugh is coming.' He also mentioned a child so I wondered whether he had a girlfriend with a child of her own as I hadn't heard Kathleen talk about being a great-grandmother. But I let him go on talking. He said they would be back on the 7th January.

'How would it be then that we could get together with Kathleen when you came back? I'm

171

assuming you make the arrangements for your mother.'

'Oh, yes. She doesn't go far these days. They've changed her medication now, you know.'

'Oh, yes?' Did I know? Had Brenda mentioned it?

'She's much better now. She's much more like her old self. A lot clearer in her thinking. It was while she was on her old stuff she tore up most of the photographs. We've nothing left of my dad.'

I pictured her sitting at the top of the stairs ripping photos up and her delight in finding face down the one of her father but John needed photos of his own father. He needed a memento now Bill was dead.

'There were some of him in his younger days but I would have liked one of him about ten years ago before he became ill so I can remember him when he was fit.'

'It's a shame,' I consoled him. 'Photos are irreplaceable. Well, shall we meet when you come home from France?'

'Yes.'

'At Kathleen's house?'

'Yes, all right. Why don't you give me a ring after the 7th January when we'll be home?'

I agreed to do that provided he sorted the arrangements out with Kathleen.

'Merry Christmas, then,' I said.

'Oh, yes. Thanks. And to you,' said my brother.

We hung up.

'Well,' said Brian turning from making a cup of tea.

'Well, how about that?' 'Y

'You sounded very chatty.'

'It was chatty,' and I attempted to recall what John had said. The difficulty for me was wondering whether to reveal our meetings with Brenda. We decided to contact John soon after the 7th January. In the meantime we could decide what to tell Kathleen and John when we saw them.

Chapter 11

A Surname Revealed

We were looking forward to seeing Kathleen again and were pleased to see John's car parked outside his mother' house. She greeted us at the door and was obviously delighted to see us. John was on tea making duties. He had phoned twice since his return from France making sure we were all right with the visit, telling us his mother was aware we were going and had taken very little prompting about who I was. Later a further call to say she preferred it that he was to be there. Paul wouldn't be there as he had his own problems. I didn't say we knew anything about that.

I walked into the sitting room while Kathleen greeted Brian. The first thing I noticed was a photograph frame on the wall unit where my Christmas card had stood on our first visit just over a year ago. The frame wasn't unfamiliar but the photo in it was even more familiar. It was of me. The one I had sent her of my sixtieth birthday. I stood up to examine it feeling inordinately pleased and not a little touched.

'It doesn't always live there,' she said as she came into the room with tea and saw me looking. 'It's just for this special occasion.'

We spent quite some time talking separately, Kathleen and I talking together and John and Brian. Kathleen talked about having boys. She asked if I had boys then remembered I had before I had time to reply. Boys were best she concluded. She didn't really want a girl.

'But you had one, didn't you?'

'Oh, yes but I didn't bring you up did I?' She went over the names of ours and we talked about how hers didn't have middle names but ours did.

She talked about Bill but couldn't remember how long it was since he died. I said we were sorry to learn of his death.

'He's sleeping you know,' she said wistfully. 'He died of pneumonia. They put him by that open window with the door open. They shouldn't have done that. But I suppose it wasn't really that that did it.' She considered the implications of dying of pneumonia and draughts for a moment, part of her torn to find a reason for his death and the rest knowing draughts weren't really the cause of the illness. She returned to this theme a time or two during our visit and each time assuring us, or herself, that he was sleeping.

Brian and John talked about Bill, too, but then John told Brian that it hadn't been his idea that he made that first phone call in June, but Paul's. He would have left things alone but Paul thought it would be wrong for his mother if they just ignored my existence. The phone call on Christmas Eve had been at the prompting of his wife, who is called Lynn. It was she who had speculated we hadn't made any further contact because the brothers had just left at the end of that first meeting and no more had been done. Perhaps we were thinking they or Kathleen wanted no more to do with us. Lynn wasn't there to have a cup of tea with us as, although retired, she still worked part-time some days and this was one of them. May be she would be there another time. John leaned across, interrupting Kathleen at one point, and asked me whether I had known that his mother had come looking for me.

I did but he told me what his mother had told him.

'Twenty Darklands Road wasn't it?' he asked. I nodded. 'My granddad's buried in the cemetery at the top of that road and she persuaded my dad to take her to see the grave. It was all a pretext really because she wanted to see you.'

Kathleen took up the tale. 'I wanted to see you. I must have told Bill something and went off by myself for a walk. I saw the two little girls who said did I want them to tell your mother I was asking for you. I remember there was a pram.'

I was a bit old for a pram by this time as I was four-years old.

'A dolls' pram,' she explained, 'and you were pushing a pram with another little girl.'

That would be my pal Alison and me. We pushed our prams with our dollies in them everywhere. John smiled.

'You would have been born by then,' I told him. 'And Paul, too.'

'Well, yes, but she came looking.' She is sharing her memories of that time with her son.

*

Alison had been my best friend. Only children yearn to have best friends and Alison was mine. She was nine months older. She had the good fortune to be the youngest of three children having a grown up brother and sister, and a baby nephew. I seem to

176

remember that her father had been in Burma during the war but Alison's birthday was the 14th August, somewhere around VJ Day. Perhaps the Burma memory is wrong. However, she and I were inseparable in our pre-school years.

We played all day making up plays to perform to our parents and putting on dancing shows in her garden, which had a natural 'stage' in a grassy stepped area. We bought net with our pocket money to make the tutus and practised to my Swan Lake records. We played at horses in my garden by getting out boxes from the shed and placing them all around as jumps. Neither of us could ride but we knew all the correct neighs to make, how to hold the imaginary reins and how to kick our legs like ponies. We pushed our prams around the pavements and along the road, a cul-de-sac, tucking in our doll-babies and soothing them when they cried. Older, we rode our bicycles up and down the road and to the shops to buy sweets. I went on holiday with her family to stay in a caravan in Abersoch in Wales. I don't recall if she came on holiday with my family and me.

It was she who taught me about shoplifting. We would stand very close to the children's penny delights in Waller's news agency and she dared me to take something. Terrified I lifted a penny bubble-gum and a yellow sherbet saucer. She derided me that I had taken so little but I gave them to her, as I couldn't bear the thought of eating what I had taken without paying. I didn't do it again.

Alison went to school before I did as her birthday fell in the year ahead of mine. Our relationship changed. She made new friends and

177

brought them home to play. Eager to meet her new friends I went over the road to play when I saw them come but they made fun of me as I hadn't started school and didn't know the ropes. Gillian was her new best friend now. Gillian lived on a road around the corner from ours. Her garden was long and had a shed at the end of it. We all three played in there once after school until a sudden change took place that I hadn't spotted. They went out through the door and locked it behind them. I knocked loudly and asked to be let out. No reply. Perhaps some distant giggling but I could have imagined that. I shouted loudly to be let out and banged on the door. No reply. I cried. No effect.

An eternity went by. I threatened to break down the door with some garden implement and knocked hard on the door with it. The door opened. They let me out. I ran home. I didn't play again. Eventually I was old enough to go to school myself but Alison and her friends gathered in a circle and mocked me.

'What's your name?'

'Margaret Kay.'

'Margaret Kay? Piece of cake!' The group took up the chant all together. 'Piece of cake! Piece of cake!

I realised I could ignore it, fortunately. Ever the pacifist, I walked away and found new friends of my own.

*

Kathleen had two photograph albums beside the settee where she was sitting and she reached for them. Together we looked through them. They contained some of the wedding photographs Brenda had loaned me but I didn't say I had seen them there. There were many of holidays abroad with Bill. She was confused about where they were but the backgrounds of palm trees and beaches suggested Spain.

'She's always been looking at photos when I call. Let's hope she doesn't go tearing any of these up.' Kathleen looked sheepishly at him and we continued to turn the pages.

When John and Lynn had been in France over New Year their son Hugh had been with them and taken his girlfriend who does indeed have a child of her own. That cleared up that little mystery.

John left shortly afterwards and I felt able to ask Kathleen about Zygmunt.

'Tell me about him,' I prompted.

'When I close my eyes I can picture him clearly,' and she reiterated the story of the cinema queue and the offer from the sisters of being able to stay when Bill was on leave, whilst still continuing to visit these girls when he had been posted and was no longer stationed in Nottingham. She had no further recollections about Zygmunt, though. I asked her if she knew how he had come to Nottingham, whether it was before the war or during it. She didn't know. Perhaps he had never talked about these things. I should have asked her if she knew his rank. I could do this some other time, I think. What had surprised me though, was at the mention of his name she had said, 'Zygmunt Roziak.' No hesitation. None of the firm censure that we had heard before:

'You're not getting to know his other name. I don't want you tracing him. Anyway he'll be dead.'

Brian asked her what she thought about the fact that we had found her. Her face lit up. There was no doubt we had done the right thing. 'I'm delighted.' And she took hold of my hand and squeezed it.

She asked us to tell her how we had found her. We told the tale again and included the detail about Sue Tomlinson, the Sheffield social worker. This time she remembered her. She remembered making the phone call to her and where she'd put the initial letter. 'It's upstairs in a book,' pointing to the ceiling. This is what Sue had told us nearly two years earlier. Her tablets are certainly bringing clarity of mind that we hadn't seen before.

I wanted to know, too, how she had handed me over to the adoption agency in 1946. I wanted to learn how she knew what she did about Darklands Road and about Mr and Mrs Kay and how it could be that my father knew about her and about Zygmunt's nationality. It was a mystery to her, too, though, as all she could remember was that the offices had been at the top of Norfolk Street. She had no recollection of the process she had undergone to have me adopted or how she and Bill travelled with me from Leicester and into Sheffield town centre. She remembered Bill had handed me over, but as hard as she tried other memories would not come.

When I left Kathleen I told her I would be going away on holiday in March and that I would be in contact when I came home early in April.

*

Two evenings later I decided to write to the Polish Catholic Club in Nottingham. I knew that it existed as I had worked close to the building when I was in Nottingham. I asked directory enquiries for the address and wrote to them asking if they were able to help in tracing Polish Air Force personnel stationed in Hucknall during World War ll.

I never received a reply from my letter. Whilst we were on holiday in Orlando staying with friends we ran another search on the Internet and came up with the same sites about Polish Air Force squadrons during the war and also an e-mail address of someone who has a record of personnel from Poland who died in the war. I e-mailed him and a reply came straight back that he had no record of anyone of that name who had died in WW11 so he said I must assume that Zygmunt had survived the war. I knew this, of course, but it was worth probing further.

What do I want from this search? To know he existed, I think. To find out something about him, if records exist and, guided by Pam's earlier Internet search, see if there is a photograph of him from the war years. Will I show this to Kathleen if it does? I'd ask her if she wanted to see it. I think Pam will be unlucky. 'When is our trip to Poland?' Pam asked in a note in her Christmas card. She loves to travel as we do, but dream on, Pam.

*

March10th 2007 – Diary entry

We have been staying, first of all, in Canada with my cousins. Les, Margery's brother, with his

181

wife Audrey, went to live in Canada in the early 1950s. They have two sons who have five children between them and the eldest has three stepchildren as well so there are plenty of grandchildren for Audrey and Les to enjoy. They all live in easy distance from Burlington, a small town on Lake Ontario, and, despite the freezing cold weather in March, we managed to see most of them. I am their family. They are mine.

Apart from quality family time we managed to see Niagara Falls again but this time in the winter. Much of it was frozen, particularly on the American side and what appeared to be huge lumps of meringue with a soft dusting of icing sugar lay below the falls. Long icicles clung to the side of the rock as water, usually deafening like thunder, trickled down the side. A spectacular site in any weather.

Whilst we were staying with Audrey and Les I took time to tell them about my search for Kathleen. I was aware they knew something about it as Margery had been keeping them up to date in their weekly telephone calls. They were fascinated, very supportive and understood my need to find my natural mother. Les said as Margery had earlier to me that they never saw me as an adopted child only that I was the child of their aunt and uncle and therefore their cousin.

We flew from Canada to Florida, leaving behind minus temperatures in Toronto to arrive in warmth in the high seventies. We had travelled to the airport in coats and scarves and needed shorts and tee shirts in Orlando but as we had four suit cases to negotiate and two carry-on pieces of luggage we had to wear the cold weather gear.

We stayed with friends at their holiday house near the Disney parks. We managed to visit Sea World seeing dolphins and killer whales performing, and had a day out with them at the Kennedy Space Center. *(I bought tee-shirts for the boys there as a souvenir which had printed on them: 'I used to be an astronaut but I got fired for moonlighting' which still makes me smile when I see them wearing them.)*

I told our friends, too, about what had been happening to me. Because they spend six months of the year in Florida, I had not spoken to them before about my search. They were very interested and pressed me to tell them how I had felt when I first talked to Kathleen on the phone and then when I met her at the gate to her house. They were fascinated about the number of coincidences that had occurred in the search.

After ten delightful days we hired a car and drove further south to a resort called Venice Beach. We stayed in a hotel where our neighbours were staying and enjoyed five lovely days with them. We left Orlando airport at the end of our trip arriving in Montreal for a one night stop-over, in freezing temperatures once more and were able to see the old town and port. We enjoyed it that they spoke French, not English, and practiced ours with waiters and shop assistants but didn't enjoy being out and about in sleet at minus three degrees.

*

Once home, I phoned Kathleen as I had promised when we were together in January, on several occasions. There was no reply so I phoned

John to see if she was staying with him. There was no reply from him and I wondered if he had taken Kathleen to France for Easter. Brian's mum and Margery came to stay for a few days and also Jack, our four-year-old grandson. We returned mum and Margery then drove to Scotland to take Jack home and stayed with Rob & Lisa for four days in the hotel. It was family time and we enjoyed it especially as Jack had a new puppy and was excited to see her again.

Chapter 12

Mother's in Hospital

When we returned there was not much left of April, the warmest since records began in the 1600s, and I rang Kathleen again. No one picked up so I rang John's number. He answered and was pleased to hear from me. No he hadn't taken his mother away. He and his wife had been away in the Lake District for the weekend but the reason his mother had not answered my calls was that she was in hospital.

We talked for an hour but his news was disturbing. Kathleen had been hearing voices. He had gone to see her and tried to persuade her it was all nonsense but she had persisted. Eventually after she had phoned him in the middle of one night he went round. Following some lengthy discussion about the existence or not of these voices he allowed her to put on her dressing gown and slippers and go down the road in pursuit of the voices, whilst he drove slowly after her. She made two trips down the road and back to her house before he insisted she came in but she grew awkward and aggressive and would not go inside the house. The time was after two am and she was creating a noise in the road so in desperation he bundled her into his car and took her to the accident and emergency department of the Northern General Hospital to ask for help. They were sympathetic and admitted her at once.

They ran tests and found that she had a small ulcer in her stomach and that her haemoglobin levels were not as high as they should be. They tried for a few days to regulate this and in the meantime the hospital, or perhaps Kathleen, managed to lose her teeth. It was disconcerting for John to see his mother without her teeth. He never had and she talked to him at visiting time with her hand over her mouth. She confessed to him that in all her married life to his father he had seen her without her teeth only twice. He guessed that in sixty-four years it would have been illness, which caused the two occasions. I explained that without teeth to support the facial muscles around the mouth everyone looked different from their real selves. Most people were unwilling to look at themselves in the mirror as they looked so unlike their usual image. He asked if I had any teeth like his mother. I laughed recalling previous conversations with Kathleen and told him that I too dreaded being without my teeth. I couldn't believe I was having this conversation with my half-brother. I never talked about my teeth with anyone except Brian and then only rarely. John had taken Kathleen to the hospital dentist to get new teeth and had been for two visits for impressions. He thought she had not been eating properly whilst she had no teeth, as she couldn't chew effectively. The day they were due to go for a final fitting, Kathleen had fainted on the ward.

This, they thought was due to the low haemoglobin levels. There is a correlation between not eating properly and low levels of red blood corpuscles. They gave her drugs to increase the level and monitored this carefully. The danger level is seven (Paul didn't know what this counted) and Kathleen's level had fallen to 7.3 and then 7.2. At seven a blood transfusion is advised. Kathleen is, of course a Jehovah's Witness so this would be out of the question although John had talked to his father about this several years before he died and they had decided that they would over-ride this if ever there were an issue in Kathleen's life that called for such a decision. It hadn't come to this as when she had the new teeth fitted and began to eat properly, the haemoglobin level rose to over eight. But the voices persisted.

As I listened to John talk about his mother's health I began to realise he was telling me this as much to let me know I had a medical history as to let me know about her health. The history of dementia was worrying. First there was Paul and now his mother. My mother. So long I had been in ignorance. Now a new truth is unsettling.

John asked me if I felt I had made the right decision in finding my mother. I had, I told him. He wanted to know more about how I had gone about finding her and what was on my birth certificate. I told him what I had attempted to tell Kathleen the night we met and told again the story she had told me about the connection with Nottingham. Kathleen still is in touch with Elaine Cooper, one of the daughters of the family in Bulwell, John said. As I began to tell him more and as he said he had things to tell me, I realised it would be better to tell him face to face. This was after all the story of his mother's wartime indiscretion and was perhaps difficult for him to come to terms with coming from me. We agreed to meet.

*

I woke on the following Wednesday feeling excited that I was going to meet John.

I've got brothers, you know,' I told Brian with a grin.

'You're pleased with that idea, aren't you?' he declared and I was. John had said his wife wouldn't be available to be there too as she was working. Brian had an early morning meeting on the Wednesday and it pleased me to be seeing John by myself.

When I arrived he was mowing the lawn. We went into the house and he put on the kettle. He seemed nervous as he busied himself in the kitchen. We made small talk about France at first and when he offered me a drink he said, 'Thé ou café?'

I smiled. 'Je voudrais une tasse de thé, s'il vous plait.'

'Uh oh,' he said.

'Je voudrais,' I explained. 'I would like.

'Right.' he said. I don't go anywhere without my French CDs, now. When I'm in the car...'

'...you play them as you drive,' I finished. He nodded.

'I've got them free from the Daily Mail,'

'Have you tried the Michel Thomas CDs?' I asked. He hadn't but he had heard of them.

'Someone else told me about them and said they were very good.'

We settled down to the tea and I asked about Kathleen but there had been no better news. John had told me that the staff at the hospital wanted to discharge her. The arrangements they, Paul and he, had made was for Linsey, Paul's daughter, to live at her grandmother's house for a while. Paul had bought a new flat screen television as he thought Linsey would need one whilst she was at her grandma's.

'He's spending his money like water at the moment,' he said. I looked blank. 'Well the prognosis for him isn't good.'

I knew it wasn't. I had been looking at the details I had downloaded from the Internet for dementia but I couldn't tell him about it, as I would have had to say it had been Brenda who had told me about this in the first place. I replied in a non-committal way and he went on to explain how Paul had been of late in the way he was forgetting things and how his motor skills had slowed. Shuffling is a symptom. His father, Bill, had died of this disease in July last year.

'But,' he went on, 'they have reassured us that it isn't hereditary. It's coincidence they have the same illness. The specialist John had been consulting regarding his father was now Paul's specialist and had told him he knew of only one other case where the disease occurred in the same family and that was a brother and sister.

This has led to the view that it is environmental.

'The only place I can think of that my dad and our Paul used to go that I didn't was the allotment. Could it be the water from the stream or something in the soil? We'll never know.' John said that Paul had taken up driving again.

'Is this a good sign?' I asked. 'Has he been able to get insurance?'

'Er, well. I did it for him on line as he isn't very good on the phone anymore.' He smiled ruefully. 'He'll be OK. He was an advanced driver.'

We talked for a while about France, learning French, our families, our interests and occasionally about our mother.

I find it so hard still to say that. He laughs each time I hesitate over it. It's different for him. He's only had one mother. I can lay claim to three if I count my mum-in-law who has been more like a mother to me since mine died and whom I call mum.

John mentioned the photographs Kathleen had been tearing up. Her excuse for doing this was that when she is dead that will be one less job for John to do but he repeatedly tells her that she is tearing up his memories. The family ones are precious although some of the photos are of views they, she and Bill, have taken whilst on their holidays and don't mean anything to anyone who wasn't there.

I had brought with me the file I had made about my tracing 'my mother' with the documents from my birth certificate with his mother's name on it and the address where her auntie Jessie had lived in Leicester – 'She's been to see my mother in hospital, you know,' he told me.' I looked amazed. 'But she'll be dead, surely.'

'Oh yes, but my mother told me she'd been,' he laughed. – to various bits of correspondence which eventually brought Stuart, the Nottingham social worker, to our house, to the letters I wrote to Sue, the Sheffield social worker, enclosing the five photographs and finally to the photographs I acquired through his cousin Brenda and had copied. It made quite a lot of information for him to take in and he asked me whether I thought it had been worth it.

'Oh, yes, without doubt,' I said without hesitation, smiling at him.

'Me, too,' he murmured.

I excused myself and went off to the bathroom but resisted the temptation to slip into the bedrooms and look around feeling this would be an intrusion. On my return to the kitchen I looked at my watch and found the time had sped onto one o'clock. Brian and I were picking up Joseph from school and we would need to be in Swadlincote for just after three o'clock.

'I need to be going,' I told him.

'Why don't you come with me?' he asked. 'It seems a shame to come all this way and not to see mum.'

He had a point but time was running out. 'OK,' I said, 'but I'll need to phone Brian as he will need to pick up Joseph,' and I explained the arrangements we had made.

We set off in his Vauxhall and as he turned on the ignition a voice said, 'Quelle heure est-il? Il est une heure.'

I laughed loudly. This is just so me. He turned it off after a while and drove to the Northern General finding, unusually a parking space straight away. We walked from the car into the old red brick Victorian building and climbed up the stairs to the ward.

Kathleen was sitting in an easy chair by her bed. She looked forlorn. Despite the fact she was dressed well in a pretty floral print, her hair was dishevelled and she was talking to someone who

191

wasn't there. She appeared to mutter and then putting her head to one side, to listen.

'That'll be the voices again,' said John as we strode onto the ward. Her face lit up at the site of John and she held her arms up to him for a hug. The she spotted me. Her face lit up for a second time as I took hold of her for a hug. And as soon as we sat down in front of her she began to tell 'her voice' that we had arrived. We chatted and she told me she hadn't seen me for a while. I made some excuse and regaled her with details of my holiday. I looked well and quite tanned from my time in Florida. She offered us a piece of chocolate from a bar John and Paul had taken her the day before and we munched contentedly.

A doctor arrived holding a clipboard, wearing a white coat with the obligatory clip-top pen in the pocket. She looked about seventeen. What she said and how she spoke would have filled no one with confidence that their relative was being effectively cared for. I chatted with Kathleen whilst she spoke to John but I kept one ear on the conversation. The main impression conveyed was the hope that she could be discharged as soon as possible but John was insistent that they should make sure they had prescribed the correct medication to suppress the voices and regulate her blood pressure. Still not satisfied by her responses, John agreed to come in the next day and talk to another doctor, more senior, he hoped.

We left together turning back to wave as she waved weakly from her chair. I suppressed a sudden unexpected need to cry by biting my lip. Travelling back in the car, Brian phoned and said he was off to pick up Joe and would see me at home.

John talked about how they were going to manage when his mother came home. Linsey, Paul' youngest, would come to live in the house. I suggested this was quite a responsibility for a twenty-year old with no experience of caring for the elderly but he said they had to try something. The alternative was to put Kathleen into residential care and he wasn't prepared at this point to let that happen. I told him about my own experiences with my mother when she had become confused and how we had tried to find somewhere appropriate for her to stay. He didn't look too impressed but sometimes these things just have to happen for everyone's piece of mind.

*

My mum, reaching a stage in her life where she was becoming increasingly frail and confused, agreed to go into respite care in a local residential home. At first this would be only for three weeks at a time in order that Brian and I could go on holiday. She thought it was splendid because she was so well cared for and because she had no decisions to make. Ever gregarious she always had made a friend by the time we returned.

As time went by and her health deteriorated we suggested she consider looking at full time residential care. She agreed she would try it for a fortnight after which we would review what she thought about it. We knew she would be celebrating her ninetieth birthday during that time so we organised a party for her on the 11th May and invited her niece and her husband, Brian's mum, the grandchildren and some friends. We were to have lunch in a local restaurant.

We had ordered a birthday cake. Regrettably we never got to eat any of it.

When my dad died he and Mum were living in Holbeach in Lincolnshire, moving there as Dad had had a few heart attacks and the idea of living on the flat rather than the traditionally steep hills of Sheffield held quite an appeal. They had twelve years of wonderful retirement but after his final heart attack and ultimate death in 1986, my mum felt very lonely and wanted to move closer to us. She bought a bungalow in our village and settled down to a new form of retirement, belonging to clubs where she played cards and the Over Sixties, which enabled her to go on coach trips to local beauty spots.

Just as is happening to Kathleen, as the years took their toll she began to grow more and more confused and after a while a peculiar thing happened. Our roles reversed and I became the parent and she became my child. A once independent woman, in control of her life, she could no longer make decisions and handling money became a terrible trial. She phoned often to ask us to change the television channel, as she couldn't remember how to do it. Over the phone, we could hear her, frustrated, pressing the buttons, which were actually those on the telephone in an attempt to change the channels on the television.

She became increasingly confused and then she had a little stroke and became even more so. She was on the phone several times each evening with requests for the same information or for help with some aspect of her life. We would drive round and sort out whatever it was. Brian taped up all the buttons on the television remote control except those for the five channels and the volume control but it was still a mystery to her. The volume on the television would be up so loud that the next-door neighbour would rap on the wall. My mother rapped back with her shoe.

'Two can play at that game!' she said. But she was confused about why the neighbour rapped at all and it made her miserable.

We would go rushing up when she phoned to say she was being plagued by ants. She had a horror of all flying or crawling insects. The windowsill would be thick with ant repellent surrounding just six little corpses. Because we wanted to care for her and felt responsible for her well-being, we cleaned her house every Saturday morning, took her shopping, looked after her garden, kept her company and generally looked after her in her own home.

An unfortunate incident occurred while we were out one Sunday visiting Nick for tea. When we arrived home at about 10.00pm there were fourteen messages from my mother on our answer phone. She had noticed wetness on her bedroom carpet when she had gone through for something. She phoned to tell us. Going again a little later, the carpet was wetter still. She phoned to tell us. She phoned all through the evening until we could phone her back. We asked her what the matter was and she told us about the carpet. We said we'd be there in two minutes. She had no idea that a water pipe in the loft above the room had burst and was slowly pouring water onto the ceiling, which was then cascading around her bed. We immediately called out the emergency plumber.

'Why didn't you press the red alarm button on your phone, Mum? Or the button round your neck?' Like many of the elderly in our area, she was connected to a Nottingham-wide service, which provided support for the elderly in their own homes. When she had accidentally pressed either of her buttons there was always immediately a cheery voice on the other end, 'Are you all right, Mrs Kay?' They would have advised her of what to do or come themselves to help her. 'I don't like to bother them.' was her reply.

We settled her in to residential care on a Saturday. I visited every day after school, just as I did at home. On Friday the staff had called her doctor as she had a tummy ache. By Saturday morning when I called she was very ill and hallucinating. She could see two cats that walked across her dressing table. One black and the other white. She wasn't keen on cats although had once owned one before I was born to ensure there were no mice in the pantry: an even greater dread. She could see flies buzzing in clouds around her room. 'Can you hear these flies?' I asked her.

'No,' she said after a moment, 'but they are there.' Her hands were clammy when I held them.

At my insistence, the matron called the doctor again and he came straight away and called an ambulance as her blood pressure was very low. Holding hands in the ambulance, off we went to the City Hospital, where they stabilised her with a fluid drip. They told us they would operate on her tummy when she was stable and to go home. I told her we would cancel her party and get people to come again when she was well. She held my hands and told the doctor I had always been a good daughter. I laughed, in embarrassment as much as anything. She became a bit cross that I should laugh. I realise now she was thinking things needed to be said in case she wasn't to pull through, but still found difficulty in forming the words; in saying things. Saying things, as I have thought afterwards, meant owning up to the possibility of death and neither of us were prepared to do that.

We went home, Brian and I phoned everyone, and then went to bed. At six o'clock the following morning the hospital called and said she had taken a turn for the worse. We got up and left straight away. On the intensive care ward someone else occupied the bed we expected her to be in. The doctor took us off into another room and we both knew then she hadn't pulled through. He explained the circumstances of her death but told us she had died in the early hours of the morning. It isn't policy to tell people over the phone that their relatives have died. A nurse brought her glasses and her jewellery through to us and asked us if we would like to see her. Straight away, I said I wouldn't.

'She doesn't look as you might imagine. The thing you'll notice is that the ties we put around her mouth to hold the breathing tubes in place during the operation are still in place.' Suddenly, I wanted to see her very badly. She was laid on the operating bed in her nightdress, covered up, but with her arms laid loosely over the covers. Her mouth was bound in the way the nurse had described but she was still my mum. My little mummy. I burst into tears weeping momentarily. Mostly with shock, I think, and then I sat down beside the bed and held her hand, cool now but not deathly cold.

And then I told her off. 'What are you doing here, hmm?'

She never liked to be a nuisance to anyone and here she was occupying a bed and not coming home with us. But it didn't last. I touched her hair, which was always beautifully quaffed and blue-rinsed, like the Queen's, and despite what she had been through, looked barely out of place. The skin of her cheeks was as soft and as downy as it ever was. We had a little chat and I told her to be a good girl. I laid my head on the soft skin of the inside of her arm. I said goodbye to her and kissed her downy cheek. Brian and I left, certain that she was in better hands now. We drove home. We cancelled the party and organised a funeral. We took the birthday cake to the Over Sixties after the funeral. Some of it had gone a bit green underneath but I'm sure they'd have found a way to slice that off.

A short time after Mum's death I went into the loft to look for her Last Will and Testament. With her will I found she had left a sealed envelope with a note she intended me read after her death. She wrote that I was her precious daughter and no one could have had a better child. It was too late to tell her but I believed no one could have had a better mother.

*

Returning from the hospital with John, I got out of his car and we stood together on the pavement outside Kathleen's house for a few moments longer, feeling   difficult   about   how   to   leave   things.

Remembering he had said they weren't a huggy-kissy family, I decided to ignore it and told him it was all right to kiss his sister. So he did. I drove back home down the motorway.

A few weeks later I had a phone call from John to tell me Kathleen had been discharged from hospital and allowed to go home. The arrangement was that Paul's daughter Linsey would live in the house with her grandma whilst Paul and John continued to visit and do the shopping or take her out. I felt uncertain at the wisdom of this but felt it was not my place to comment.

*

I phoned John after some time to see how things were progressing and as he was out spoke to Lynn, his wife. She felt in no doubt that the arrangement with Linsey wouldn't last long as she was only young and had social needs like any other. If she wanted to go out with friends, John or Paul had to stand in. Grandma was restless and would often be up in the night disturbing Linsey's sleep. Grandma could sleep in the day but this wasn't a luxury Linsey could afford, as she had to be 'on watch.'

Lynn, although we hadn't met, was voicing concerns I felt myself. Also she expressed a sense of grievance that John was spending so much time with his mother when there were tasks at home he could be doing. She had no doubt that John was a devoted son and gave him credit for being like that but also felt there were other areas of his life that were being neglected. I sympathised. The compensation was that as Linsey was at Grandma's they could spend time in

France without feeling guilty. Kath sounded very pleasant on the phone but I don't know whether we'll ever be destined to meet. I asked her to say exactly where their house was in France and when I came off the phone Brian looked it up on the roadmap. It is to the east of our route from the ferry ports but, you never know, we could find ourselves visiting them in time.

*

I decided to visit Kathleen at home and phoned John to make arrangements for several days with no answer. We were going off to France (for the fourth time this year!) and I wanted to pop up to see her before we went. In the event of no one answering I phoned Kathleen directly and she answered the phone immediately.

I expected that if I heard a female voice it would be Linsey's and I was prepared to say who I was, knowing that John had briefed her about me when she first went to stay in case I turned up unexpectedly. I don't know what he said to her – 'grandma had a bit of a fling in the war!' perhaps – nor am I aware of her reaction. It struck me as odd at the time that a father or uncle should have to tell a child about a grandparent's indiscretion. It's usually the other way round in that a father tells his mother that his daughter is having a baby but isn't married and waits for the outrage – or not. Actually, we told Brian's mum that Robert and Lisa, as yet unmarried, were having Jack. Of course, she took it all in her stride as in retrospect we should have known she would. Linsey probably did the same. Later John would tell me that Linsey had reported that one evening Kathleen said to her that she had once had a beautiful baby girl. Suitably primed, Linsey probably just murmured, 'Did you, Grandma?'

But the voice on the phone wasn't Linsey's and I asked Kathleen if I could come and see her the following day. She said she thought so but just needed to consult the white board on the kitchen wall. As I waited I could hear voices in the kitchen and pictured the wipe-clean board. I had seen it when I went to visit John there and he made me a cup of tea. There was a phone number on it of a lady called Elaine who lives somewhere in Nottingham and would have met Zygmunt. I remember Kathleen saying she had been a teacher in Nottingham. She is still on touch with Kathleen. I was wondering if she could tell me anything about Zygmunt when a male voice came on the phone.

'Hello,'

'Hello, it's Margaret. Is that John or Paul?' I could tell it wasn't John but I needed something to get into the conversation.

'Paul.'

'I was wondering if I could come up tomorrow and see your mother'

'It's not convenient. Tomorrow's not convenient.'

'Oh.' I felt a bit let down and didn't know what to say but he rescued me.

'Could you come on Monday?' I said was sorry but I couldn't as we would be in France by then but I would phone again and make some other arrangement when I came home. He said goodbye and rang off.

Not convenient, eh? I don't suppose on the whole that I am very convenient.

*

We went to the French house. On the Monday I phoned John but no one answered. A day later the phone rang and there was John. How had he got my number? I hadn't been able to leave a message, as he doesn't believe in answering machines. He explained that his 1471 facility had picked up the French number and Kath, a computer literate lady, had brought up the Pages Jaunes on the internet and found our listing thereby discovering the phone number that matched. I was impressed.

I began to explain my conversation with Paul. 'Our Paul said it wasn't convenient, I understand,' he said.

'Mm...yes,' I admitted, 'but he did suggest another day.'

'He hasn't told me why it wasn't convenient.'

'I suspect, as it was a Friday morning he would be taking your mother shopping.'

'Our mother.'

'Well, yes.'

We left it at that. They, Paul and himself, had begun looking for some suitable residential care for their mother as the arrangement with Linsey couldn't last forever and as she continued to hear the voices and felt disturbed and confused by them, they felt full time care would be the best option. I could tell he wasn't happy at having to make the decision but felt resigned to it. They now had the task of selling the house but would first have to clear it. No easy job. I recalled my own experience of this.

*

Shortly after my mum died we went to her bungalow to begin the job of clearing her things. It is a heart-breaking process for any family, going through personal effects and finding little mementos that a parent has kept. I knitted two egg cosies in yellow wool when I was about six as a Christmas gift for my mum. They were poor things as all my efforts at knitting had been but there they were. Too sentimental to throw them away she had kept Thank You notes the boys had written to her and my dad; unused lace hankies beautifully folded; cuttings from the Sheffield Star of when Brian and I had been married. I wandered about the sitting room touching things I treasured. The first thing I gently wrapped in tissue paper to take home was an elephant; a brown Indian chap that had been part of a much bigger collection of my dad's. It would be placed beside a lighter African one which had once been grey but my father had washed him as my mum thought he looked grubby and, cheaply mass-produced, the colour washed off. Now he's a genuine white elephant. From inside her china cabinet I took my aunt's bone china, gold leaf decorated tea service, which my mother had treasured but never used. It stands in my china cabinet, still unused, far too precious, because using it would most likely mean I'd break it. It has become a family heirloom but we have sons and they most probably won't want it when we've gone

203

because they will think it's so old fashioned let alone the fact that it's not dishwasher safe. Most of her little bowls, often holding sweeties found their way into my china cabinet. I'm talking of the past, eight years ago, and forgetting that we didn't own a china cabinet then but had to buy one to accommodate the new additions. Of her jewellery I picked out her platinum and amethyst ring my dad bought her and wondered if I should wear it alongside her wedding and engagement ring I had put onto my little finger the day after she died. I look at these little rings every day and think of her small hands. I decided to put the ring and several other pieces away safely for the time being.

We asked the boys to come along with their then wives to choose anything by which they would like to remember their Nan. They chose ornaments and jewellery and a picture or two. A little time ago whilst looking in one of Robert's kitchen drawers for a knife I came across a cruet wrapped in tissue paper, the old fashioned sort where the little chromium salt and pepper pots sit on a small tray alongside a mustard pot with a blue glass container in it and a small spoon. I bought it for their silver wedding gift when I was eleven. Robert probably remembered it from his own childhood visits to his grandparents, as well as the purple tumblers, three only left now, that sit in his glass cupboard but which we still drink from when we visit. Nick had things but Diane who, remembering my mum well, still treasures things she chose and they stayed in her house when the marriage broke up. I feel sure that if I squirreled about in his personal drawers Nick would have some memento of his own.

The French house has many of my mum's bits and pieces. In the kitchen especially there are knives, plates and serving dishes, which give me pleasure to think they were hers and it would delight her to know we were still using her things. A friend staying with us recently commented she had a cheese knife like ours. 'Was it your mother's?' I asked her. 'Oh, yes,' she said.

*

John said he would let me know when Paul and he had found somewhere for his mother to live. In a short time they settled on a residential community for the elderly not too far from where she had lived.

Chapter 13

A New Home for Kathleen

On returning from our holiday I phoned once more to John to suggest I go to see his 'our' mother. (Must try harder to bring 'our mother' or better still just 'mother' into my vocabulary.) He described her as healthy but unsettled. She was finding it hard to settle into her new home and readjust to a new life. She has tried to escape once or twice he told me. 'They found her in the local Spar grocery one time,' he went on. 'It's because she's well dressed. She'd gone out with the visitors, someone else's, of course, and walked to the shops nearby. The shopkeeper must have phoned the reception and they collected her. They're considering putting her in the 'secure unit.' It's on the floor below where my mother is and they do lock the residents in. But it costs more to do this.'

'Are you selling the house?' I asked him.

'There's no rush. My dad left her well provided for. Not lots, you know, but enough to pay for her care for a while.'

'What's the place like?' I wondered.

'Oh, it's great. Our Paul and me, we looked at quite a few places until we settled on this one. It's quite state of the art. It's only been open for three or four months. There is a Sky TV connection in each of the rooms. She doesn't need it because she finds four channels more than enough to cope with as it is. The new TV Paul bought is installed there and it gets quite a good picture. Good enough for her at any rate. And there's a phone point and a room for computers with an Internet connection.

'An Internet connection?!' I couldn't imagine why elderly people would want to be sending emails.

'It's for the future,' John explained. 'There will come a time in a few years that people who have been using the Internet regularly will want to be living there.'

We laughed at the prospect that people who become easily confused could be able to use such a facility but we should be careful about this facetious attitude as it could come back to haunt us.

'Anyway, she seems to be getting on better now. I have to tell her that my dad has died as she thinks he will turn up at some time. 'Gone to sleep' as she puts it. As long as I keep taking her through it, you know, the funeral and all that, she remembers.'

'I need to know how to find her,' I told him and he gave me the name and address of the home.

'It's not a home. They don't call it a home. They refer to it as a residential community. It's the modern way.'

'I'll not phone you when I've been unless I think there's something particular to tell you.'

'OK.'

Driving up to Sheffield on a warm July afternoon I was looking forward to seeing Kathleen and when I had passed the turn off for her house I turned left off the Sheffield Parkway and following John's careful directions easily found the residential community in Hazelthorpe.

The building was impressive: warm red brick and large modern windows. The reception area was wide and welcoming with a hairdressing salon off to one side. A day centre lay straight ahead. The building smelled fresh and new paint-clean. A care worker who knew Kathleen was playing bingo in the lounge upstairs took me through double doors and up a flight of stairs. The door at the top of the flight opened onto a small lounge are where a circle of easy chairs had been turned inwards so everyone could hear the numbers being called. Someone had just won so the game was as good as over. Kathleen was sitting with her back to the door. She turned and saw me and her face lit up with pleasure.

'Oh, it's been a while since I saw you but I'm so glad you're here.' She looked genuinely pleased.

The nurse took both of us down the corridor to Room 40. The door bore her name, printed clearly with a sense of permanence. We went in and I sat on a high backed chair, which matched the rest of the furniture in her room: a single bed with a peach duvet, beige carpet, peach patterned easy chair, a chest of drawers and a small bedside table. The ensuite bathroom was hidden behind a closed door. The window, which made the room airy and bright, looked directly onto a garden with tall silver birches and sycamores and a grassy bank and then further onto a road of semi-detached houses or flats. Cars passed quietly as we watched.

Producing some family photographs I had brought I showed her a recent picture of Jack and one of Joseph taken with Nick and Debbie at our house. All are smiling or laughing. I pointed out that the two young ones were her great grandchildren. She pondered this for a while taking it in slowly. And this one is your grandson I told her pointing to Nick. She looked closely, carefully scrutinising him. I really wanted her to say she recognised him or could see Zygmunt in him. I really wanted to hear that.

But she didn't say that. She said, 'I think I would know that high forehead.' She ran her fingers over Nick's face where his hair was receding slightly. 'I think I would know that face. He's very good looking, isn't he?' That would please Nick as it pleased me.

I went and made some tea. Only two doors down the corridor from her room was the kitchen. It had everything in the cupboards from cups and saucers to tea and coffee pots and the surfaces contained containers of tea, coffee and sugar. I filled the kettle and switched it on. In a full sized fridge I found fresh semi-skimmed milk. I poured it into a jug, made the tea and carried it on a tray to her room. Sitting companionably we enjoyed tea and biscuits together.

She asked me something that made me think she hadn't quite grasped the point of my visit. She had only boys she said. Two boys, no girls.

'Except me,' I said.

'Oh?' she looked vague.

'Except me. I am your child, aren't I?' I persisted.

'Oh, yes,' she conceded. 'Burton on Trent.' A flicker of recognition but not of joined up thought.

'That's right,' I continued.

'Has Bill met you?' she asked.

'Er, no. There was always the problem of who you were going to tell him I was. He has met me but only when I was a tiny baby and he carried me to Sheffield and handed me over.' A flicker of real recognition now. 'You were at your Auntie Jessie's.'

'Oh, yes. Out of the way,' she smiled.

Painstakingly, conscious that I had to raise my voice and others in the corridor might
have heard our conversation, I went over the details of Bill coming home to find her pregnant and then standing by her until she had me and the time came to give me away.

'Twenty Darklands Road.'

'That's right,' I smiled.

'I came to find you, you know, to look at you.'

'Yes.'

'And those little girls. They weren't you but they knew you and where you lived. 'Shall I go and get her mother?' they said.''

'It's perhaps a good job they didn't, isn't it?'

'Yes, perhaps it is.'

I left after another half hour and drove away in good spirits. A care worker had come to get Kath, as they all call her, for tea in the dining room, another brightly lit room off the kitchen but open to a wide space that was part of the corridor. She was insisting she came down stairs to see me off but with John's warning sounding in my ears I said it would be better if she didn't go down stairs but instead sat down with the others for her tea. I didn't want to be responsible for another 'breakout.'

I drove to Margery's and picked her up to come to our house. The next day the three of us were off to Scotland to stay with Rob and Lisa whom we hadn't seen for over a month. The journey to her house from Hazelthorpe took just over ten minutes. I was surprised to find how close it was. I told her about my visit and she surprised me by saying she would like to go with me one day to meet Kathleen. I'd have to ask the 'boss'.

As soon as I got home I rang John.

Nothing to report but I just wanted to say how splendid the place is. She was alert and chatty and seemed quite settled. No talk of going home or feeling confused about where she was.' He was delighted.

*

I asked Brian to go with me the next time. I wanted him to see where she was. I phoned John, who had just returned from his French house, and suggested the following day and a time. He said he would be there in the morning and I said we would be there before he left all being well.

We arrived a little late just as he was leaving and met him in the car park. He looked well and relaxed after his holiday. Brian shook his hand and he accepted my kiss without a murmur.

'She's not so well today,' he said. 'She's more confused than she was yesterday. I'll go back up with you.'

He turned and we went into the building as he signed us in then up the stairs. She was in her room and was delighted to see us and equally delighted that John had returned. We had a hug and asked after each other's health, looked around the room and out of the window at the view, Brian exclaiming how pleasant everything was.

I went off to make the tea again and Kathleen came with me. She let me get out the cups and put the kettle on then slipped into the dining room, empty now as lunch was a while away. I tried to keep my eye on her, as she seemed to be making for the door. But she didn't leave the room. Instead she stood and talked to someone in an intense manner but, of course, there wasn't anyone there. It was Bill she was talking to. She was telling him about my visit and then listening to what he said. When we went into her room with the tea and John had produced a box of chocolate biscuits he had brought from Normandy, I mentioned her hearing voices again.

'   It's me dad,' he said. 'It's been going on all morning. Once I've talked her through everything, the funeral and that, she remembers he's gone.'

'Bill would like to meet you and he's coming soon,' she told me convinced it was the truth.

'If you want to meet him,' said John, 'you'll need to bring a spade.' The irreverent macabre humour made us laugh but I didn't look to see if Kathleen was laughing.

Brian and John continued to chat about France and preferred routes across the Channel whilst Kathleen and I talked about holidays. I told her where we had been so far this year.

'Did you meet John in France? Didn't you see a sign on his door?' Confusion. I ignored it.

'No, no. We met him at your house. Him and Paul together.'

After a few moments we had the same conversation again.

John got up to go, kissed his mum, me and shook Brian's hand. Then he was gone.

I had brought our photograph album of Rob and Lisa's wedding, which contained some excellent pictures of both Nick and Rob. She enjoyed looking but there was no sign she recognised anyone from her past in either of their faces.

We spent an enjoyable time with her and delivered her into the care of the care workers who insisted she sat down in the dining room to what looked like an excellent lunch even whilst she was insisting she came downstairs to show us out. She knew Bill would be there wanting to see her. After a while she gave up on that idea. Bill had told her he couldn't come.

Before Brian and I had set off for Sheffield the post had brought us a surprise. A letter from the Polish Air Force Association with news of a Zygmunt Rosiak, based in Britain from 1939 who in 1944 had become a pilot.

Part 5

Poles Apart

Chapter 14

Some Polish History

I remember when I first heard the name of my natural father, Zygmunt, or Sigmund as we thought at the time, in Kathleen's house. She was unwilling to say his second name as I might go looking for him. 'And anyway he'd be dead.' 'Of course we wouldn't go looking for him!'

But…

It's so enticing to try to follow up what you know.

What do I know?

From my father I know he was Polish, had been an airman during the war; wasn't Jewish and was most probably Catholic. From Kathleen I learned in addition that he had become a pilot, had liked going dancing to the dancehall in Hucknall, was called Zygmunt with a surname that sounded like Roseac or Roziak, seemed to have been based in Hucknall for quite some time as he had been able to form a relationship with my mother and was taken home to meet the James family members (sisters/mother) in the house in Middlewood in Sheffield suggesting an affair rather than a one night stand.

From Pam, my helper extraordinaire in my search for Kathleen, along with her husband Alan, they speculated he was possibly a trainer in Hucknall as he was able to spend enough time there to meet my mother on several occasions. This was borne out by the fact that his name does not appear in any of the

Polish squadrons that flew with the RAF from 1939 until 1945 listed in detail on the Internet website.

It is surely the prerogative of all adopted children to romanticise how their natural parents might have looked and, no exception, I had romanticised a notion of my natural father from the time after my dad had given me the information he had gleaned from the adoption society. Oddly, before I knew this information I hadn't done this so much. I had never really wondered who my natural father was. I guess this is as a result of a contented childhood and a secure upbringing. But now I decided he would have been tall and handsome with dark eyes, which doubtless would have contained a gleam for my mother. I am tall, so he must have been. I have brown eyes, so he must have had them. I don't look Polish, according to Stuart, my social worker from Nottingham but he *has* to be wrong. Many Poles have brown eyes and dark hair. I must look like my natural father. This is especially true now I have met my mother and find that there are quite a few bits of me that are still seriously unexplained. His feet probably turned out a bit, too. And there still remains the mystery of the Polish ears.

My original thinking had been that I wouldn't try to do anything to find my natural father but curiosity has gripped sufficiently to change my mind. When I worked in Nottingham I had to drive by the Polish Catholic Society in Sherwood Street to get into the car park at work. Knowing for many years that my natural father was Polish, but with no knowledge of the Nottingham connection, I would occasionally speculate that they could be of help if I ever wanted to trace him but had absolutely no idea how set about this. One of the many coincidences in my search has been that I was conceived in Nottingham. (Yes, this is still speculation as I could have been conceived in a big over-stuffed feather bed in an upstairs room in Middlewood, in Sheffield, but let's be sensible.)

Knowing about the Hucknall connection, on the 21st January this year, I wrote to the Polish Catholic Club in Sherwood Rise, Nottingham asking for information. I told them that I had recently learned the name of my natural father who had been a Polish airman in Nottingham during World War II and that I had been an adopted child born in 1946. I told them I had traced my natural mother who had had connections with Nottingham during the war. After sixty years, I told them she had little recollection of precise details except his name: Zygmunt Roseac or Rosiak or either of these names spelled with a 'z'.

Recalling that he had been with the Polish Air Force based at RAF Hucknall certainly until August 1945 when I would have been conceived, it might be presumed he returned to Poland not knowing he had fathered a child. My mother recalled he had been a pilot and that he was about three years older than she, which would make his year of birth about 1920. I said I hoped this was sufficient information for them to be able to identify Zygmunt and asked them for advice about how I should go about tracing him. Several months went by without my hearing anything.

On the morning Brian and I were setting off to see Kathleen in her residential community a letter arrived in the post. The envelope had a bright red franking mark saying Air Force Association

Charitable Trust. Brian had recently donated some money to RAFA and we assumed the letter was an acknowledgement of this. The part missing from the top of the envelope franking was 'Polish.'

As usual we were on the last minute and as I had said to John we would try to be in Hazelthorpe before he left there was no time to read the letter thoroughly. As I drove up the A38 Brian read the details from the letter.

It was in reply to mine of the 21st January 2007, seven months earlier sent to the Polish Catholic Club in Nottingham but instead of a reply from Nottingham it must have been passed on to the Polish Air Force Association. The letter gave documentary proof that Zygmunt Rosiak had actually existed! This was an exciting moment but I had none of those feelings that I had had on learning Kathleen was alive. The relationship I had with both my parents was very close. My dad in particular was so proud of me, always protective and loving that I felt that no other man could ever take his place. My search for Kathleen had been motivated, not by any sense of loss, but the need to reassure her she should not feel guilty about me. More so than it had been with Kathleen this search for Zygmunt was just a matter of curiosity. I was researching a piece of history not trying to find flesh and blood.

The Polish Air Force Association had only a small amount of information, they wrote, but was able to give us the address of the Ministry of Defence in Ruislip, Middlesex where we could write for more information. Enclosed with the letter were two documents. One seemed to be the service record of

220

one Rosiak, Zygmunt. The format was a ledger entry. It contained quite a lot of information but all of the headings and most of the information were in Polish!

We managed to decipher that his date of birth was 29th December 1916, which made him four years older than Kathleen remembered. His nationality was stated as POLSKIE'. He will be ninety years old. This all seems a long shot and the chances of his being alive are a bit remote. The form might be asking for place of birth and this is stated as: OTMIANOWO woj: POMORSKIE. Other information that was of interest was what appeared to be a record of his education. It looked as if he had been educated in 1934 at some unidentified L'ecole supplementaire at Aubervilliers, near Paris. In 1936 he went to Szkota Rolnicza – Bnesi Kujawski. Does this mean he had two years from 18 to19 being educated in France followed by a year back in Poland? The form seemed to indicate that he spoke two other languages: English and French.

The reverse of the form was quite informative because we were able to make an educated guess at some of the headings. Zygmunt appeared to have joined the Royal Air Force in 1939 as a radio operator. Had we interpreted this information correctly? How had he arrived in Britain? In 1943 he started training as a pilot. On the 18th October 1944 the entry states he became a 'tuytur pilota.' This surely bears out our speculation that he was a pilot trainer in Hucknall training other Poles to become pilots. This must have been what kept him in Nottingham and allowed him to have the affair with my mother.

I wrote to Pam in an e-mail headed 'Pack your

bags we're off to Poland!'   However, the service record also contained an address in the UK.   This wasn't RAF Hucknall but RAF Station Faldingworth, near Lincoln, where he must have been stationed. With the service record there was a copy of his members' card for PAFA showing his progress beginning as a radio-telegrapher, then pilot then 'plut Sgt' (Sergeant Pilot?) then two further entries that have been obscured.   Two locations are given as Skipton on Swale, which is in Yorkshire, and RAF Burntwood in Lancashire.   There is also an address of 22, Goldsmith Hill, Upper Wortley, Leeds 12.   I would remember this address in the future but at that moment I was unaware of its significance.   A date stamp gives his last contact with the Association as 15th August 1949.

Should we go and sit outside the house at the address in Leeds thinking what we might do next? Perhaps not.

What I have done instead is to alert Pam by e-mail to the fact we have these addresses and the information and ask her what she would do next.   I added a rider about packing her bag. The destination could be Leeds, Maltby, Skipton on Swale.   Who knows?   You never know, perhaps she has an Internet search tool that will produce Zygmunt alive and well, aged 90, living in Yorkshire just waiting to be discovered. More realistically, because Pam's mother, who has had a serious stroke in recent years, and is being cared for in her own home near Pam and Alan by care workers who are from Poland, I have posted copies of the material sent by PAFA to Pam in the hope the care workers can find the time to translate the headings on the forms and the entries, too, so we can have a clearer picture of Zygmunt Rosiak.

I have a friend who is a firm believer in the notion that we are all, all humanity, connected in some spiritual way with one another, as we are all God's children. Others believe in an idea of six degrees of connection between everyone in the world and if we continue to seek them out all the elements of our lives will be revealed. Who can tell? But Brian and I live by the tenet that we never ridicule what we don't know or understand.

What I have also done is to write to the Ministry of Defence with a copy of the records sent to me asking them if they have more information and whether they are willing to translate the Polish language entries for us. We await events.

*

On the reverse of Zigmunt's service record appears this entry:

| 300 DYW 28.5.45 | | plut | pilot |
| 300 DYW | 46 | plut | pilot |

At this stage Brian and I can only guess that 'plut' refers to pilot until we hear from Pam's mother's Polish carers. But the reference to 300 we instinctively feel is the squadron he was attached to for the last two years of his wartime experience. I looked on the Internet and found a website that contains all manner of interesting information about the Bomber squadrons the Poles were attached to during the Second World War: www. geocities.com/skrzydla/300 containing a 'Brief History of No. 300 (Polish) Bomber Squadron written

223

by Wilhelm Ratuszynski, the site offers fascinating information about the formation of the squadron and the daring deeds of the pilots from 1940 until the disbanding of the squadron in 1945. The information included here is taken from this useful site, informed by my interpretation of Zygmunt's record.

The 300 Squadron was the first Polish squadron to be formed. It consisted of Polish airmen who arrived from France early in 1940. Zygmunt's service record tells us that he was educated in France during 1934/5 when he would have been 18 and 19 years old. Perhaps this is significant in giving him access to the UK, as he would probably be able to speak fluent French after a year in the country. The pilots of the time were sent to Redhill in Surrey with the navigators and the gunners going first of all to Redhill then later to Hucknall, near Nottingham. An order dated 14th March 1940 was issued that RAF Hucknall was to be a Polish Training Unit as part of an Operational Training Unit of the RAF. The unit was called the No. 300 'Masovian' Bomber Squadron and the task of the RAF was to convert the skills of the Polish crews to those needed by the RAF bombers. They began by flying Fairey Battle light bombers.

The Poles of this squadron erected the first Polish Air Force flag on English soil on 1st July 1940. An honour for the squadron, a month later they received an unexpected visit from HM King George VI. He spent time chatting with the crews about their experiences in France and about the Polish campaign.

Later in the same year the squadron made the first bomber raid of the Polish Air Force in Britain on German barge concentrations around various French

224

ports in Normandy. Successful, they continued to bomb a variety of targets in occupied Europe including Antwerp.

After a disastrous return from a bombing raid the squadron was introduced to a new type of aircraft: the Wellington Mk1 and the squadron's number rose from a little over 200 to nearly 400. They continued despite loss of life to complete fifty-five successful bombing raids.

During 1941 they continued to bomb targets in Germany including Berlin wreaking in part revenge for the relentless bombing of Warsaw and London. Aircraft now included the more powerful Wellington Mk IV. The number of sorties rose to four hundred and forty one although casualties continued to rise, too increasing significantly during 1942. The squadron dropped their bombs over Germany major industrial cities such as Manheim, Frankfurt, Dusseldorf and Hamburg. They also flew over Italy bombing Turin and Milan. A new operation of laying mines was begun in this year, namely and still, inevitably casualties and losses continued to rise. The Wellington MK X, a better aircraft arrived in April 1943.

The squadron continued to fly bombing raids over ports and industrial centres whilst also laying mines in the open waters around the entrance to French ports. On one occasion during 1943 the No 300 Squadron was the subject of a wonderful commendation from Bomber Command C-in-C for their vital and important work in the war effort. The commendation was from Air Marshall Harris, Bomber Harris.

"Heartiest congratulations to the whole personnel of Squadron 300 of the occasion of laying last night in a painstaking fashion, their two-thousandth mine. It is a most valuable contribution towards winning the war and affords further proof of the splendid spirit of cooperation animating both our Air Forces. I am proud of you. HARRIS"

Shortly after this it was decided to convert the squadron to Avro Lancaster, a four engine heavy bomber. Some crews continued to fly Wellington bombers whilst others trained to fly the Lancasters. Successes continued but not without the price of dreadful loss of life and aircraft.

Throughout the period from 1941 to 1943 the squadron had been based in a variety of places starting at Redhill in Surrey, moving to Bramcote in the West Midlands, then to Swinderby and Hemswell in Lincolnshire. In 1944 HQ Bomber Command decided to move them to RAF Faldingworth and this is where they were based when Zygmunt joined them. His service record states he was part of 300DYW from 28th May 1945 and certainly remained attached to them until 1946. In 1944 this RAF station offered only basic facilities but was blessed with long concrete runways and flat unobscured approaches. Polish-crewed Lancasters continued their bombing missions over Cologne and Rouen railway junctions and were directed to make their targets the enemy's communication systems across northern France and Germany. On the 12th June heavy losses were sustained during a daylight attack on naval ships in Le Havre. Many acts of bravery are recorded during this time.

On 1ˢᵗ August 1944 the Warsaw Uprising broke out. Anxiety and tension was rife amongst the Poles as they felt helpless to support their fellow countrymen and women and many still had family members living still in Warsaw. Although over four thousand flying hours were recorded over a hundred men were lost in this year.

The beginning of the final year of the war brought deeply felt sadness to the Poles fighting in Britain for the Allies. In the Treaty of Yalta Poland was offered to Russia in exchange for their support on the Eastern Front. As can be imagined, this terrible blow led to low morale amongst the Polish crews yet they just kept on going, fulfilling their duty in a commendable way. They were still flying sorties but felt despair that such an arbitrary decision could wrest their homeland and hand it over to Russia. A letter from a Polish Airmen at the time expressed their feelings:

"Just think, I and so many others knocked about the world feeling like criminals, starving, hiding in forests – all only in order to fight for...what? For this we shall never see our native town because it has simply ceased to be...It's a funny feeling but sometimes I wonder if all this has any sense. If Germans get me now, I won't even know what I'm dying for. For Poland, Britain or for Russia."

A poignant memoir from a Pilot Officer Magierowski, particularly because he perished, dying in action shortly afterwards. The Germans were fighting to the last and Poles continued to attack German cities. On V-Day although the British were wildly celebrating victory in a war, which had begun in 1939 in the defence of Poland's independence, the Poles had no such victory to celebrate.

The 300 Squadron continue to fly for a short time after the war dropping food supplies into Holland, repatriating British prisoners of war to Britain from Germany and Italy, carrying Red Cross supplies for liberated Poles in German concentration camps and carrying bombs from the dumps for disposal at sea.

Was Zygmunt involved in any of this work? The date stamp on the copy of his membership card for the Polish Air Force Association suggests he remained in England until the 15th August 1949 at least.

On the website which produced this information about Polish Squadron 300 there were some pictures, old wartime photographs supplied by members of the squadron or former RAF personnel but none of these were of a Zygmunt Rosiak.

*

18th August 2007 – Diary entry

Family life continues to be exciting. We have a new grandson. Benjamin Robert came into the world at 06.22 on 18th August 2007. We were fast asleep when the phone shrilled. The radio alarm clock read 4.45 as I bolted awake. To be fair we had asked Robert to phone when anything happened and he took us literally and phoned when he and Lisa arrived at the hospital in Dumfries.

'How far apart are the contractions?' I asked him.

'Ten minutes...well, some are.'

'She'll be hours,' I told him confidently. We remained awake unable to sleep. Two hours later the phone went again.

'He's here!' an excited Robert announced.

'Crikey, that was quick.' And we proceeded to have a conversation about what time we could get away from home and be at the hospital in Scotland. 'If we get up now we can be away by eight o'clock. Who does he look like?'

Robert described a perfect image of Jack when he was born except he had weighed eight pounds, five ounces less than his new brother.

'There is one difference though.'

'Oh, yes. What's that?' I asked him.

'We can't work out whose ears he's got. They're not mine. They're not Lisa's.'

'Oh.' A snort of disbelief from me followed by a low laugh from him.

'Looks like it's the Polish ears.'

When we saw him in the hospital a few hours later we were introduced to the new offspring by his big brother, Jack. Ben, perfect and golden, was the exact image of how Jack had looked at a few hours old. But there they were, one on each side, a little crumpled, a little pointed on the top, just like his cousin Joseph's ears, just like his uncle Nick's ears. The Polish ears.

*

Pam e-mailed on 24th August with an explanation of the Polish entries on Zygmunt's service record.

'You're not going to believe this,' she wrote, 'but I've found him.' A moment of anxiety settled over me but was soon dispelled as I read on. 'Not good news though.'

So he's dead. I think I suspected all along this would be the outcome even if she were able to trace a record him. And, of course Kathleen was right from the start. His age is against him. Ninety-one and still living is a bit unlikely. She adds something I at first don't understand: 'Looks like California, not Poland.' What does she mean?

Pam's mother's Polish carer, Zibie, was a great deal of help with the documents I sent to Pam. The service record states that Zygmunt Rosiak, was born on the 29th December 1916 in Otmianowo, a town in Eastern Poland, in the state of Pomorjkie.

This is probably akin to the departments in France or to our counties. He was Roman Catholic (like Bill and his family) and his civil status was single. His health was A/B (i.e. good.) His address is given as RAF Station Faldingworth, Lincoln.

Details of what Zygmunt would like to do presumably after the war has ended states that he wanted to stay in Britain. This indicated he did not wish to return to Poland. Perhaps his city was handed over to the Russians in the Treaty of Yalta. Perhaps he had no family in Poland to return to.

I wonder, because there is no date on it when this particular information was given on the form. Were Polish flyers asked when they volunteered what they wanted to do after the war or was it a question asked after their squadrons had been disbanded? In 1946 after the signing of the Treaty of Yalta, Poles were faced with a choice of settling in Britain, emigrating to Commonwealth or other foreign countries or returning to Poland. Yalta had sealed the fate of the Poles and they were treated most shabbily as the British government formally withdrew recognition of the legality of the Polish government in exile. Free elections took place in Poland but they were a sham and a Communist government was installed bringing about the start of the Cold War. This government was recognized by the Allies, which left the Poles-in Exile in effect a mercenary force. The RAF was responsible for the demobilization and transfer of armed combatants into what was known as the Polish Resettlement Corps created by the government of the day under Ernest Bevan through an Act of Parliament. Immediately all Poles were formally advised that all of them couldn't remain in Britain. Enrolment into the Polish Army Resettlement Corps (PARC) began. Although the British economy had been shattered and faced huge shortages in raw materials and manpower, an anti-Polish campaign by the TUC and leading trade unions turned public attitudes towards the Poles from a country desperately needing experienced combatants and acceptance to one of shunning the Poles.

The headquarters for the PARC was Hucknall. At this time the three choices were offered to the eleven thousand Poles who 'joined' the PARC. Zygmunt obviously chose to stay in Britain and I can only deduce that he was one of the successful ones as his membership of the PAFA reveals him to still be there in 1949. Another place the PARC were based was Skipton on Swale and this has been written by hand on his membership card so perhaps he went there, too. By March of 1946 the RAF had the disbandment plans arranged. All PAF fighter squadrons were relocated to Norfolk and one by one the squadrons awaited the orders to disband each of which were marked with fly-past and marches to bands. Over three thousand Poles from the PAF were repatriated and another two and a half thousand had emigrated to other countries by July 1948. However, some nine thousand managed to stay in Britain, Zygmunt amongst them. It is curious to me that he was in this country with no knowledge that he had a daughter growing up in Sheffield.

The part of Zygmunt's service record about his education suggested for four years from 1934 he could have been attending L' ecole supplimentaire in Aubervilliers. Pam's email tells me that Zibie, her mother's Polish carer and our interpreter, says they have some 'foreign' schools in Poland and this could be one but he is unsure. As we know there is a district of Paris of this name it would seem more appropriate that he actually attended there. For one year in 1936 it appears he was at a farm or agricultural college. This doesn't appear to be consistent but we only have this translation to go on. The next information, says Zibie, is about where he stayed and it looks to be his pathway to the UK in 1939 via France and then to England. This would be consistent with what we know from the website on the 300 Squadron but it looks to me that it is giving details of the languages he spoke rather than his travel route.

His rank was lieutenant although Zibie wonders if 'plut' actually means that he was a corporal. The form gives details of what kind of aircraft he could fly and it says 'not a single engine' apparently, which is consistent with what we have already learned. His work in civil life was as a manager of a shop and a pilot'; his hobby is given as 'Aviation' and what he would like to do says 'technical.'

The reverse of the form gives his record with the PAF and starts by telling us that he was a radio telegrapher from 1939 to September 1941. It isn't possible to translate what he did from then till 10th May 1943 but from then on he became a pilot under training; from the 18th October 1944 a pilot with 18 Operational Training Unit and remained so until 1946. He became part of No 300 Squadron in 1945.

Zygmunt's form also tells us that before the war he was engaged in some way with food as a salesperson from September 1936 to January 1939 then from this date to November 1939 as a manager. It doesn't state what he managed, whether it was a shop or a food-producing factory. We can only guess. But I was grateful to Zibie for his attempt to translate the document and now felt I had quite a lot more information about Zygmunt.

Having pondered over the information in Pam's e-mail I rang her. She had given me a website which I clicked on following her enigmatic 'Looks like California not Poland' message. Zygmunt died in 1969 and the website revealed that it was the

Californian death Records. And there he was. Pam had certainly found him. He died aged fifty-two in Los Angeles in the state of California on 2nd April 1969. The document contained his American social security number, which suggests he was there for some time and probably worked there. He could have emigrated in 1949, the last date we know he was in Britain, then married and had a whole heap of children. There could be other siblings. Britain had made it difficult for Poles who remained here to get employment without a lot of 'red tape' and almost impossible to become self-employed. Perhaps Zygmunt had grown tired of being shunned by once grateful Britons who paid no heed to former bravery and sacrifice and decided after three years to try his luck in America.

In my phone call to Pam she told me that she would try to find out what I could do with the social security number in order to gain access to his records in the United States, which could possibly reveal when he arrived there, what he did for a living and whether he married and had children.

Chapter 15

A Visit to Kathleen

As I was following John up the staircase of Kathleen's residential community on the day I received the information from the Polish Air Force Association, I told him about it. I said he would probably not still be alive and his mother's estimation of this would prove to be true. He was interested up to a point but, of course, Zygmunt was only his mother's 'bit of a fling' in the war and of no real interest to him. I told Nick and Robert that I had traced some details about him but neither was particularly interested to know more.

<u>*2ⁿᵈ September 2007 – Diary entry*</u>

>   *John phoned a few days ago with news of our mother. She had been transferred to the lower floor of the residential community.*
>   *'If you want to go and see her I thought you had better know,' he told me.*
>   *'That's good,' I said.*
>   *'No it's not,' he said. 'It's the secure unit. The lock up. She's been walk-about again and the staff advised that she should be moved downstairs for her own safety.' He seemed philosophical about it all. Paul hadn't visited for a few days and John was bearing the burden on his own. I felt a wave of sympathy for him. Paul's health wasn't very good at the moment, John told me. He had stopped driving again, a sure fire way of knowing he wasn't feeling well. The room on the lower floor, John said, was just*

235

as pleasant as Kathleen's previous room; it had a view of the garden and an open, airy aspect. She had decided to leave to see Bill who she was convinced was waiting for her at home. She must have walked out with visitors who were leaving, without any money and caught a bus to Crystal Peaks in Sheffield. From there she boarded a tram to the city centre and was found wandering about asking for directions to the bus stop for Handsworth, which was where she used to live. A kind stranger took her to the police station at West Bar and they were able to ring John who came and returned her to the home. It's very worrying for him and he agreed the move to the lower floor for her. I feel sad that she has become so vulnerable in the short time that I have known her. We are off once more to France in two weeks and I intend to see her before we go.

*

A few days later the Ministry of Defence sent a reply to my request for more information. They asked me to fill in a form called a Certificate of Kinship, which asked for details of the relationship between Zygmunt and myself, and to send a copy of the death certificate. But, of course, I don't have this so I emailed Pam for advice. She is still waiting to hear from her contact in the USA who will tell us if we can buy a copy of the certificate here in the UK or whether it would be better to do this in the US.

*

When I arrived at the residential community, I turned towards the reception area to sign in. After a moment my glance turned towards a group of forlorn residents sitting in armchairs in the foyer, and there I spotted Kathleen. She smiled when she recognized me, or perhaps in return for mine.

'They're waiting to see the doctor,' the receptionist told me.

'Is she ill?' I asked. I received a vague reply. She wasn't exactly ill but they had some concerns, she said, but didn't tell me what they were. I am her friend, not a close relative, so not privy to information about her. Two carers took her away through some doors, one relieving me of the flowers I was carrying with a promise of finding a vase and asked me to take a seat in the café area next to the hairdressing salon. I decided on the flowers this time partly because I had not seen flowers in her room since we began visiting there and also because I thought it about time I offered a bit more commitment to this relationship with my mother. I was going on to see Brian's mum later and so bought two bunches at the service station as I set off up the A38 for Sheffield.

After a while Kathleen joined me at the café table. She was dressed in a green floral print, belted dress and although her hair was somewhat flyaway, she looked really nice and inordinately pleased to see me. We began with small talk about how good the weather had been lately. A young woman from the home had taken her a walk around the grounds yesterday and she had enjoyed the change.

'It's delightful here,' she said. 'I'm very lucky to be here although I'm ready to go home now.'

'Oh surely not. It's more like a hotel,' I volunteered. She agreed it was what with the food being so good and there was breakfast and a good lunch every day all served by these wonderful people. 'Everyone here is marvelous,' she said. 'I'm having my hair done later. It's free you know. You don't have to pay. It's free to pensioners.'

'Marvellous. You wouldn't get that at home would you?'

She agreed she wouldn't.

'Did you meet Bill?' she asked me.

'No.'

'Are you sure? He so enjoyed meeting you. He said you should come again.' She was completely convinced of the truth of this. 'He was there at the house when you came.'

'No. No he wasn't. He was in the nursing home wasn't he? We said, didn't we, that it wouldn't be a good idea if we went to see him because if he asked who I was, what were you going to tell him? Who would he think I was?'

She looked lost. 'Oh yes, I suppose so,' she conceded.

'After a few moments she said again, 'Bill really enjoyed meeting you. You came to the house at Christmas time.'

'Yes we did. Round about that time,' I said. 'I sent you a Christmas card.'

A dawning of recognition appeared on her face as if clutching at something tangible gave her a sense of herself.

'I put my phone number in there,' I reminded her.

'Oh yes, on a piece of sticky paper. I phoned you, didn't I?'

'Right. That's what you did,' I encouraged.

'And you came and met Bill,' but she was beginning to look doubtful.

'No. Bill has passed away now, you know. He's asleep.' Grab the bull by the horns, I thought, that's what John would do. 'Bill's not here? He's not waiting at home?' Looking saddened as if hearing the information for the first time she let it go.

Then she said, 'My sister's got a baby, you know.'

'Which sister would this be?' I asked.

'Audrey. She's got a baby and I don't know how it's going to be looked after.'

'Audrey?! Audrey's got a son called Christopher who must be in his...er...fifties,' I calculated. 'It's unlikely she's had a baby!'

'Oh, no. Of course not. I've imagined it haven't I?'

'Yes, I think you must have.'

'I got up at half past six this morning. I had the carpet to clean.' She looked concerned.

'Why is that?' I asked her.

'Well, in my room the carpet needs a clean and I offered to do it for them as it will give me something to do but they haven't brought me anything to do it with yet. Perhaps they've forgotten. Or perhaps they don't want me to do it.'

'Couldn't you offer to do a bit of light dusting instead,' I volunteered. 'That would keep you busy.'

The days must be long if there isn't much to do. Kathleen is obviously a person who likes to keep busy. She looks fit enough to be cleaning anyone's carpet but I thought the whole conversation was unlikely to have happened except in Kathleen's imagination. I thought I'd change the subject and told her that John and I had been speaking on the telephone before he went off to France and I told her what he had said he and Lynn, his wife, would be doing: a week at the house to work then a week in the Dordogne staying with friends.

'I wondered why I hadn't seen him,' she sat back in her chair and looked relieved tapping herself on the chest.

'He's on holiday,' I repeated. 'Has Paul been to see you?'

'Neither boys have been,' she said but that may not be true as she wouldn't remember if Paul had been or not although thinking back to my last conversation with John, perhaps Paul wasn't able to come, wasn't fit enough to get himself there. When I talk about John to Brian I sometimes say 'Our Paul' because that's what John says. It's an expression often used in Sheffield. People call their relatives 'our' someone as a sign of affection and belonging. Kathleen doesn't use it, though, but I like to say it. 'Our Paul.' I like the sound of it. Brian tells me, 'You like the idea of having brothers, don't you?' I do. I'd rather hoped one of them would be there on this morning but not so.

I had brought the laptop computer to show Kathleen some photos of the new baby grandson, Ben. Fortunately we were sitting beside a socket outlet so I plugged in the machine and while I powered it up she watched in wonder. I showed her the photos Brian had taken and she was fascinated. I didn't remind her this time she had a new great grandson but she peered at him with such pleasure. I reminded her that the last time I had visited I had brought an album of Robert and Lisa's wedding photographs so this time would she like to see some pictures of Nick, the eldest son, getting married a couple of years ago? Yes, she would. So I ran that collection as a slide show and she was delighted as I pointed out the various relatives. She loved the colour of the bridesmaids' dresses and the design of Debbie's dress. She made no comment on whether Nick reminded her of anyone she might have known. When I put the laptop away she asked to hold it to see how heavy it was and was surprised by its weight. She thought the idea of having photos stored in that way was good as the screen gave a bigger picture than a snapshot, there would never be a curling at the edges or fading and you could save them forever if you wanted, altogether, not loose in a box.

Peering closely at the screen all the time, she was interested and completely lucid, not at all confused but asking sensible questions about what she saw or making perfectly normal observations about the setting or the wedding guests, even though she didn't know them. I thought then just how important it is to stimulate the elderly and confused. I read recently, in fact it's often in the features pages of newspapers, that as one grows old it is possible to keep the brain cells reproducing and thereby staving off Alzheimer's disease by a variety of methods. One is by having an active social life. Kathleen didn't have this although the residential community teemed with caring women who chatted and took an interest in the residents' conversation whenever they could. Brian and I have a frenetically active social life –

241

friends, travelling, holidays and, of course family
including the grandchildren to keep us on our toes.
Another way is to do puzzles. I've always liked
crosswords picking up the habit from my dad whose
reason for living on a Sunday seemed to be religiously
completing the Sunday Express skeleton crossword
and the nine-letter word game. I like all the puzzles
but have become addicted to Sudoku. He'd have
loved that if he had lived long enough to be aware of
the craze. I'm not seriously worried by the knowledge
of Kathleen's condition thinking that it isn't a
foregone conclusion that I will inherit it, but, hey, let's
hedge our bets.

After a while Kathleen expressed a need to go
to the toilet and when I had taken her had a word with
a carer asking that when I was ready to leave would
someone be there to look after her as we were very
close to the reception door through which she had
made her recent escape.

'When she comes out of the toilet I'll take her
down to her room as it won't be too long before
lunch,' she offered. Realizing she had missed the
hairdresser as we had been talking Kathleen was
content to make an appointment for the following day.
I apologized that my arrival had prevented her from
having her hair washed but she didn't mind. She
scratched her head and said she had been getting some
dandruff so needed a hair wash. 'Do you get that?'
she asked at exactly the same time as I involuntarily
scratched the side of my head. She saw me doing it as
I caught myself doing it. She was holding onto my
arm at the time and she leaned into me as we laughed
together. We followed the carer down the corridor to

her room. I noticed that she punched in a code number on the keypad at the door.

Her new room was simply lovely. Pale blue was the theme with matching quilt cover and pillowcase on the single bed, blue carpet that showed not a trace of wanting cleaning, in fact, it looked brand new, and blue curtains. The window was open a little and the view from it was splendid. This room was on the other side of the building and looked inwards onto a courtyard of paths and borders. The paths were laid in soft grey York stone paving and meandered under a pagoda and around a water feature. Grass was laid beside part of the path, beds planted with shrubs and trees were on the other side. The beds were covered in bark chippings so no weeds showed through. The pagoda was made with logs, which supported trailing plants. Beds of bedding plants still well in flower contained brash orange of marigolds, which clashed startlingly with the pinks and mauves of busy-lizzies. A fountain made from three upright stainless steel tubes of different heights ranging from about three-feet tall to over five-feet in height formed the centerpiece. From each tube, water fell in a voluptuous sheet. It made not a sound; there was no splashing just the silent movement from the top of each tube onto a gravel bed that held the rising tubes.

'Wow!' I was moved to exclaim, 'that's wonderful! What a view. Aren't you lucky to be looking out on this?' She agreed she was. 'Oh, yes, it's very good here. Like a hotel. But I'll be going home soon, I think. They'll be coming for me. Look at the bathroom.' She opened the door onto a wet-room with the shower in one corner, a high toilet and a washbasin. It was as John had suggested: state of the art. I exclaimed some more as it was lovely.

'I wouldn't want to leave this in a hurry,' I told her. 'I'd like to live here myself.'

'I just have this need to go,' she said looking sad. 'I can't explain why.' I gave her hand a squeeze.

She leaned towards me in a confidential manner. 'There's this woman.'

'Oh?' Did she mean in this place?

'Yes, she's a neighbour and I don't want to start a scandal but she's after my Bill.'

'Oh really? I shouldn't think so.'

'Oh, yes. I could start tongues wagging in Handsworth,' she confided. But then she thought again. 'How old is Bill?' she asked and when I told her eighty-six she reconsidered. 'Yes, perhaps I've got that wrong. He is very faithful and eighty-six is a bit past it, isn't it. It's me that should be setting the tongues wagging.' She looked mischievous for a moment. 'You know what I mean?' I did. We looked at the photographs on the dressing table and the window ledge of Bill and her. One where they are wearing life jackets clearly on a boat abroad somewhere, celebrating their fiftieth wedding anniversary. Another from the kitchen wall of her house in Handsworth of Bill and the two dogs and another of Kathleen and him, taken some years ago on yet another holiday. They were like Brian and me; that is fortunate enough to be able to go on jaunts around the world. 'Do it while you can, love,' is what Brian's mother tells us, 'before it's too late.'

'He's your man,' I told her. 'No one else's. Look at this one. You are celebrating fifty years of marriage. In fact you were married for sixty-four years before he died.'

'Is he dead?'

'Yes, he's asleep, you said.'

'I keep thinking he's alive.'

'Is it any wonder,' I said hoping I sounded kind, 'you were married sixty-four years and together for more. How can you just put someone out of your head after all that time? He had been part of your life for so long.' She appeared to be wondering about this for a moment when a carer called her from the corridor to come down for lunch. 'I'll come and get you in a moment,' she said smiling.

Kathleen and I stood up. 'I'll take you down and then I must go.' I had been there for over an hour and a half and was expected in a while at Stannington. I felt a sudden rush to hug her. She is so likeable. Everyone in the residential community likes her. 'You are so huggable,' I told her. We stood by the door.

She looked up into my face. 'I can see that face,' she said suddenly. I wondered if she meant she could conjure up my face when I wasn't there. 'I know it,' she continued scrutinizing me carefully, holding my arms. 'I can see it.'

'What can you see when you look at this face?' I asked looking down into her eyes and expected her to say herself.

A Polish Airman,' she said. 'I loved that face.' A beat of silence, then, 'But don't tell Bill.'

We walked together into the lunchroom the moment passing but I wanted to hold onto it like a precious talisman.

Chapter 16

Invasion in France

Summer 2007 – Diary entry

A month in France. The first time this year that there would just be the two of us, for a week at least before my friend, Mary, came to stay with us. As she flew home Robert and Lisa, Jack and new baby, Benjamin, arrived not merely for a holiday but to live permanently. A new life for them. And as it turned out, complete chaos for us. At least for a short while.

Lisa's parents had come with them to France expecting to stay in a Gîte, which I had arranged for them in a village a couple of miles away. In the first week of our stay this arrangement fell through as I learned that the Gîte was less than comfortable or clean. I felt responsible. Telling a friend about this unfortunate turn of events she provided a solution and suggested they stay with them in the cottage they rent out for the summer. All was swiftly solved but as the let would not become available for two weeks we agreed that all the family would stay with us. This meant that when the huge removal lorry plus an additional trailer arrived with furniture for two households our barn, most of the floor space and all of the hayloft, came into its own as storage. The cottage for rent was fully furnished and had no storage space so Lisa's parents' furniture remains in our barn until they have a place of their own along with all Lisa and Rob's furniture that won't go into the house.

Lisa and Robert will live in our house, our small French holiday home, with Jack, Ben and Tiny the cat with the two dogs making a home in the area of the yard between the piggeries. We never intended that our holiday home would be for permanent living so it has inadequate insulation for cold winter months and no central heating.

After Lisa's parents left us the feeling that we were all on holiday subsided and Brian and I began the process of settling them into the area. Jack, aged four, needed to be in school. Rob, Lisa and I went to see the people at local Marie to ask about admission to the nursery department of the maternelle. We were directed to a nearby village and went to see the teacher, Madame Bigot, the maitress. She showed us around the classroom, so like Jack's nursery class in Scotland, except there were rows of little beds for the little ones to have their afternoon nap in a side room and an open space with small toilets, no seats, no cubicles. Pleased with what they saw and with what Mme Bigot was telling us we asked when he could start expecting her to say next January or at least after the half term break in November. But, no, would Jack like to start tomorrow? Yes, he certainly would. His only disappointment was that some other children traveled to school on a bus but his parents would prefer to take him there in the car, particularly at first until he settled in. Everything is taught in French, no concessions to his being English. Each day he listens to story read in French so picks up vocabulary. He is encouraged to bring home reading books (at a level suitable to help mum and dad extend their vocabulary – plenty of pictures) every Friday and Lisa reads to *him – with a dictionary beside her. Day by day he is learning to speak French and, so people say, after about six months will have developed a confidence with the language that within a year will have become fluent. This is one of the reasons Rob and Lisa have moved to France.*

Next job was to become registered with a doctor, as baby Ben would need vaccinations against polio, tetanus and diphtheria so I phoned the local doctor recommended by our neighbours, then and Lisa and I went to see him. Dr Ruquois was delightful and spoke a little English, which was so helpful for Lisa when we went home and she was left to explain Ben's needs to him. The final need on the list, in the early days, was Robert's. He wanted to join a football team. This he has done and plays most Sundays for the team at Montemboeuf, training twice a week with them. His vocabulary is coming on leaps and bounds but some of it is not for polite company. They are now getting on with their lives and beginning to feel settled in the new country.

*

December 2007 – Diary entry

We spent Christmas with them in France, flying by Ryanair from East Midlands airport to Limoges on Christmas Eve and taking with us my cousin, Margery. We had an enjoyable time watching Jack open all his presents and watching Ben watching him in bewilderment at all the excitement. We were cold some of the time but each had two duvets on our beds and we had taken a lot of warm clothing. The sun shone for us on Christmas Day and as I walked down the garden for a look at my favourite view breathing deeply on the fresh air I thought how lucky I was to be in my French garden at Christmas. We all sat around the table, Lisa's parents and the seven of us toasting our good fortune and enjoying scrumptious food – the turkey was succulent even though it had arrived from the butcher's shop with its head tucked under its wing. We pulled crackers, read mottos – English as I had bought them in Sainsbury's a few months earlier – and jokes and passed the small presents to Jack and drank and laughed a lot.

Nick phoned to wish us Merry Christmas; we had had a Christmas lunch with Debbie and him, Joseph and Aimee with a turkey and all the trimmings, Christmas pudding, and yet more crackers on the Sunday before Christmas Eve exchanging our presents then. I was still wearing their gift of warm pyjamas I had asked for under my dressing gown as we were talking on the phone.

Norman phoned from Knaresborough and we talked to some of his family as well as Brian's mum, who had been very ill three weeks earlier but was now recovering. It was like being at home.

*

8th January 2008 – Diary entry

Continuing with my search for details of Zygmunt Rosiak, I have downloaded a form from the website: ancestry.com so I can apply to the Office of Vital Records at the California Department of Health Services to obtain Zygmunt's death certificate. If you *want the official record the application must be accompanied by a signed affidavit that I am the official next of kin but it is possible to obtain a certified copy marked that it is for information only. This is because it cannot be used to commit identity fraud. I don't think I need the real thing. I want to apply to find out who registered the death with a possibility that there will be an address in California. Pam is too busy to pursue these enquiries for me but if I have any success, she and her husband will like to come to California with us, no doubt. I need to find out how to send the fee of $12.*

In the meantime, whilst I ponder on American connections, I have received a letter from the Ministry of Defence. I now have a reference number to use in all enquiries with them. They can't send me the information I want as all military personnel records are held in confidence under the Data Protection Act. The 'subject of the record' has to give permission for the information to be used – impossible – or the official next of kin. Who can this be? Perhaps they already know but as they know I'm not they have sent me a Certificate of Kinship form to complete. They require proof of death. This will need me to send my request to California. However, I fill in the form, tell them of my difficulty in obtaining the death certificate, and tell them I have no proof of kinship or if he has left a widow. I also enclose the printout from Ancestry.com giving Zygmunt's name, date of birth, place and date of death and his US social security number. I hope for the best.

The reply comes in a very short time. The MoD would like to inform me that the Internet details are enough to disclose information regarding my natural father's military service under British command and would I send £30. This I have done.

I have also sent off the request to California, not with $12 but a cheque for £7, the sterling equivalent. Last week we were dining with Ann and David, Brian's cousins who were in at the beginning, on the night I met Kathleen and are always interested to be kept up with current events. Ann used to work in a bank and brushed away my problem of sending US dollars and suggested instead that I send the cheque in sterling.

So, I wait for details from the MoD and information from the records office in California. What would excite me most at the moment would be if there was a photograph amongst his service records. I want to look like him. I want my children to have some resemblance, about the eyes, possibly.

Chapter 17

A Family Gathering

Kathleen had spent Christmas with John and his family. This I learned when I phoned him on our return from France. I thought about him on Christmas Eve because that had been the day he first phoned me a year ago. I wasn't able to talk to him until after New Year's Day as he had been in France at his house for New Year. Christmas Day for Kathleen, for our mother, had not been very successful, as she had slept for most of it, including during the meal. John thinks the residential community gets the drug dosage wrong from time to time and at these times Kathleen is not herself. She had had a fall recently. Finding her on the floor of her room John picked her up. Asking her why she was there she told him she had been climbing over the rocks with Bill. She wasn't hurt (or wet!)

On my last visit, though, she was lively and delighted to see Brian and me. We took the laptop with photographs of the children opening presents at Christmas and told her of the French house. John joined us after a while and out came the photos again.

I had visited a few weeks before Christmas and taken my cousin Margery. She had asked me some months ago if she could come and see Kathleen so I asked John what he thought. He had no objections but did wonder if it would be confusing for her. And so it was but not more than she could cope with.

Kathleen was sitting in the lounge when we arrived. Dozing in front of daytime television with a group of other ladies, she opened her eyes as we arrived.

'That's her,' I said to Margery.

'Yes,' she said, 'I knew straight away.'

I felt pleased. She thought we looked similar. Brian doesn't see any likeness. I'm pleased to have a second opinion because I need to look like someone, to have specific characteristics reappear in me.

'It's round the mouth, the chin,' Margery said. 'And the hair.' The good old salt and pepper.

We went to her room and Margery exclaimed as I had done how lovely it was and how pleasing the view of the garden was from the window. I explained to my mother that Margery was my cousin. I felt quite odd doing this. Earlier, Margery had said, 'I'd like to see your mum,' without any feeling of awkwardness, as my mum had been her Aunt Dot but here was another mum who was no relation to her, well at least, not by blood. So, here was my mother. We talked first of all about children and Margery told her she and Fred hadn't had any. Kathleen told her she had two boys – no mention of a girl, though. None of this was uncomfortable. John arrived after a while so introductions were held again. We chatted like a family. What's so unusual about that? I can't remember our conversation but what stands out is that Margery and Kathleen faced each other in easy chairs, John sat on the bed and I perched on a small stool at Kathleen's feet. Even though John is younger, I felt I was the child.

*

Brian and I continue to visit my mother at her residential home. Twice in the last three occasions John and Paul have been already there. Always delighted to see me, Kathleen smiles and is welcoming but Paul has stood up straight away and looked agitated. Then, he has gone off down the corridor towards the door with John in pursuit to put in the security code so he can go and sit in the car. Brian and I feel guilty about being there but John is very reassuring and tells us that Paul, unlike ourselves, can see his mother whenever he wants to, as long as, that is, John is available to bring him in the car. His dementia is worsening. He feels embarrassed that he is unable to carry out a conversation easily and rather than try to face it out, prefers to be elsewhere. He knows who I am and I would love to form a relationship with him but it is not to be. It's just another thing where I am a year or two too late. I feel I look a bit like Paul although it's probably nothing more than being tall. Tall genes are most commonly passed on through the mother's side so it stands to reason we might have characteristics in common as Bill wasn't tall at all and of course John is Bill's double. Paul has been unshaven and has an air of neglect about him. When we come out into the car park with John I smile and raise a hand towards Paul but he smiles vaguely and just nods. It's very sad, as the day I met him no one would ever imagine his health could go down so rapidly.

The last time we went there was no sign of either of my half-brothers. John must be in France. But there was Kathleen sitting in a comfortable chair in the foyer waiting to have her hair shampooed and set. Feeling slightly alarmed as she has this reputation for leading The Great Escape, we went straight over to her and sat down beside her. As ever she was thrilled to see us and recognized us straight away.

'What a coincidence!' she declared. 'Do you come here for your hair doing?

'Brian, head shaven (by me with the Babyliss) on a number one every six weeks, quite firmly said that he didn't. But she meant me so I told her I might have a trim!

We sat and watched as the two hairdressers took ladies from the seats and placed them by washbasins; put ladies under the dryers; and set rollers in their hair. A lady at the side of me, plainly a resident, toothless and in her eighties, told me that she hoped they wouldn't be too long as she had the children to collect from school! I expressed no surprise and quietly agreed with her. We told Kathleen that it wasn't such a coincidence as we had driven from Burton on Trent especially to visit with her. It seemed a jolly morning and we did a lot of laughing. She got on to the subject of Brenda at the mention of Burton and I told her once again that we had met her and her husband Al.

Kathleen once more asked if we'd met Bill. Instead of struggling to tell her the truth I just gave in and said that he'd been upstairs one time when we had called and she looked pleased. I have taken a lead from John on that during a visit a time or two before. He said he does the same as it becomes too stressful to have all the details of a memory in place to talk about when it's just so much easier to go with the flow and agree, even if Kathleen's version is far from the truth.

What is in her mind, no one really knows so it seems kinder to let her have her version of events to think and talk about and not rock the boat by being pedantic.

Eventually, Kathleen went into the salon and sat down to have her hair washed. We waited and chatted together and I disappeared to find a vase to arrange flowers we had taken and put them into her room. After a while she emerged looking refreshed and stylish. She always looks splendid when we go. She never expects us so it is her normal look. When we were waiting with her she pointed out a hanging rail with some of her clothes on which must have been returning from the laundry. I recognized a dress and a skirt I had seen her in. She looked slightly bewildered until she realized they would be returned later to her wardrobe washed and ironed.

Going to Hazelthorpe reminded me that I had not heard from the Ministry of Defence for a while even though I know that they cashed my £30 cheque in April. I must pursue them for the information on Zygmunt. I still haven't heard from America either.

Chapter 18

A Polish Air Man's Past Revealed

A phone call to the MoD at Ruislip reveals an administrative error. The lady there tells me with much apologizing that she has dealt with my case but put the papers back in the drawer instead of in an envelope for the post. When I made myself known at first I said my enquiries were about Zygmunt Rosiak, pronouncing it as it looks – Ros-i-ak. 'Oh, yes' she say not missing a beat, 'Zygmunt Roshak'

Is that how it's pronounced?' I asked her.

'Yes, Roshak.'

'I haven't heard it said before,' I told her. I felt pleased that I had had to ask or I would never have known how it sounded.

*

The papers have arrived.

The covering letter apologized again for the delay in sending them to me and told me that they were happy to enclose statements about my father's military service in the Polish Forces under British command during WW11. The envelope was quite bulky, as she had sent all the available documents. Enclosed was an extract from 'Indeks Represjonowanych' regarding Zygmunt's deportation to Russia in 1939. Deportation to Russia?! This was something quite new. I quickly scanned all the pieces of paper delighting in some and putting others aside as they were in Polish! Here, though in my hands were

257

documents that held his signature and even a fingerprint. Sadly, however, no photos.

There was a summary document which revealed he was Flight Sergeant Zygmunt ROSIAK number 704560, born on 29th December 1916 at Otmianowo in the Parish of Pyskowo, district of Wloclawek, county of Pomorze, Poland. His parents were Jan and Maria Rosiak and her name before marriage was Kuczynski. These people were my grandparents and would never have knowledge of a granddaughter in England. His father remains as his next of kin on all his forms throughout the period so remained alive for the duration of the war, at least. His parents were Polish and, like him, Roman Catholic. The form gives his civilian occupation before Army Service as an Agriculturist. He served with the Polish Forces under British Command from 15th August 1942 until 8th January 1947 and went on to serve with the Polish Resettlement Corps from 9th January 1947, relegated to Class 'W' Reserve on the unemployed list until he was finally discharged, relinquishing his commission on honorable discharge two years later on 9th January 1949.

His conduct is described as Very Good in a document called a General Conduct Sheet where ten entries testify to the fact that he has "nothing to report," from 11th September 1943 to 14th April 1948 under the column 'Offence'. They refer to his active service, of course, not to his conduct with a married woman in Hucknall!

His military service began o11th November 1938 whilst he was living in Otmianawo. He joined up for active military service and took part in the 1939

September campaign in Poland. The campaign began on 1st September 1939, the outbreak of World War 2, of course, and continued to the 20th September. The brave Poles had held off the Nazis for twenty days until they were overrun. Zygmunt was with the 14 Infantry Regiment, Frontier Defence Corps and around the 20th September, the Russian authorities arrested him. As he was of Polish nationality he was deported to the former USSR in 1940 although the exact date and place or places of the deportation within the former USSR aren't recorded.

On the basis of the Sikorski-Maisky (Polish-Soviet) agreement of 30th July 1941 Zygmunt was released for the purpose of joining the Polish Armed Forces, which were being organized in 1941-1942 on the former Soviet territory. He enlisted in the Polish Army on 15th September 1941 and was posted to 14 Infantry Regiment, 5 Infantry Division.

Together with other Polish Army units he crossed the Soviet-Iranian frontier and was evacuated to Iran. This was how he came under British command with effect from 15th August 1942. He was then transferred to Iraq where he was trained as a wireless operator. Up until this time he had been a soldier, not an airman but on the reorganization of the Polish Army in the Middle East he was assigned to the Polish Air Force in the UK. The 21st May 1943 was the date he joined the Polish Air Force under British command.

He had the rank of Flight Sergeant and in his trade of pilot had a variety of postings:

21.05.1943 – Air Crew Training Centre, RAF Hucknall

11.09.1943 – Polish Initial Training Wing, RAF Brighton

15.02.1944 – No.25 Polish Elementary Flying Training School, RAF Hucknall

18.05.1944 – No.16 Secondary Polish Flying Training School, RAF Newton, Nottinghamshire

26.10.1944 – Polish Air Force Depot, RAF Blackpool

02.11.1944 – Polish Air Crew Training Wing, RAF Morecambe

08.11.1844 – No.18 Operational Training Unit, RAF Finningly

02.12.1944 – No.71 Base, RAF Lindholme

28.05.1945 – No.300 Polish Bomber Squadron, RAF Faldingworth, Lincolnshire

These dates are fascinating. He was in Hucknall, home of the fateful dancing, in 1943 and 1944, time to get to know Kathleen, a young woman married just over a year with her husband away fighting in the Middle East for a few months, but he doesn't seem to have been there at the time of my conception, July or August 1945. However, the Lincolnshire bases aren't too far away if transport was readily available. After bombing raids over Germany the lighthearted moments of dancing and much more, with a pretty girl would have been precious.

Zygmunt was involved in the demobilization of Polish Forces under British command, which occurred gradually over a period of at least two years, enlisting in the Polish Resettlement Corps/RAF (PRC/RAF) on 9th January 1947 serving in the UK until he was finally discharged on 9th January 1949 on completion of his two year contract. He was entitled to two medals although there is no record of whether he received them: the Polish Air Medal and the British Defence Medal: The War Medal 1939 –1945.

The documents, although not very extensive, which bear the heading Indeks Represjonowanych concerning Zygmunt's deportation to Russia, are in Polish and may take some time to have translated. Although they seem to be forms with his name and family members on them, they also contain several sentences of information, which may prove interesting in creating a picture of his movements at that time.

The Polish Resettlement Corps (RAF) document dated 7th March 1947, actually paints a more human picture of the man who was my natural father. The entries have been completed and signed in his handwriting. At first the form asks for his name, place and date of birth, his religion, and marital status so reveal no new information although his full address is given as RAF Skipton on Swale which is near Richmond, in North Yorkshire, where my dad, in the RAF, was stationed in the war before he was sent overseas. I am wondering now whether my dad whose job was to talk planes down as they came in to land after flying sorties was actually a wireless operator.

Zygmunt's form says that he has been enlisted in the PRC (RAF) and provisionally entered in the trade of pilot. In the second part of the form there is space to enter a description of the recruit completing the form: details such as height, weight, wounds, scars distinctive marks indicating congenital peculiarities or previous disease, chest measurement – girth when fully expanded and range of expansion in inches – colour of hair, eyes, complexion, size of head and of boots. Maddeningly, not one item has been filled in. On turning this form over again I notice that there seems to be a penciled note scribbled on the top as an afterthought, so probably not when it was being completed, which says 'Eming to Canada'. It's barely noticeable but does seem to be an indication of his intentions.

The accompanying attachment has more information. It tells us that as a pilot he flew 80 hours in Wellington bombers and 370 hours in Lancaster bombers as part of the Operational Training Unit 300. Whilst at Skipton on Swale he clocked up 700 flying hours making his last flight on 1st December 1946. Under special qualifications including service jobs other than aircrew it says Trained as W/OP Ground in the Polish Army although it doesn't explain what this was. There is information about his education. He was in primary school for seven years followed by 4 years in secondary school where he achieved 'Half Matric'. It doesn't give any details about the subjects he matriculated in but it does state that he has French as another language confirming what previous documents have revealed. His civil job is given as 'Working with father in wholesale food stores for 5 years'. The entry 'Agriculturalist' probably refers to this. Does this entry suggest his father had a business?

His spare time activities are given as – keen on swimming and tennis, is learning English, likes reading serious books, prefers variety theatreand goes to cinemas with dancing. I'm still smiling as I read this over again. Finally, he is keen on motoring and does running repairs. He sounds a very interesting man: sporty and cultured.

An odd question is: Expecting to marry? He writes 'No' Dependents? No. Details of his hometown is unclear as it states London Area, Yorkshire, which could be Skipton on Swale and then, oddly for this time, Hucknall in Nottingham. Was he still in Nottingham in 1947?

His future wishes are expressed as preferring work in meteorologist section as he learned something of this during pilot training. Under further notes it says: 'In Army at beginning of War – Transported to Russia in July 1940 – employed on labour (does this refer to hard labour?) but only on odd jobs for about a year – In August 1941 he joined the Polish Army in Russia and was trained as a Wireless Operator – Sent to Iraq in April, 1942 and after about a year volunteered for the Air Force and was sent to England – has had interview with Labour Exchange who stated that he could be trained as a textile worker.' Not too close to his desire to work as a meteorologist, then which apparently he was very keen on. Nottingham was known for the extent of its hosiery industry at that time although it's much depleted now. Perhaps despite everyone being asked their preference textile workers were needed most.

We learn a little more about him over the page through the Board's general Observations: 'F/L (not flight sergeant but this is probably an error) is an N.C.O of medium height and build. He is very smartly turned out and throughout the interview was most cooperative. He has expressed a preference for work as a meteorologist assistant and as he seems intelligent and has had a fairly good education he should do quite well at this. His experience of meteorology is confined to his aircrew training. He expressed no desire to remain in the service. His writing of English was described as very good. His spoken English was declared good and he was able to express himself well. I feel that he and my dad would have got on very well. They share some interests, although not the participation in sport. They were intelligent, liked reading serious books, going to the theatre and the cinema. My parents had a season ticket for the Sheffield Repertory theatre and used to go each week. Before the war they went to the cinema two or three times a week. My dad was very keen on motoring and had a car and a motorbike from an early age. And, of course, they had the RAF in common, which would have kept them reminiscing for many hours.

A year later, on 8ᵗʰ April 1948 Zygmunt signed form 2925 referred to as Alien Identity Certificate, which gave approval for his release from the Polish Resettlement Corps for employment by the Ministry of Labour and National Service. Here he is described as Flight Sergeant Zygmunt Rosiak, Height 5 feet 7 inches. Not as tall as I had imagined, then, but an inch shorter than me. His complexion is described as 'dark' and his eyes 'grey'. Oh dear. I was convinced they would be brown. Do two sets of grey eyes make brown? I do hope so. His hair is brown, like mine but I still think I have Kathleen hair. He has no marks or scars. There is an address given where he 'is proceeding': 27 Water Street, Leeds 2 and the local office of the Ministry of Labour and National Service is in Leeds, too, at the employment exchange on West Street. His expected employment is as a Presser with Sassoons Tailors Ltd, Victory House, Samuel Street, Leeds 1. Zygmunt has signed the document with a bold flourish with the loop of the R framing the top part and half the down stroke of the Z.

And so he left the Polish Resettlement Corps to start a new life in Leeds in, by association, the textile industry. He could have been wearing his demob suit as the note on the form tells him that if he doesn't take up the work as specified and approved by the ministry he will be liable to pay back any temporary release benefits given to him or be entitled to another civilian outfit.

One final document of interest is a record held by the RAF, which is Airman's/Airwoman's Record Sheet for Active Service. All the information we have about where he was stationed, the dates of the service are listed, from May 1943 to January 1947. Also given are assessments of his character throughout his service. All twelve entries from September 1943 to April 1948 describe him as 'VG'. There is an entry for 14.4.48, which details that he was released to industry and given a clothing warrant for £42.8.0. Perhaps, then he bought his own demob suit from Sassoons Tailors Ltd. He would have looked smart and well turned out, of course.

His address in a note at the end of the form at June 1949 is given as 22 Goldsmith Hill, Upper Wortley, Leeds 12. It is the same as that given on his Polish Air Force association membership card.

265

Another hand written note at the top of the form made me gasp. It says: Granted British Nationality 22.2.50. There is a final note saying 'Auth:- H.O. letter R.23627/x D/D 24.3.50. I can't guess what this means but both dates are an indication he was still in the UK.

A document towards the end recommends that he should receive the Defence Medal for his service from 1.3.42 in the Polish Army East of Suez through service at all the RAF bases until 8.5.45. I hope he received it.

So here we have a man of exemplary character, culture and intelligence who liked to dance and caught the eye of a young married woman at a dance hall in Hucknall, Nottingham. He had an interesting war, which he was lucky enough to survive despite being deported to Russia, flying dangerous missions and probably spending some time training others to fly. He wasn't as tall as I had imagined; he didn't have the brown eyes, but together my mother's and his created mine. Without a photograph the Polish ears haven't been identified but I remain convinced he is the source of them, present in two further generations now. I think I would have loved to know him and would have been very proud of him had our lives been different.

There are nineteen years of his life remaining, knowledge of which should reveal what he was doing in Los Angeles in 1969. I have looked again at the entry of his death from the Internet records. I know I wrote that it was 2nd April 1969 but on closer inspection, because Americans write month then date, I now see that the entry reads 4th February 1969. On this date in 1986 my dad died. On this date Brian's father died ten years later. Coincidences still abound in this story.

*

I try to phone the office in California to see why they haven't let me have Zygmunt's death certificate, perhaps his papers are stuck in a drawer in the Health and Human Services agency in the State of California, but am thwarted by automatic messages.

Chapter 19

A Surprise French Visit

Summer 2008 – Diary entry

Yet another holiday in France in what has proved to be the wettest August in the UK for sixty years. Thank heaven for the little French property even if it is still occupied by Number Two son and his family. In spite of that it's still wonderful to spend time with Rob, Lisa and the little boys. The baby, Ben, didn't recognize us and whimpered when we arrived but after a day or so he had adjusted to our presence and clung onto our legs to pull himself up and walk around using both us, anybody else available and the furniture. Jack swung himself into our arms and gave us the biggest hug he could find. We enjoyed celebrating Ben's first birthday on the 18th August, which was a low-key family affair of presents in the morning and tea later in the day with sandwiches and a birthday cake with candles. He knew something special was happening, as he was the centre of everyone's attention for most of the time.

We had been to the méchoui in Massignac meeting up with French neighbours and English friends. The day dawned cloudy and in anticipation of rain, which never came, the organizers had put up two marquees on the recreation ground where tables were being laid for about six hundred people. When Brian and I arrived to write our names on the paper tablecloth to reserve sixteen places one of the committee members was up a plane tree with a chainsaw taking off branches whilst below him was a group of six Frenchmen giving advice. As we watched a lady walked across the road from the car park just as a branch crashed onto the road missing her by inches. Oh la la! She wasn't best pleased and uttered some words of criticism gesticulating towards the man who remained in the tree offering words of apology. We were struck by the difference here from how such a job would have been undertaken in England. Mindful of health and safety, there would have been hard hats for everyone, a safety net, closing of the road in all directions and twenty-four hours' notice of the work being done. Mais, bof, c'est la vie: she wasn't hurt so they just continued to saw. The tree looked neat when we arrived for our lunch two and a half hours later and the lady was smiling as she served some of the courses. As ever we ate well and long.

We managed to see all of our friends in the Charente at least once and spend time with Norman, Brian's brother and his wife, Sue and their daughter, son in law and grandson, out for a holiday, having a meal with Rob, Lisa, Jack & Ben in the local pizzeria for Norman's birthday. Margery, my cousin came out for a week, flying to Limoges bringing with her a week of lovely weather, which enabled us to show her some of the sights such as a day out in Angoulême, another in Brantôme in the Dordogne, lunch in La Rochefoucauld, a run round the local countryside and a meal with family, in particular Lisa's mum and step-dad. On the way back to the airport in Limoges we stopped at a splendid relais for lunch in the heart of stunning Haut Vienne countryside followed by a visit

269

to Maison de Porcelain in Aix-sur-Vienne. A walk and a sit in the sunshine beside the wide and slow-moving river completed the outing. She didn't want to go home and we were sorry to see her go.

Just ahead of Margery's stay Robert had a stroke of luck. He had heard that a local restaurant, Dutch owned and run, was looking for a new chef. He presented himself to the owners and told them what he could do. They loved him. After his two-day trial he has been given a contract. He and Lisa are also looking at buying a house, which will complete their circle as they will have been living in France for almost a year and their life is beginning to come together.

*

When the time arrived for us to leave and as we had booked an early morning crossing from Caen to Portsmouth on the Saturday morning we set off after lunch on the Friday, three days after Jack started school again. Instead of driving directly to Caen we took a detour when we got to Argentan in Normandy towards the town of Flers. Not far from there is a little village called Fleuriac. In this village John, my half-brother and his wife Lynn have a holiday home. The chances of finding the house or of finding them out there for a holiday were remote but at least we would have seen the village and the area, which we could talk about the next time we saw him at the residential community. Our mother is always wondering whether we have seen one another in France.

The countryside as we drove along the main roads towards the village was delightful, the views long and rolling. We found the village with little difficulty and turned towards an English pub on the right but noticed a church on the opposite side of the road so turned around towards it. We drove along a lane with smart permanent looking houses on it and thinking they certainly weren't holiday homes turned round again until we reached a lane signposted to the Marie. We drove down this lane and up the other side of the hill when Brian remarked that John had told him his house was on a hill. We came to two cottages and stopped in front of the first.

'Get out and read the letterbox,' Brian instructed.

'Daniel Deroux,' I read.

'There's an English car in the next drive,' he pointed out. 'John's got a new car.' I walked up the lane and read an English plate on a Ford Mondeo. A little to the right of this was another letterbox. It was painted green and read: 'Newcombe J & L'

'Oh, my God, we've found it,' I shouted raising both my thumbs. I walked back to the car and got in. What were the chances of that? You can look forever to find people in France, as there is no system in French villages of addresses that contain house numbers or road names.

'What shall we do?' we asked at the same time.

'Drive up the lane and turn round,' I suggested so he did and pulled up again in the lane in front of the house.

'Now what shall we do?' he asked.

'Oh, come on. Let's go and knock. What's the point of coming all this way and not doing anything about it. We can't just drive away. What would you think if it was them and we found they had been to look us up and then driven off?'

'Right' he said, 'Let's do it.' So we walked up to the front door of a charming little stone built cottage with lots of land and a lovely view over the surrounding countryside and knocked at a newly fitted varnished wood door.

John opened the door and his face was a picture. Despite his surprise he asked us in and welcomed us. Lynn, however, looked non-plussed.

'Who's this?' she asked, 'I don't know these people!'

I stepped towards her and holding out my hand said, 'I'm Margaret.' She shook my hand as recognition of the name dawned and in the French way, I leaned forward and kissed her cheeks. Our spectacles clashed. She was, she said later, only four feet eleven to my five feet eight so I had to bend quite a lot.

John looked amazed and delighted in turns and said to his wife, 'You know who this is don't you?' She did. But Lynn was quite alarmed that we had arrived without warning and at a point that they had packed into boxes things they would need to take with them the following day for a trip to Bayeaux to stay in a Gîte with the object of sightseeing in Normandy. They had just finished eating and the detritus of the meal was evident in the room. John, however, began moving boxes from the other room saying come in here; we'll be more comfortable. So we followed him into the room pursued by Lynn and sat down on a sofa. He disappeared for a moment and returned with a bottle of cabernet sauvignon and four wine glasses.

All the while Brian and I protested we hadn't come to disturb them, wouldn't stay long. They had only to say it wasn't the most convenient moment and we'd go. We reiterated the idea that it was by sheer chance that we had found the house, and what coincidence that we had found them on holiday there anyhow. 'What's the chance of that happening?' I wondered aloud.

I told them of our tour round the village in search of their house and how we had seen large, smart houses on the road leading from the church. 'You'd know that wouldn't be ours then, wouldn't you?' murmured Lynn.

There were pauses as we made small talk about houses in France, the best Channel crossings, and eventually got onto the subject of 'mother.' We said we had been to her residential community in the week before we set off for France – over a month ago and they realized they had been in France then, coming home just after that and they were in France now for a second time this month. I told them about the hairdressers and the remarks of the lady sitting next to our mother worrying about picking up her children from school. They laughed. I told them too how Kathleen found it an amazing coincidence that I had turned up to have my hair done at the same time. They laughed at that too. And when I said how worried we had been that she was sitting near the reception in the entrance given her predilection for escaping, Lynn told us about how mother-in-law had been found in the local supermarket and again in

273

Sheffield town centre before being brought back again by the police.

'The home didn't let us know until quite late that she was missing. It was after ten at night and too late for us to do anything about it. It was just lucky that the police had her and brought her back soon after. She's famous for her break outs.' Lynn laughed.

I laughed with her at the memory of what John had told me before and then she suddenly said, 'Oh! You looked just like your mother then.'

'How do you mean?' I asked turning towards her.

'It's just her look. It's about the mouth and the chin. It's just her.' I felt a sudden surge of delight.

'You don't know what that means to me,' I told her and turning to John said, 'Already I love your wife!' Then we were all laughing.

Lynn wanted to know how we had traced Kathleen and Brian and I gave her the story of the Long Search including the contact with social services in Nottingham and Sheffield and how Kathleen had contacted Sue Tomlinson after she had received her letter. I told her about how Kathleen had known about twenty Darklands Road and how my father had known her name, about the Polish airman, and the address in Sheffield we had gone to look at when we first began the search. She was as amazed as we had been that they had been able to know these things given the secrecy of the event at the time. She agreed that it was probably an address where Bill's parents had lived at the time. She knew from Kathleen that she had made the visit to Darklands Road meeting with some little

274

girls and asking after me. She realized what an ordeal it had been for her mother in law to give up her child that she was still feeling it and hankering to see how I had turned out as much as four years later. I agreed and reminded her that she would certainly have already had John and most probably Paul, too.

'I think it was a pretext that she told Bill that she wanted to visit his father's grave at the cemetery between Crookes and Crosspool as she would have known full well where Darklands Road was. She must have been hurting very much. Would Bill have known from the start? Do you think she wrote and told him she was pregnant?' she asked.

John didn't know. 'I shouldn't think so.'

'What a shock to come home and find out,' Lynn said. 'When were they demobbed in the Middle East?'

We didn't know, of course, but it wasn't unreasonable to suspect it could have been quite late in 1945.

'Suppose it was December,' I proposed. 'I was conceived in August so she would be at least four months by then and showing.'

'However did she tell him?'

'She just had to do it right out. He said he wasn't bringing up some other man's bastard and so she had to give me up. They stayed together and soon had John. There's less than a year between us. She thought he was very brave,' I told her.

'Well, I certainly don't,' she said adamantly. A woman of strong opinions, this one. I must have looked amazed, as I had just accepted Kathleen's version of events.

'Well, I don't. It would have been a lot braver to decide to keep you. John's mum had been sent away to keep her out of the way when she began to show…'

'Yes, to her Auntie Jessie's in Leicester.'

'Oh, she lived in Leicester did she? Well so much the better. It wouldn't have taken much to come home with a baby that was to all intents and purposes theirs and just get on with things. As it was it broke her heart and it was just a sop that he said they should have a child of their own, to keep her happy. It's a good job it didn't take long to get you, John.'

Brian said, 'Well, to be fair, it was more likely the pressure of Bill's father, a Roman Catholic that forced Bill's hand.'

'Mmm,' she considered for a minute and conceded that was probably the case. 'She did say that she had had an affair, didn't she, John?'

'I'd like to think I wasn't the product of a one night stand, conceived round the back of a bike shed at the dance hall in Hucknall…' I was just going on to say '…or in a big feather bed in the house in Middlewood when I caught her looking at John.

She said to him, 'Are you all right, love?' He had got up to open the windows as the room had grown warm whether with the red wine being drunk or the hot air being generated by this seamy talk or whether, indeed he was finding all this a bit hard going. Brian caught my eye at this point saying silently you're going a bit too far. I had got carried away with my tale and was behaving somewhat insensitively.

'It's very odd all this. It makes me see my mother in quite a different light,' John said smiling ruefully. What did you think when you first saw her?'

'I thought she was lovely. I still do. She's funny with a quirky sense of humour. She came out to the gate to meet us and that was when I saw my mother for the first time in sixty years. It was a very odd feeling.' He looked away wanting to say something but not finding the words.

'It was weird the day he found out, you know,' broke in Lynn. 'He used to pick me up from work and this time he was very quiet and I thought he had had a bit of a spat with his mother because sometimes she was nasty to him and it used to upset him.' This was something new, as I couldn't imagine her being nasty but then why should I, as she had not behaved like that to me. How sad as it seemed to me that John was a very caring son.

'I asked him what the matter was and he said she had told him he had a sister.'

'I couldn't believe it, continued John. 'She had been telling me some funny things for a while about a sister, about someone called Margaret who had a house in France. I just thought she'd got muddled up with the fact that we have one. She gave me quite a lot of detail and then repeated it in a way that made me realise she wasn't making it up and then she told me she had had a baby during the war and given it up. I felt quite shaken. I asked her if it was something our Paul should know about and she said it was but would I tell him? I had to take him on one side and tell him.'

'How did he react?' asked Brian.

'Like me really. He didn't want to know. It's not the kind of thing you want to know about your mother. It's just not.'

'And at that time your father was still alive,' continued Brian.

'Yes, but he didn't know anything about anything. You sent the Christmas card.'

'Yes,' I agreed. 'That was ironic wasn't it? We didn't know of course that she was a Jehovah's Witness.'

'Well,' said Lynn. 'We used to send her one anyway.'

'Then there was a letter wasn't there?' said John.

'Do you mean one I wrote to her? Yes.' I told them that after she had stopped getting in touch with the social worker the trail went cold, sort of speak. I sent the card after a friend of mine in similar circumstances suggested it would be a way to reawaken the contact. Then after we had spoken on the phone – she said she was a nosey woman and couldn't resist phoning the number on the post-it, you know - ...'

'What did she say on the phone?' asked Lynn. 'Did she know it was you?'

'No. Well, I don't think so. After she explained about the card and said something about a possible contact from caravanning days she actually asked what contact we had. And I said the contact was the 10th April 1946 and she said, Oh. And then she said, 'Are you Averill?' And I said I was. So she said I think we should meet. And we did. But after that when I wanted to see her again I wrote to her and reminded her of our earlier meeting.'

'I was in the house when that letter came,' said John. She opened it and put it in her handbag so when I had a chance I copied the address and the phone number, although I didn't read the letter. That's why I was able to phone you but I knew who you were by then. She'd told me.'

'Then there was Brenda,' broke in Lynn.

'Oh, yes, I've met Brenda,' I told her.

'Yes, I understand so,' she said. 'I had to tell her at the funeral but I had the impression that she already knew. My mother had told her before. It wouldn't surprise me that she knew before I did.' He laughed.

'In fact we think Pat knew before you,' said Lynn. Pat?

'A friend of John's mother from the Jehovah's Witnesses. We think she told quite a few people from there which is funny really given what a straight laced lot they are.'

John recalled a conversation with Pat and someone else from the Jehovah's Witnesses group who when he overheard them talking were mentioning 'Margaret' so it seemed to him the word had got about. 'Half the street knew and probably all before me!' he added. I wanted to giggle as I recalled having to speak quietly on the brown velour sofa in Kathleen's living room when we were first talking in case the neighbours overheard.

Brian told them of some of the coincidences we had discovered in our search for Kathleen: his cousins Ann, Margaret and Charles and his aunt and uncle living in the house across the cul-de-sac, the fact that we had been going to see Ann and David on the night I met Kathleen, Middlewood and Hillsborough where he had been brought up just streets away, Firth Park Grammar School where he and Paul had attended albeit at different times. Even French houses.

After a time John went out of the room taking Brian with him to see the house and the work he had done on it. Lynn and I talked of Paul and his illness. He was suffering quite badly now from loss of memory and motor skills and John having to give a lot of his time to his brother. Lynn was disapproving of Paul's children, as they did nothing to help their father, letting instead the responsibility fall to John.

'John's mother registered the birth in Leicester did she? Or in Sheffield? Why didn't she just have you adopted in Leicester? Why did she have to come back to Sheffield with you?' I explained what I knew and why I thought she had done what she had. It seemed the most practical thing. She said Kathleen had told her I was Maureen. Or was it Averill. Both, I said. She wasn't too fond of either, she said, but perhaps Kathleen was thinking of a French connection when she named me for a month. We laughed at that. She was interested to learn what we had been doing to trace Zygmunt so I told her of the American connection. She already knew that so I said what the papers had revealed about his looks: that his eyes weren't brown but grey and we had an inconclusive discussion about whether two sets of grey eyes made brown.

'Perhaps there were others,' she hooted, something she probably would not have said if John

280

were still in the room but she didn't say it seriously. We were both laughing, even though I felt a bit embarrassed when Lynn said, 'Oh there it is again, the same laugh, the same look.'

'Do you mean Kathleen?' I asked.

'Yes. It's uncanny.'

'That means so much to me because unlike you who can look at yourself and say that you are like your parents in various ways and John is like his in others you can see the same characteristics repeated in your son. It's Hugh, isn't it?' She agreed it was and told me that although she is four feet eleven and John is about five six, Hugh is five feet eleven; so there go the tall genes again. 'I can't do that. I don't know who I look like but knowing from you, who knows my mother so well and has done for years that I am like her, is just so precious.' She looked pleased as she stood up to close one of the windows as the wind was beginning to rise. So I told her all about the Polish ears: Nick's, Joe's and now Ben's.

'There may be pointed ears on the James side of the family. I don't know.'

'In a way I don't want there to be but in another I'd like to know. I shall appoint you the official sleuth to examine the ears of the family.' At this point John and Brian returned with Brian saying what a good job John had made of converting the bedroom. He was very proud of the bathroom, which leads off the lounge as it was beautifully tiled on the walls and the floor with white painted *lambris*, the tongue and groove common in French houses, on the ceiling and a large shower in one corner.

It looked very professional. He's good at DIY.

'Would you like a guided tour?' he asked.

'Yes, please.'

'Don't take her in the lumber room,' begged Lynn but she was not to be spared the indignity of a newly found relative inspecting the unfinished work.

John led me up the elm staircase and once in the bedroom explained what he had done to renovate it. It was a lovely room in daffodil and cream, which had a ceiling with oak beams in the sloping eves and a view over the countryside from the Velux window, all this complemented by bed linen of pale yellow. He explained how he had brought the wooden flooring on several trips in his car, as it was too heavy to bring all at once. He explained how he had put beading around the edge of the skirting board to finish off. Once or twice he broke off to say, 'You're not interested in this, are you? But I'm going to tell you anyway.'

'Oh but I am. You'd be surprised at what interests me.'

Then out of the blue, 'I like your hair like that.' I must have appeared amazed. 'All blonde.'

'Do you? That's very nice of you to say so.'

'Not with that red, though. This makes you look younger. I didn't like the red. You don't mind me telling you do you?'

I have a hairdresser, Kathy, who I have been going to for the last fifteen years. She is a lot younger than I am and likes to set the trend. And I like her to set it with me so in recent years I've had short funky, spiky hair styles, which have been enhanced with colours; first a bit of blonde then more blonde bits with red bits. Très chic, n'est pas? But no, apparently not to John's taste. Now I just have two colours of blonde, which have become even fairer with the sun from this holiday.

'Er, no, of course not. How many glasses of red wine have you had?'

He didn't answer me but we looked into each other's eyes quite intently as if to discover what we could about our relationship. Brian often says I like the thought of having a brother and he could like the notion of having a big sister, especially one that isn't afraid to turn up on his doorstep unannounced.

'I told Lynn she'd like you.'

'Did you?'

'Yes, but she said she wouldn't. You would, I said. She's bright like you.'

'Well, we haven't stopped doing this,' I indicated with both my hands repeatedly knocking my fingers against my thumbs, the sign for chattering, 'since you left the room.'

'I knew she'd like you.' I missed the moment to ask him if he liked me. Brian thinks he does. He went on to explain how he had laid the balloon water tank on its side in the wall space below the eves.

'You'll not be interested but I'm telling you anyway.'

'Lead on, MacDuff,' I said as he crossed the landing to show me the room that he was to work on next and we discussed whether to leave the lambris wood stained or paint it a light colour.

'Paint it white,' I advised, 'it will lighten the room.

'Lynn says she'd like it daffodil like next door with a bit of green to set it off. I just do what I'm told.'

283

'Well, that'll look lovely, won't it?' I ventured.

We went down the stairs and joined Brian and Lynn. Shortly after, when we realized we'd been there nearly three hours we left.

Lynn and I kissed cheeks mouing simultaneously in the French manner. Brian did the same then shook John's hand. I got hold of my brother and said, 'You can give me a hug. Hugs are ok.' And so they were, tightly held and sheepishly smiling.

*

No mail from America when we returned, unfortunately. I've decided to write a reminder letter as the blurb from the California Department of Health Records says their turnaround time to deal with requests purports to be twelve weeks. I've been waiting over twenty; I tell them in a polite letter enclosing a copy of the original application form. Every morning I come downstairs to the post on the mat longing for my letter from America. I believe it will help to produce a final chapter in my life of discovery.

*

John phoned today. He was calling from Hathersage in Derbyshire sheltering under the boot lid of his car from the pouring rain, which has been a feature of summer 2008 in the UK, even though now it's officially autumn. He was about to go walking over Stannage Edge, a fifteen mile hike, something he does with a friend once a month. It was just after nine in the morning. I was surprised at the earliness of the

284

hour as it is not a time my feet have often felt the bedroom carpet in these days of casual habits in retirement. Don't get me wrong, if there's something to rise early for I'm up with the lark, as I am in order to take Joseph to school on two mornings a week. Today Brian was already away up the motorway to see his mother as the builders were coming to talk to her at two o'clock about renovations to her flat in the sheltered accommodation where she lives in Sheffield. He'd gone early as she had phoned yesterday to say she had suffered an asthma attack and struggling desperately to get her breath had called the doctor who gave her a nebuliser and a prescription for relieving the symptoms of what he thought was a recurring virus.

With no one to go for the prescription Brian's brother thought it prudent they go in the morning to help out and before the builders arrived.

John's phone call held doom and gloom, too. Kathleen had fallen at the residential community and was now in Sheffield's Northern General Hospital suffering from a fractured hip. She was being operated on today and would expect to leave there to return home in just over a week. He had visited her in at home yesterday morning with Paul and found her very dopey in her speech and quite confused. Hours later he was called to the Northern General to be told of the fracture and that they will be putting in a metal plate with a wiggly joint of some kind to aid mobility.

'How did it happen?' I wondered.

'She said she'd fallen down the stairs,' said John but as we both know there are no stairs to fall down as her room is on the ground floor. 'She was actually on her back on the floor in the room. I suspect they had been giving her drugs but I don't know what for.' The last time this had happened was when she had been hearing voices and muttering seemingly to herself but it was as though she was talking to Bill.

'She has fallen before, hasn't she?' I was reminding myself, 'In the kitchen at Handsworth? When I first met her there were crutches.'

'Not in the kitchen. She didn't fall in the kitchen. It was out on the road. She'd gone to see our Paul and tripped over the pavement. A neighbour called the ambulance and then she was given a walking frame and later on, crutches.'

'Was her recovery so rapid then?' I asked, as I was amazed at the speed of her intended return.

'Yes. The surgeon this time said that it was a routine operation common in old ladies like my mother. They do them all the time and it doesn't take longer than three quarters of an hour.' Amazing.

Even more amazing was that she had signed a form giving her consent to a blood transfusion in the event of her needing one. Given her devotion to Jehovah this was a surprise.

'She'll have forgotten,' said John. 'Anyway, *I'd* have signed it if she hadn't been able to. But she won't need it. They said it was just routine. I'm letting you know in case you decided to go to Hazelthorpe and found that she wasn't there.'

I told him where Brian had gone this morning and that I hadn't gone with him as we have Joseph after school and wouldn't get back in time to collect him.

'My biggest fear is that she catches something whilst she's there,' said John sounding concerned.

'You mean like MRSA?'

'Yes.'

Even so, John wasn't asking me to go to the hospital, but said he would let me know when his mother came home and tell me how she had got on. Feeling grateful I thanked him and hoped he had a delightful walk, despite the rain, in one of the most beautiful places anywhere in the country.

Chapter 20

A Communication out of the Blue

<u>*10th October 2008 – Diary entry*</u>

We are planning a trip to New Zealand in the new year of 2009. January 18th to 15Th February, to be precise. As Brian will be 70 in 2009 we thought we would take a special holiday and invited Malcolm and Lesley our friends next door to come along, too. Without a second thought, they jumped at the offer and we have been planning it on and off since last May. The tickets for flights have arrived and hotels in Hong Kong, a three-day stop over there, and Auckland, Wellington and Christchurch at various points in the holiday have been booked. We have also booked a couple of trips in Hong Kong: one to see the island and harbour during the day and an evening trip to have dinner at a revolving restaurant, Restaurant 66, which includes a river trip with unlimited bar. We are hiring a car to tour New Zealand. As we begin to book bed and breakfasts in North and South Island, we're getting excited.

*

An extraordinary e-mail has arrived in my inbox.

Subject: Zygmunt Rosiak; From: Mitchell-Smith.

Colin Mitchell-Smith appears to be a man responsible for keeping alive the memories of those in the RAF/PAF 300 Squadron who lost their lives in

WW2 via an organisation based at RAF Faldingworth, Lincolnshire.

He writes that he is sorry that he has no information about my father as yet although, if he was at RAF/PAF Faldingworth a photograph of him may be in the Parish church although he is not named in them. Would I be able to recognise him? Er, no. But would someone else know him? Colin goes on to say that there are new outer gates, window, plaque, candlesticks and memorial books in the church as well as the memorial and personal plaque on the airfield.

All this is a mystery to me as is the information that in a proposed memorial service to be held to the memory of the RAF300 (Polish) Squadron that served in Fladingworth to be held at a later date they will be burying parts of more aircraft lost from the base.

I e-mail straight back telling him that I would be interested in more details of the memorial service and ask him if he has written as a result of my enquiry to the website of the PAF 300 Squadron. He has. I can't remember when I was first looking at the site, perhaps when I was writing about the exploits of the Polish aircrews earlier in the year. His reply tells me that as he is of an age that still remembers 'pony express mail' he doesn't spend a lot of time searching the net but he just happened to be checking what had been said about Faldingworth when he came across my enquiry. What had I said? I guess I just asked if anyone remembered him or was able to provide any information as I was making a search for my father. The memorial service is to be held on 19th September 2009. Quite a wait then. It's October 2008 now. It isn't the first. It's an annual event, apparently. It's held in Faldingworth and the village hall there has a display of photographs.

Lunch, available in the local pub, is followed by the service held in the afternoon in the church. After that, held on the airfield, there is a dedication of additional aircraft parts in memorial. The occasion is rounded off with a reception in the local primary school next to the church where tea and cakes are served and perhaps even more importantly folks can chat. People go home after that or they can go to the pub for n evening meal and more chat. They will probably need to stay for the night if that is their choice. Colin makes it all sound delightful. But it's not just a local affair. The Defence Attaché from the Polish Embassy comes along usually with the Consul General from London. They have even had the past Polish President. Most excitingly the BBMF Lancaster makes an appearance, as it has done on numerous occasions. Last year they had a Spitfire and a Hurricane 'beat up' the village. Is that a fly past? Or a strafing? Wow – some excitement indeed.

He had told me that they have a handout sheet of the past events and other things they have done and as it has too many pictures to send by email would I give him my address so he can send it by post? Fascinated, I did just that.

I e-mail once again to tell Colin about my discovery of Zygmunt's death and my request to America for his death certificate. I tell him too of all the different RAF air bases he served at in his time with the PAF. One of the handouts Colin has attached to his email is about the memorial itself. It's not just a ceremony, of course, but also a concrete structure that can be visited at any time. The base is constructed, literally, from concrete blocks broken up from the old runway, perimeter track, aircraft standings and buildings at Faldingworth. These broken structures represent the broken lives and tragedy of war, a poignant reminder. Inside the base are placed small parts from some of the aircraft of 300 Squadron lost from Faldingworth. These parts are buried with some soil from the Masovia area in Poland. The crew names are on a notice board at the side of the memorial and it is thought that they would have taken off for the last time on the runway where the memorial stands, as it was the main East/West runway. From the base rise three columns of stone that came from the Lincoln Cathedral quarry, which represents the Cathedral itself, as so many aviators knew it as a landmark. It also has a metaphoric purpose in representing hope for the future rising out of the destruction of war.

Between the uprights and the base there is a stone plaque whose inscription states to whom the memorial is dedicated. Behind the memorial is an old windsock post. As a reminder of today's living world, a world that must be preserved, some trees have been planted. There is still some room for others to be planted with a dedication plaque if people want to do this.

A few days later the material too large for email arrived by 'pony express'. There are pictures of the gates to the memorial, how and where these were made and to whom they were commemorated and also how the stained-glass window was designed dedicated with the words 'For our and your freedom' in English and Polish. The dedication on the plaque on the runway reads:

'300 Sq' POLISH AIR FORCE 1944-1947
1667 HCU RAF 1943
TO THOSE
WHO WHEN TYRRANY THREATENED
FLEW FROM THIS RUNWAY
SOME NEVER TO RETURN
AND THOSE WHO SUPPORTED THEM
ON THE GROUND
WE REMEMBER YOU ALL

A plaque accompanying a tree planted at East Kirby to commemorate all who flew with the Polish squadrons in bomber command reads:

IN MEMORY OF
ALL THE AIRCREWS OF THE
POLISH BOMBER SQUADRONS
WHO FLEW FROM LINCOLNSHIRE
AND ALL THEIR GROUND SUPPORT

The tree is a Canadian maple. It was grown by a past resident of Faldingworth from the seed of a tree outside the house of a Polish pilot who flew from Faldingworth who went to live in Canada.

Included too are photographs of previous ceremonies and those who attended them. One such took place in 2001 in Pont d' Ouilly in France, another the dedication of the gates at All Saints Church in Faldingworth in October 2005, a further tree planting in March 2005 in memory of crew of a Lancaster bomber lost in the Baltic Sea dedicated by the sister of the pilot. The Polish Consul General and Defence, Military, Naval and Air Attaché appear with several other uniformed personnel in a photograph from September 8th 2007 laying parts of three Lancaster bombers at the memorial. Juxtaposed with this is a BBMF Lancaster flying over Faldingworth. This undated but no doubt associated with the report of Colin Mitchell-Smith's 'beating up' of the village. In 2004 Jerzy B Cynk presented the village primary school with the official history books of the Polish Airforce at War 1939-1945. Earlier, in July 1998, they had been presented with a badge from Blackpool PAFA. Heading the brochure is a poignant black and white photo taken in 1946 of the final fly-past of Lancaster bombers before the unit was disbanded.

Perhaps most moving is a sheet headed: All Saints Church, Faldingworth Memorial Porch Outer Gates. The photograph shows clergy of differing denominations attended the ceremony on Saturday 8th October 2005: the Bishop of Grimsby, the Polish Roman Catholic priest for Lincoln and Scunthorpe the Methodist minister and the Rector of All Saints Church. The gates, constructed in hand forged steel, were made in Hackthorn Forge to a design showing the RAF and PAF markings with the letters BH. Depicted above this is an impression of the runway. There are arms sweeping upwards from different parts of the world, Poland and Britain, to join in prayer as they pass through a door, which is depicted in the gate itself, into the next existence. Wings carry the onlooker skywards for those who returned, Zygmunt of course, with a half wing either side of the door for those who didn't. The gate commemorates the sacrifices made by the whole of the 300 Polish Squadron right down to the individual in commemorating the coming together of peoples to join in a common cause and in some cases the marriage of Polish and British men and women. Many people and organizations contributed to the making of the gates but there was one main donor. She is not named in the leaflet but her father flew from Faldingworth and like so many, Zygmunt included, had been a prisoner of war in the USSR. He was later shot down to be a POW in Germany. He married an English girl, whose name was Beryl. His name was Henryk Jachacz. Coincidentally the initials of the 300 Squadron are also BH and if an observer looks through the gates when the inner doors are open he or she will see the stained glass window across the church framed in the outer gates. The English side is on the West and so too the letter B for Beryl; the East side is Polish as Poland is East of Britain. Henryk was Polish and the letter H is on the East side.

The stained -glass window commemorated a few years earlier in September 1999 replaced a plain glass window, which had been known as the Polish window. It has two crosses, which stand central in the main panels: the one on the right representing the Christian community of Poland; the one on the left Great Britain. Ribbons flow back and forth around the crosses representing the coming together of two peoples. A rose and a cornflower represent the people coming from their own country's soil and of love lost and found, their position near the crosses representing

the great sacrifices made. Above all is a sunburst symbolizing the fact that we are one people under one sun. There are some sharp edges in the shape of the sunburst depicting the pain and suffering not only of those long gone from this life but also of those left behind. There is the Polish Air Force and the Royal Air Force roundel representing the Polish and British airmen and women. The famous words 'For our and your freedom' in English and Polish are on the ribbon. 'To 300 Squadron and all their comrades' is across the bottom of the window with the 300 Squadron badge in the bottom left corner. Although the 300 Squadron is specifically mentioned, as this Squadron was at one time the only Squadron on the base, the word 'All' also reminds people of all their other comrades in arms. The cooks, the ground crews, the admin staff and so on as well as all those other Squadrons that helped all the forces win freedom. The glass is in parts transparent and so allows the landscape and the sky to be seen, thereby showing that the love and friendship depicted is for today as well, and not just the years gone by. Apparently, the RAF Battle of Britain Memorial Flight did the village proud with a special fly-past of the
Avro Lancaster.

The 19th September 2009 seems such a long way away so Brian and I decided to go and take a look on the next Sunday, weather permitting, so I emailed Colin to thank him for sending all this interesting material and to tell him of our impending visit. He emailed in return that next Sunday wasn't the best choice as it was Remembrance Sunday and he would be very busy on that day and unavailable to show us all there was to be seen.   I phoned him. He sounded very RAF - military-like with clipped sentences and long vowels and very pleased to hear from me. He explained the drill for him on Sunday and we agreed to postpone our visit until the 23rd November when he would be less fraught. We must take a camera.

Chapter 21

An Hour with Kathleen

I went to see my mother last Thursday phoning ahead to the home the previous Monday to see if she had returned from hospital. She had but was quite frail and had already had another small fall because the dementia made her think she was fit and well and could walk properly so she was forgetting to use the frame the hospital had sent.

Having taken Joseph to school as we had had him to stay the night before, I set off up the A38 just after nine o'clock. I was by myself as Brian was visiting his mother. I arrived too early at 10.30 so sat a while reading the paper – front page news in The Times of Barak Obama's triumph in America's presidential election. Why was I doing that? I kidded myself that it was because I didn't want to be in the way of breakfasts, pill dispensing and bed making but it's really because I don't know whether I could sustain a conversation with Kathleen for more than an hour in her current mental state if John doesn't come.

I went in at quarter to eleven and looked at the visitor's book before signing it, as John does, to see if anyone else was there or had visited in the previous few days. No sign of John for a week or so, so I guessed he would be in France again but instead someone called Roy had visited already this morning. No coward like me. I remember when we were visiting Kathleen one time a caller named Roy had phoned asking her if she wanted a lift to the church.

She'd put him off in favour of spending more time with us.

Down the corridor the door was closed, her name missing from it. I asked a carer whether she was there. She wasn't too good today I was told. However, I went with the carer into the room and found her still in bed. The room smelled strongly of urine but no one said anything.

She lay in bed looking pathetic but her face brightened as soon as she saw me and a hand came from under the covers to clasp mine. She told me of Roy's visit and I confirmed with her that it was the Roy of Jehovah's Witnesses. If proof were needed on her duvet was a copy of the latest Watchtower. Having brought flowers I cast my eyes about the room for a vase but without luck. After she had remarked on the vividness of the fuscia-coloured gerbera I put them on the floor. I had brought with me the set of photographs I had received from Brenda and had had copied. First of all, I showed Kathleen the photo of her wedding. She looked at it with wonder, as the photo is without doubt a good one – clear and sharp despite being a copy – and named everyone in it.

'That's my daddy!' she exclaimed.

'Yes it is.' I agreed

'It's' so sad, you know,' she declared.

'Sad?'

'He died yesterday,' she said with absolute conviction of the truth of her statement.

'Oh, dear,' I sympathized. 'What a shame.'

She looked at the other two wedding photos with continued interest and then,

'Is it raining?'

I turned to look out of her window into the courtyard with the fountain, now stilled. It was a typical November day, misty and damp.

'No, not raining. Not now anyway. It was wet on the motorway with spray and quite misty, too. It's foggy now, here.' I recalled when I first came off the motorway earlier that morning that I had run into fog almost straight away.

You've come by car, then?'

'Yes, I've driven up.'

We continued with the photographs, Kathleen pointing out Sidney and Ernest as husbands of her sisters.

'That's Brenda,' I placed my finger on a small child held in the arms of her mother, Kathleen's sister, Gladys.

'Oh, yes. Yes, of course. I don't see anything of her now. She's not been here, you know. Do you think she knows where I am?'

'Oh, well, I should think so. I think she'd ask John' I floundered.

'Is it raining?'

'No not raining. It's foggy though'

'Have you come by bus?'

'No, I've driven up today. Up the motorway. From Burton on Trent.'

'Oh, yes.' A momentary flicker of recognition. 'From Burton. Near Brenda's.'

'Yes.'

'Is it raining?' She wriggled in the bed in discomfort pulling at a cushion, which was under her right leg under the duvet.

'No it's foggy.' Desperation now. 'I've got some more photos to show you.' And I fished in my bag pulling out a photo of John, as a small baby, sitting on our mother's knee, she with a head of strong dark curly hair.

'Is that a perm?' I asked.

'No, no, no; all natural,' she smiled. I produced a photo of her with Audrey and Sidney, which provoked a discussion on where it might have been taken. Both sisters were wearing bright fuscia jackets.

'That must have been the fashion,' she ventured her brow furrowing. 'Where's Bill?'

'He must have been taking it,' I volunteered. 'It looks as if you were in Chatsworth Park or some park in Sheffield nearer to home.'

'Mmm. Yes, but where is he now? He's supposed to be coming here today as I'm going home. He's coming to fetch me. Do you think he'll know where I am? He won't mind if I'm a bit late, will he?'

At that moment a carer came into the room.

'Still in bed, Kath?'

'Yes. But I'm not comfortable. The bottom of my back hurts.'

'You'd be better up, you know,' the carer said sternly. 'It's nearly lunch time.'

A non-committal nod from Kathleen. 'It's been raining in this bed', she said.

'Oh dear. I'll get Personal Hygiene.' And she left smartly to be followed in a short time by a young woman.

'I'll leave you to it,' I said and wandered off to find a vase for the flowers in the kitchen. Still no success. I stood by two carers who were going through paperwork muttering darkly about different patients and who lowered their voices to exclude me although I did overhear ill-tempered grumbling about not having information about draw sheets or incontinence pads. That'll be Kathleen, I thought, speculating that before she went into hospital she would have not had that sort of problem but after about a month away for the operation on her hip her ability to control her bladder could well have deteriorated. How sad. Will I come to that? Who knows?

I returned after a while to the room where all was now well but still carrying the flowers thinking they were neither use nor ornament. I was voicing the problem whilst standing in the doorway of the room before Personal Hygiene left having settled Kathleen into her armchair when a cleaner in the corridor came up to me and said that in his room they had lots of spare vases; would I like him to get me one. I would, and he left to fetch it.

'How kind,' I said to Kathleen. 'They must all like you here.' She agreed. She had been dressed in a green cotton print dress and a matching cardigan. Her hair was a little disheveled but looked all right.

'Green suits you,' I told her.

'I've got a lot of green,' she said. 'I like that green spotty thing over there. What is it?'

I glanced towards where she looked and saw the flowers.

'Err, it's nothing, actually. It's the wrapping from the flowers.' We looked at one another and laughed raucously. She knew she'd made a mistake but somehow it didn't matter. The cleaner arrived with the vase and I stood to take it from him.

'She's had a visitor already today,' he said.

'Yes, I know.'

'My dad was in the…er…you know.' He looked slightly embarrassed signaling towards the Watchtower, which had been placed on the chest of drawers by the door. 'At Intake. Are you?'

'No. Are you?'

'No. No. Not at all. Each to his own, of course,' he murmured, afraid of giving offence. He left to begin hoovering the corridor.

'Bill will be coming to get me soon. Will he know where I am?'

'Oh, I should think so. But it's lunchtime in a while,' I said. 'Better to have that first, don't you think?' I prompted.

Kathleen needed the toilet after a while and I attempted to lift her from the chair to make the five paces to the ensuite. I couldn't move her and quickly realized I needed help. Running down the corridor I found a carer who came immediately to assist Kathleen into the toilet. She told her how to get up using the walking frame, by pushing down on the grips on the top and pushing up. She did as she was told and rose slowly to standing. She found putting the frame ahead of her difficult and was told to roll it forward a few paces and catch it up. She did this and I waited until she was safely back in her chair. As she was sitting well and no longer lying down I got out the laptop and showed her holiday photos from the summer, which included the grandchildren. She cooed with delight especially at the ones of baby Ben looking golden and innocent whilst full of mischief.

I looked at my watch and was amazed to find it was almost one o'clock. So much for thinking an hour would be enough for her. Lunch loomed. A carer arrived as I thought to take her down to the dining room but instead she sat on the bed, stared frankly at me and said, 'I hope you don't mind me asking you but have you known Kath long?' An odd question, this.

'It depends what you mean by long. I've known her for two years but actually all my life.' An odd answer, too.

Susan, the carer as she introduced herself, asked if I knew anything about a baby.

'That's probably me,' I said.

'Well, no,' said Susan. 'This baby died in a fire.'

'Should we be talking about things in front of...er...you know.' I felt it was somehow an imposition to be discussing things in front of Kathleen as if she wasn't there. I felt that I needed to tell this carer who I was and how I knew Kathleen.

'It's better to say things now because there are times when she gets very distressed and we need to know what to say. She's been getting upset about this baby and if we're saying there never was a baby and she knows there was, even if it hadn't died in a fire then it's worse for her for us to keep on denying it.' I understood what she meant so I turned in my chair and spoke directly to my mother.

'You know when I come here to see you?' I began. A look of intent concentration. 'Turn up like a bad penny?' A nod. 'Do you know who I am?' Confusion but no response. 'Do you know that I'm your daughter?' No response but the dawning of a smile. 'Do you know that you're my mum?' A look of rapture but she didn't say anything. I began to wonder about the wisdom of telling too much. Susan needed more help. 'I was adopted after five weeks but only managed to find my mother about two years ago, before she came in here,' I told her. She seemed overwhelmed by the information.

'Isn't that wonderful,' she breathed hugging the papers she had in her hand close to her chest.

'I think if there had been any truth in a baby having died in a fire John, my half- brother would have talked about it to me. He was the eldest of her children before I came along and he found himself as a middle child. Quite a shock for him, don't you think?'

'Yes, it must have been. So you've managed to find your mother. How did you do that?' she asked.

'It's a long story, too long for now but I used social workers to make contact. You can't just turn up on your own at some unsuspecting person's door.'

She agreed you couldn't and asked if I would mind filling in a form they gave to family members, which would help them in their work with dementia sufferers. I was only too delighted to do it and took the papers from her. I hugged Kathleen and said goodbye as Susan took her off in the opposite direction to lunch.

I sat in the foyer and looked at the questions on the form. Apart from the usual name and address the form asked for relationship to the resident and name of mother and father. For the first time in my life against mother I wrote: Kathleen Newcombe; against father I wrote: Zygmunt Rosiak.

I couldn't help feeling a tinge of disloyalty so I wrote that Dorothy and Edward Kay had adopted me in 1946. Under former addresses I wrote 20 Darklands Road, Crosspool. Where asked I wrote the names ages of my sons and the work I had done in my working life. Driving home when I thought about it again I regretted I hadn't written anything about former names, as there wasn't a place. I hadn't put that I used to be Averill.

Chapter 22

A Visit to Faldingworth

Sunday the 23rd November dawned icy cold and blustery. Drizzle had fallen in the night turning to a thin coating of ice on the wall tops. There were vestiges of frost on the stone slabs in the courtyard, which is our back garden. The sky was heavy with promise of snow. Definitely not the best of days to be wandering around an exposed airfield but we had promised Colin Mitchell-Smith we would be with him by midday so we wrapped up warmly and set off to Faldingworth.

We found the church easily and parked outside to wait for Colin to appear. Snow, now just beginning to melt, had fallen in the village overnight and lay quite thickly in un-cleared side roads. We weren't surprised, as we had been driving through slush since Lincoln. Getting out of the car at the sight of someone leaving the church we walked towards the entrance and saw immediately the gates commemorating the two nations, Poland and Britain. Colin appeared in moments and invited us into the warmth of the church. Hardly warmer, but at least out of the biting wind. Showing us the stained glass window he pointed out the significance of the images then took us briefly outside again to show us the effect of looking at the window from the closed gates and indeed, as we had read in the information he had sent us the two seemed to join as one to the glory of the fallen, both RAF and PAF personnel, and the living. The window contained a red rose, the emblem of Britain and a cornflower on the Polish side. Did I know what this represented, Colin asked? I didn't. It was the flower all Poles remembered when asked if there was a flower to represent home, as they grew in profusion in the hedgerows of Poland, countryside apparently so like our own.

A cabinet had been placed in front of the window into which had been placed two leather-bound books. In these were many photographs of the ceremony in the niuring which the window had been commemorated and also of members of the 300 Squadron with their planes or on the airbase during the nineteen forties. Zygmunt could well have been one of them as although quite a few were named, many weren't. Two heavy candlesticks made of polished lead stood on the cabinet and Polish people in memory of their loved ones had provided these.

Colin asked us if we would like to look in more detail at the books. The best thing to do, he suggested, was to see them at our leisure at his house over a cup of tea later in the day. As it was now lunchtime we agreed to meet him in an hour.

The Coach and Horses provided a splendid Sunday roast lunch. In the pub there was a photograph of the last fly-past over the airbase after the end of the war; a fleet of Lancasters in formation. I looked hard at this and experienced a curious feeling. Zygmunt Rosiak would have been at the controls of one of these planes.

Picking Colin up from his house an hour later we drove off to the airfield along narrow country lanes. As we approached the entrance the road became severely potholed filled now with water from the melted slush. He pointed out hangars and the officers' quarters on the approach road. We continued around the perimeter on the old runway until we came to where this joined the main runway. Stopping the car we sat for a moment looking at the memorial. There was the base of concrete pieces topped by three pieces of stone rising up like three fingers.

'Ready?' asked Colin.

'Ready.'

We got out of the car into the biting wind determined to blow us over, snatching at our breaths. The area is so exposed, flat fields on one side of the memorial, the main runway ahead. Not a tree to break the force across the landscape. Colin explained that pieces of Lancaster had been buried beneath the concrete wall.

These had been found around Faldingworth airbase indicating that some planes had crashed on takeoff and so too others after limping home. A small stone plaque engraved with the number found on the sides of the planes had been placed over where the bits of the plane had been buried. Each is buried with a handful of Masovian soil brought from Poland. Small plants grew in the spaces between. The flagpole for a windsock was positioned into the earth behind, the earth reclaimed from a farmer's field the beginnings of a garden mulched with gravel and laid out in a semi-circle surrounded by small shrubs. There were gaps in the shrubs where deer had strayed in and eaten them. There were the three stone pillars representative of what pilots could see of Lincoln Cathedral when coming home to Faldingworth. The stone had come from the same quarry that those making repairs on the cathedral use. When we returned to the car and drove a couple of hundred meters we could see the cathedral in the distance.

'There are only two towers on the cathedral,' Brian remarked.

'Actually,' Colin explained, 'there are three. Of the two smaller ones, one obscures the other from this angle.' And as we looked back through the rear view mirror the same occurred on the memorial; three became two. We continued to drive along the main runway and at the end got out of the car once more.

'This is where they took off from,' Colin said. I stood facing into the wind, my face obscured by my scarf as I pulled it over my ears, and looked down the runway, experiencing once more that strange feeling. He was here. In 1945 he was here with no knowledge that more than sixty years later a daughter would be standing on this spot. The wind made my eyes water. We drove off for the last time.

Arriving at Colin's house we were able to see photographs in the books from the church. Many depicted Polish aircrews but no Zygmunt Rosiak. Colin looked at some of the material about Zygmunt's war that I had received from the various sources. As we drank our tea Colin produced his pièce de resistance.

Carrying it from another room he brought a photograph of the type of my old school photo from 1962; one where everyone on the front rows is sitting with those behind them standing in tiers of increasing height for two or three rows. But this wasn't a school photo. It was one of 300 Squadron taken in 1946. Staring out at me from over a hundred men was my father. I scrutinized it trying to narrow down the faces by ignoring all those who didn't have three stripes on their jackets – he was a flight sergeant – those who looked too young – he would have been twenty-seven at the time the photo was taken – and anyone who didn't look dark haired. An impossible task. Many of the men had a moustache, which obscured their faces somewhat.

But I felt privileged to be looking at this document; it was clearly a treasured record for Colin. He asked whether I thought my mother would be able to recognize him but after all these years and given her state of mind at present it seems unlikely. He offered to send it to me on disk but I waited in vain for its arrival in the Christmas post.

However, wanting to help further Colin did give me an address of the person who at the moment is chairman of the branch of the Polish Air Force Association in America and on getting home I wrote to him telling him I would appreciate any help he could offer. Colin also suggested I could write to the National Archives Office at Kew where the RAF Station Records might be held and there was a possibility of a photograph being available. That would be a treat. I will get onto it before we go on holiday to France in a few days and certainly before we go to New Zealand in January.

*

5th December 2008 – Diary entry
Disappointing news from America. The chairman of the Polish Air Force Veterans Association in America has written to say that they have no record of Zygmunt

being a member. The chairman had called one of the members in Los Angeles who said he had no recollection of Zygmunt either although he was able to say that he was listed as in the register of members in Great Britain as Flight Sergeant with the No. 300 Bomb Squadron. His date of birth was given as 29th December 1916. His record noted that no further details were known. The letter told me that the records of the Polish Air Force personnel are held at the Polish Institute and Sikorski Museum in London. I telephoned them to ask if they had any records and the lady there told me to write to her with copies of what I had already. I asked if there was a chance they held photographs. The answer is yes.

*

My intention was to make my enquiries before the trip to New Zealand but time overtook me.

When we came home I hoped that in the pile of mail for the month might be the reply from the California record office but no. Still waiting. The person at the Polish Institute had suggested I sent all the information I had on Zygmunt so they could check with their records to see what they held. When I looked at all the stuff I had accumulated there was too much to copy. Some of it was on foolscap sized paper rather than on A4 so my facility here was too small and the cost of having a company do it made me think it would be worthwhile just to send it all to London. I bought a big jiffy bag and sent it by registered post. The following day a man from the Institute phoned to say everything had arrived safely. What a change from the American offices! The only downside was that the search would take three months. But at least I know that and won't be watching the post uselessly. The suggestion is that I go to their offices when they know what they have as photographs are held on microfiche. Imagine scrolling through faces of the 300 squadron and seeing for the first time one that could look like me!

*

Margery was eighty three a few days later and we went to lunch but decided to call in on Kathleen on the way. No familiar cars in the car park so I thought that we'd chosen a day when the brothers weren't there. But, delightfully I was wrong. They were in the corridor talking. John looked pleased to see us and Paul just smiled although, unlike the earlier visits, he didn't leave.

"Toilet problems," said John indicating the open door of the room.

"Ah," I said and mentioned the conversation on my earlier visit in which our mother had told me it had been raining in her bed. He laughed and we went in. Kathleen expressed the same delight to see us but she clearly wasn't well and after a struggle to have a normal conversation or what passes for normal on these occasions as she seemed unable to hear any of us properly, we talked amongst ourselves. Brian talked to Paul about our weekend in Sheffield and he managed to make some response although there was a lot of smiling and nodding on his part and no volunteering of information. Kathleen apologising, asked me my name as she had forgotten it. I think, too, she has forgotten who I was despite knowing me

312

at first. I think she recognises my face. John and I talked about France. I told him about a nostalgic trip to Sheffield we had just made to celebrate our Ruby wedding and about the New Zealand trip. It will be his and Lynn's Ruby wedding in June this year. They haven't yet made any specific plans to celebrate.

Kathleen began to talk to her voices. She had been unwell for a few days according to John.

"They ring me when things are bad," he said. "I haven't been coming as often as I've had the house to do."

Kathleen's house had been on the market for some time but in the economic downturn, especially after one or two potential sales had fallen through he had decided to rent it out.

"But that hasn't proved as easy as it might," he volunteered. "To get a tenant the house has to meet certain criteria so I decided to put in a new bathroom and modernise the kitchen. I've been busy for a few weeks and there isn't enough time to do it all and come here and to take our Paul to his hospital appointments." I murmured my understanding. "But," he went on, "things are looking up as we've suddenly had an offer and if we accept it I won't have to finish everything and that'll make more time."

He certainly has a lot on his plate. Everything falls to him. For instance, we've never seen Lynn when we've been visiting as she always seems to be at work. That's normal as she works in the day and John visits whilst she is at work but I wonder if there have been occasions when Kathleen has been less than polite to her so she has left it to John. Who knows?

313

For a while we watched Kathleen deep in conversation with the voices. I hope it's with Bill but it's hard to say and quite hard to watch to be honest. She's not there, in the room with you. She's somewhere else.

I generally go when it's like this," said John. He was being practical and sensible but I felt a little sad. We got up to go anyway and the four of us trooped out into the corridor without a second glance. Poor lady. Perhaps she'll be better the next time. In the car park John settled Paul into an open-topped Jaguar.

"What's all this?" smiled Brian. John's little indulgence apparently. Paul was smiling as he pulled a car rug tighter around his knees.

"Keep warm, you could get chilly in there," I told Paul as we said our goodbyes. He smiled and waved as John, after a hug willingly given, drove off with a discrete toot of the horn. I felt sadder. Dementia is a cruel illness. It steals people away.

*

Part 6

The American Connection

Chapter 23

The Death Certificate Reveals More

Arriving back from a couple of weeks in France, I glanced idly through the post. There was a letter from Colin Mitchell-Smith from the RAF/PAF Faldingworth Memorial organisation with a programme for the memorial event in September. I already have this on my calendar and we had every intention of going. There were several envelopes from the Reader's Digest Association who assured me I was a whisker away from winning the £250,000 draw and would I like a cheque if I win or the money transferring straight into my bank. Needs some thinking about, does this. And then I spotted it.

An envelope with a red franked postage mark giving the price of the stamp as $1.24; the letter from America at last!

On the envelope I read The Department of Health Services, Sacramento. I opened it with care. And there it was: a certified copy of the death certificate for Zygmunt Rosiak. I had written again to the Records Office in April before we went away to try to shame them into dealing with my request as urgent. It was my second letter following the original, in the year I had been waiting and I had asked them what on earth had been holding things up. It is important to me I told them as the people in my family I am hoping to trace aren't getting any younger. It must have done the trick.

The dates of birth – 29 December 1916 – and death - 4 February 1969 were correct as was his social services number and his place of birth. The cause of his death had been threefold. First of all on the 6 January 1969 he had been diagnosed with septicaemia; then on 1 February he had seepage of fluid in the lungs, what I imagine could be pneumonia; and finally on 4 February the illness which killed him being Pemphigus Vulgaris. I had never heard of it so went onto the Internet to look it up. Pemphigus vulgaris is a serious skin disease that causes blisters and is more serious than most other 'blistering' skin conditions which if not treated can be fatal. Before treatment became available, most people with pemphigus vulgaris died. It's very painful but these days, most cases can be controlled with treatment which is usually with steroid medicines and other medicines to suppress the immune system. Poor Zygmunt. It sounds quite awful and very painful. I'm hoping it's not hereditary.

The death certificate gives details of his funeral director and where he is buried. He's in the Forest Lawn Memorial Park which while looking on the Internet for a website I discovered is the final resting place of many Hollywood greats such as Telly Savalas, Liberace and Stan Laurel. He's in illustrious company. His job before death was a self-employed milk distributor for a retail dairy, the Superior Dairy. His address is given as 6349 Barker Avenue, Los Angeles where he died and lived with...his wife. Who is or was his wife? Grace Leland Rosiak. Well. Not surprising, he was married. Not very surprising either is that his nationality is given as British, not Polish. This is the

318

proof of the pencil note on the top of his PAFA record. It would have helped him with his emigration to Canada.

I kept the certificate and pondered on it for a while then I emailed my friend Pam, my genealogy guru for some advice about what to do next. I gave her all the details and she wrote back in under half an hour that she could find no trace of Grace's death and suggested I wrote to the Memorial Park where Zygmunt is buried and asked if anyone else was buried with him. Also, she wrote, I could ask them to tell me of any likely newspaper which would carry an obituary giving any details of the next of kin. She had searched for details of marriage but could find no record in the USA. Of course, she continued, it could have taken place in Canada. The alternative, though, is that she is still alive.

I thought about the name Leland. It's not very usual, not like Clarke, so I put Grace Leland into Google to see what came up. There was a Facebook entry for a Melanie Leland living in Leeds. I looked closely at her picture. She is only a young woman. Leeds, though? I looked up the papers I still had for Zygmunt, those that I hadn't sent off to the Polish Institute and Sikorski Museum and found his record card for the Polish Air Force Association. The last known address in 1949, was in Leeds: 22 Goldsmith Hill, Upper Wortley, Leeds 12. He would have been working in the tailor's shop in Leeds at that time.

I emailed Pam with my find and wondered to her whether Zygmunt and Grace had married before leaving for Canada. How could I find out if he married her before they left the UK, I asked? A short time later I received this reply:

'Grace, Ziemunt (yes, note the spelling) and Melanie Rosiak sailed for Canada, destination New York on the Samaria on 28 September 1950. Grace was aged 22 and Ziemunt, 33 and their daughter Melanie, one. Their UK address was 22 Goldsmith Hill, Leeds 12. He was a Presser.

And there staring out from the page at me was the Leeds address that had been available from the first information from the Polish Air Force Association. Would Pam have been able to find Zygmunt much sooner if I had thought to pass it on to her? Who knows? But she probably needed Grace Leland's details to inform the search.

Melanie was born Leeds 1949 March qtr. Mother's maiden name Leland. Marriage Leeds September qtr 1948.

Pam suggested that if I went on line I could send for both these certificates from the General Record Office in Southport so then she would be able to trace Grace's family in the census records back to 1911. But I won't do this as I have no interest in Grace's family, only Zygmunt's. Only my own. And here I have a half-sister, Melanie, three years younger than me. Pam's email went on:

'Melanie Rosiak married Julian Holdsworth on 12 May 1973 in Los Angeles. She was 24 and he was 25.' She continued, *'Now check this out. Julian is Professor of Math, Vice Chancellor for Research and Dean of Graduate School. He got his PhD at the University of California in 1973 and BA at Sheffield University in 1969.'*

Pam supplied a website for Julian and an e-mail address she had taken from the faculty website.

'I wonder if Melanie went into Education or if they met at Uni – funny if she went into teaching, too? Up to you – you may want to e-mail him and see the response. If the response is good then you will probably be able to get all the information you want from Melanie. Keep me posted – fingers crossed that enough water has flowed under the bridge and they can handle the discovery. It may be good to go through Julian first as he can pave the way, hopefully.'

Her final bit of information was that Julian was born in Middlesex.

After some overnight deliberation, I wrote an email to Julian to the address Pam had given me from the website for Julian's University and waited anxiously the following day for a reply. There was a further email from Pam giving me the address of the Holdsworth's in a town called Ardmore in the state of Nebraska. Brian and I put Ardmore into Google for a map of the States to see whereabouts it was. Then a reply came from Julian's e-mail address but unfortunately this was only a mailer-daemon message telling me the delivery of my message had failed. So, Pam's discovery of their address was perhaps a pointer that I should write to Melanie directly. I tried to imagine how it would be for her to receive my letter but couldn't. It has been forty years since her father's death but her mother is still quite probably alive. She will only be 81; younger than my cousin, Margery, currently in Canada staying with her brother for a month and younger than Kathleen, my mother, currently in a world of her own.

All that happened occurred before Zygmunt met Grace and he probably had no notion he had fathered a child. Who knows? He would have hardly been likely to tell a new girlfriend he had had a relationship with a married woman either, so no one is likely to know of my existence. I didn't know of my existence until three years ago!

I adapted my e-mail which had begun Dear Julian to read thus:

'Dear Melanie

I have some unusual information I want to share with you. You will not have heard of me but I think quite strongly that we are related. I am hoping that you are the daughter of the late Zygmunt Rosiak who died on 4th February 1969 of septicaemia and Pemphigus Vulgaris and who married Grace Leland in Leeds in 1948. Zygmunt was born in Poland on 29th December 1916 and during the Second World War, after deportation to Russia, came to the UK to fly with the Polish Air Force. I have in my possession details of his war record as a flight sergeant, where he was based and where he trained other Polish pilots, and details of his demobilisation in 1945, which I have obtained from the Records Office of the Ministry of Defence at RAF Northolt in Middlesex. I am currently waiting for more from the Polish Institute and Sikorski Museum who hold the Polish Air Force Archives. You may wonder why I have taken the trouble to research this information.'

I explained how I had applied to the Record Offices in Sacremento for the death certificate and what information had been revealed about her mother, Zygmunt and herself on the Internet. I continued:

'Well, I'm hoping, Melanie, that you are my half-sister. There may be others. I have no details of further births registered to Grace and Zygmunt. I understand that you may need some time to take all this in but to all intents and purposes this affair took place in Nottingham and Sheffield during the War and was before he left to live and work in Leeds. He probably had no idea that he had fathered a child.

I realise this may come as a bit of a shock to you and your family and I apologise for that but I am interested to learn more about Zygmunt and his life in America. I would particularly like to see a photograph.

So, can you help me, please?' I closed with:

'Yours sincerely and with every best intention.'

As indeed I have. I don't want to rock their boat but I would love to share with Melanie what I know of her (our) father and look at family photos of her growing up with Zygmunt at least until his death. He was 52 in 1969, over ten years younger than I am now but it would show him as an older man. I would like to see photos of him in the era when he knew Kathleen. He would have been in his early thirties or late twenties. An interesting comparison would be to see him in his late thirties and look at him together with photos of my sons now. Does Nick really have the Polish ears?

Another waiting game now. I didn't occur to me to put my e-mail address on my letterhead, only my address so Melanie will have to write back, presuming she wants to, so I will be watching the doormat for yet another letter from America.

*

21st June 2009 – Diary entry

I went to see Kathleen yesterday. Her delight at seeing me is a joy to behold. She was in the lounge, not in her room, talking to herself. The voices are still there. But she recognised me straight away and her little face lit up like the sunlight on a June day.

She knew I had come from Burton and asked me, perfectly lucidly about my journey up the motorway. She wanted to know where my hubby was.

'Playing golf today. The weather is so nice he wanted to get out there on the golf course,' I told her.

We smiled and giggled and held hands like children. Human contact is so important when you *are alone. No brothers today. A carer told me they had been earlier in the week so John isn't in France. I felt a vague sense of disappointment at this. I had taken a small tea rose in a plant pot to brighten Kathleen's day and it certainly did the trick. She exclaimed over it.*

'It will last longer than flowers,' I said and we looked at the number of buds still to come out. She agreed and suddenly reverted to the car journey.

'Burton on Trent. Yes, Brenda lives there. I haven't seen her here, you know.'

No, I know.'

'And you've driven here today?'

'Yes.'

'In your own car?'

'Yes. It's a beautiful day out there. Warm and sunny, you know.'

She did know and commented on the silver ball in the garden on which a fountain of water played soundlessly.

'Have you been to my house?' she asked suddenly.

'Err, no,' I said wondering what had prompted this.

'The boys will be there, now.'

'Will they? Are you sure? John isn't in France?' Too many questions, I think, from me.

'Oh, they'll be there,' she said worriedly. 'They're only little.' Oh right, a blast from the past, then. I thought I'd steer away from that subject.

'I've brought you some photos to look at,' I said and took from my bag an electronic picture frame. But the trouble was that there was nowhere to

plug it in. One of the other visitors, someone's son, suggested I took Kathleen to her room. A carer, agreeing, got up from sitting on a stool close to another resident to help.

'I'll bring a wheelchair for you, Kath,' she offered and walked off to get one. A wheelchair? I wasn't aware she needed a wheelchair but as she began to stand I could see what a struggle walking was going to be. I wasn't sure this was going to be a good idea but the carer reassured me and continued to offer the chair to Kathleen. But she wasn't having any of it.

'I don't need one of those,' she insisted.

'Come on, Kath, it'll be better in the chair.

'No, I can walk, thank you,' and she set her face in refusal so the chair was put to one side in favour of a walking frame which she clung to with force in order to stand up. We both took hold of her arms until she steadied herself. Thereafter began the slow and painful process of walking the short distance up the corridor to her room. Her balance wasn't good and she needed the wall to lean against sometimes steering the walking frame, which was wheeled, into the wall. But we managed and eventually arrived at the room. 'Is this my room?' she asked the carer, but then realised, 'Oh, yes, that's my bed, isn't it?' We laughed, as indeed we'd been laughing during the process of walking up the corridor.

'We do nothing but laugh,' she told the carer.

'Is it you or me?' I asked. She looked blankly. 'Is it you or me who's funny?'

326

'Oh, me,' she said suddenly getting the joke. There was more laughing which in turn took the breath away that she needed for the effort she was making. When we arrived she needed the toilet urgently so was bundled into the bathroom by the carer as I looked around the room for a place to put the little yellow rose. I sat it next to another pot plant in the room, an orchid with veined petals deep pink and waxy. John's, I guessed. There were some flowers in a vase, too, but they were almost dead as they had no water.

I plugged in the electronic picture frame and the first few slides rolled round. The first were of London and when Kathleen was settled again, I explained that Jack, our six year old grandson living in France had wanted to come to London to see Big Ben.

'You know the clock that appears on TV at the start of the ITV news? Well, he sees it in France along with that big house where the Queen lives and wanted to see them both...' I stopped as the slides continued their show realising that I was actually talking to myself. Kathleen was talking to someone else in her head, mouth going soundlessly. Was it Bill? I continued as if it wasn't happening giving a commentary on the slides. Suddenly, the pictures of Jack and his little brother, Ben, cute as a box of delights, came on and they took her attention.

Kathleen said, 'Ooh, isn't he lovely; look at all that blonde hair. Look at the curls.' And he is lovely with his head covered in a halo of wild blonde curls that he is refusing to sit still for long enough to have trimmed. He was wearing a pair of Mickey Mouse *blue and white striped pyjamas and was playing on the field at the back of the property with Jack trying to put a stick into a molehill. Then she was telling the voice about it or about something else, mouthing a conversation only she was privy to. So quiet was she that it was hard to tell what was being said. Then I heard 'Audrey' and 'Sidney' (her sister and brother in law) and 'smacking too hard' and 'you'll murder him if you're not careful.' I looked hard into her eyes and she suddenly focussed and smiled at me. 'I'm talking to myself, aren't I?'*

'Where are you?' I asked but she just smiled and turned away to where the source of her voices emanated.

'Come back,' I demanded but she couldn't. I chatted on about the rest of the slides, Robert opening his birthday presents and the little boys helping him, while she mouthed to herself events in her life from a long time ago, sometimes cross but although her tone changed she didn't raise her voice. I held her hand for a while just letting the slides do their own thing when she suddenly said, 'Those roses are yellow in the sunlight. There's more to come.'

I agreed with her and we sat on as she whispered to herself just once or twice coming back into the room to be with me saying things she'd said earlier about the journey and coming by car. It was as if she was in a darkened room groping to focus when suddenly a light was turned on and a lucid moment arrived.

Moments later the light went off again. The morning wore on and apart from our hand contact we could have been in different rooms.

328

I began to watch the clock as I needed to be in Stannington to have lunch with Brian's mum. I let a little more time elapse then turned towards her and said I should really be going. She came round once more returning to reality suddenly. I hugged her goodbye and kissed her cheek. She is so loveable. I left her sitting alone in her room, knowing she would have to make another epic struggle back to the dining room in less than half an hour. I felt guilty that I had forced her to move from her comfy chair in the lounge just to look at a few photos of people she doesn't know. I I told the staff at reception as I signed out that she was on her own and they said they would tell the carers. I drove off feeling a bit tearful and wished I had Brian with me.

*

A cheering phone call from John helped dissipate the guilt. He had been to visit mother and seen the roses. He asked her where they had come from and she couldn't remember.

'What roses?' she had apparently said as she thought they were chrysanthemums.

So he had gone off to look at the visitors' book and seen that that it had been me who had signed in earlier in the week. He reminded her I had been and she remembered the visit. But the conversation snippets I described are a regular occurrence. It's usually Audrey and Sidney.

She had been much better that day; no muttering or voices, thankfully. She was well enough to know she still had a house and thought he had come to take her home. Unfortunately, depending how one looks at it, there is no longer a house as John has sold

it. There will be more funds to pay for her keep now, which should be seen as a positive thing. It also relieves him of the added work of having to renovate the house for rent.

I asked him why he wasn't in France and unfortunately his wife, Lynn, wasn't well. She has a heart condition stemming from high blood-pressure and they had already cancelled two crossings to France and a visit to the Pyrenees. They are hoping to go in September to mark their Ruby wedding which is actually in June. They have had poor luck this year as well as whilst they were at their French house in January Paul's carer had contacted them to say that he had been losing a lot of weight and they were worried about him. As a consequence they had come home so John could take him to hospital. There was little sign of resentment in his voice, only resignation. Paul has two children who seem to do nothing to help their father. After a series of appointments he was given the all-clear. Weight loss seems to be a part of the illness.

'None of those where my mother is, seems to be fat,' he observed. And it's true.

I went on to tell him of my luck with my search for information about Zygmunt. He listened attentively whilst I told him about Melanie and that I had written to her. 'A half-sister, eh?' he said. 'They're mounting up.'

'There could be more. I don't know if she has any brothers or sisters.' He laughed. It was up to Melanie to reveal anything more.

Chapter 24

The Polish Ears Revealed

An amazing discovery in the post today from the Polish Institute and Sikorski Museum. The Polish ears have come to light.

An envelope arrived with some documents much sooner than they lead me to believe when I sent them my papers on Zygmunt. They are all in Polish and when I phoned to ask was told they were about his time in Russia. One is two sides of A4 written in his own handwriting about his experiences. But the most exciting contents are two photographs. They are of Course No. 30, presumably as part of Squadron 300, forty-six air men in four rows of eleven or twelve all wearing forage caps and battle-dress uniform. Their names have been added by hand by the Museum so across every chest is written a name. And there on the front row bottom right is ROSIAK. The second photograph is a blown up version of the original with only eleven of them on it so the picture is larger and clearer. A sheet of paper attached to these listed everyone's surname with their first names added in a different coloured ink and other notes such as a date of birth. Also hand written is Newton, which I guess means RAF Newton in Nottinghamshire and the dates 18.5.1944-18.10.1944. This tallies with the records from the MoD at RAF Northolt. He was there from 18th May to 18th October 1944.

My first impression was to see a handsome young man whose eyes and nose looked very familiar. I covered his mouth with my hand and looked closely

at the upper part of his face. I took out the photo of myself, my passport photo at twenty that I had sent to Kathleen before we met and covered the same part of my face and, to me, they seemed strikingly similar. And as I peered closer, under dark hair partly obscured by his forage cap, was a right ear slightly curled over at the top with an uneven bumpy edge. I hoped Brian could see it, too, and that he didn't think I was being too fanciful. I phoned Nick right away on his mobile but had to leave a message. 'This is mum. I've found the Polish ears.' Enough information to intrigue, I thought. The Polish Ears revealed at last.

No longer a haphazard guess but a reality.

He has just been to see it. Obscuring the names with lengths of paper I showed him the blown up version so he had fewer faces to choose from. He bent to look closely for a few moments then he said, 'Him.' Right first time, bottom row right hand side.

'How did you know it was him?' I asked thinking he would recognise himself in the face.

'He looks like Rob,' he said without hesitation.

'He looks like you, too,' I told him and I scrutinised the two framed family photographs, one of Nick, Debs, Aimee and Joe and the other of Rob, Lisa, Jack and Ben that usually live in the sitting room on the china cabinet. Nick's face is fatter than usual there but he has lost some weight recently and as both boys have a strong family resemblance, similar features, similar build, it's not surprising they could both look like something like their paternal grandfather.

'Perhaps,' he said.

'Well, we think so don't we, Rosiak,' I told the photograph after No.1 son and his dad had gone off to play golf.

It would be good to have other photos from Zygmunt's life in America as well as to share this one with Melanie. Let's hope I haven't long to wait.

*

Arriving for dinner on Saturday, friends Lesley and Malcolm, the friends we went to New Zealand with, looked at the photo. I showed it to Lesley covering the name in case she should remember it from our conversations whilst on holiday. She looked a little anxious, 'I'm usually not very good at this,' she admitted. 'He looks like Robert,' I prompted after a moment.

'Oh in that case, it's this one, bottom right.' Bingo. No hesitation. Got it in one.

I took the photo to my hairdresser, Kathy, this morning. We have a close relationship. Same process but I covered nothing up as she wouldn't remember the name. I told her it was a photo of my father so she spent a while peering at all the faces.

'He's only about twenty-seven,' I told her. 'Think about my boys when they were younger.'

'Is it this one, he looks like Robert?' Result.

Brian is cautious. He doesn't want me to be disappointed. But I know it's him. And the more people who confirm my suspicions, the more he will become the man who gave me life.

*

As no letter from America arrived I began to have doubts that I had posted it so I sent it again adding my email address to the letter heading. Each day letters drop onto the mat and I rush to see if anything has come but still nothing. Has Melanie received my letter? Is she ignoring it? Is it all over?

*

Late one night when I should have been making my way to bed, on a whim I looked at the e-mails. And there was something in the inbox.

Sender: Michael Rosiak. Subject: blank.

Michael Rosiak? Michael? My letter to America was to Melanie. The email said:

"Hi Margaret. This is Michael Rosiak writing. I am Melanie's brother and although your letter does not indicate that you know about me, perhaps I am your brother as well! I am in England visiting family and will be there until Saturday and might be able to visit you in Burton upon Trent if you would like to do that.

I am fifty-eight years old, born in Montreal, Canada on January 2 1951 and have lived in California most of my life. I have a most amazing girlfriend named Yoli, who is with me. We've been together a long time. This is our 3rd trip to England together. Yoli and I are looking forward to meeting you, if we can pull this off.

We are glad that you made contact. Melanie and I have only one concern that I'm sure you'll appreciate. We both feel that it would not be in mom's interest to find out about this relationship that dad had before they married and would request your help to keep that confidential.

Can you tell us about yourself and your history? I've read the letter and wonder about the other things that you've done (work, marriage, children, etc?) and what you're doing now.

If you would like to get together, I have a cell phone with me (he gave the number*) which also has a voice mail. If you can call you can leave a message or simply reply to this e-mail as I check them each evening."*

I have another brother. I have a *Rosiak* brother. When I read the sender of the email as Rosiak it seemed amazing and I could barely take in all he had to say. I had expected a sister. And now I have a brother as well. I whizzed off a reply:

"Goodness me! What an amazing piece of luck that you are in the UK. Thank you for getting in touch. I feel a bit overwhelmed. Where are you? A bit about me. I'm 63, married to Brian for forty years and have two sons, Nick aged 39 and Robert, 37. They, too, have sons. Our grandsons are Joseph, 9, Jack, 6 and his brother Ben, nearly 2. I retired three years ago. I'm an English graduate and taught the subject in secondary school until 1999.

I also had an interest in vocational education and worked as a consultant until my retirement six years later. I love keeping fit and go to the gym 2 or 3 times a week. I am learning French. (I've been learning for 9 years. Some information I have on

Zygmunt tells me he spoke French. Is that why he went to Montreal when they emigrated to Canada?) When we visited Montreal two years ago we were able to speak it there. We have a holiday home in France and like to go there when we can. We like long distance travel and visited New Zealand this year. We have been to Toronto three times as I have cousins who emigrated there in the 1950s. Is that enough?

Since I wrote to Melanie I have received a photo of Zygmunt from the Polish Institute and Sikorski Museum. He is in uniform and is part of a training unit of 40+ other Poles. I'm sure you'd love to see it; that is if you don't have it already, of course. I have lots of stuff that the Ministry of Defence has supplied me with, which I'm sure would be interesting to you. I would not dream of making any contact with your mother, you can be assured of that. To me, finding out what Zygmunt looked like has been amazing. He looks very like our younger son, Robert, who has yet to see the photograph as he lives in France. Nick picked him out very quickly not because he looked so much like himself but because he looked like his brother.

Where are you staying? How can we make contact before Saturday? Ring me as soon as you get this. It's a bit late to ring now – 12.45am..."

This was Thursday 16th July 2009. There followed a series of e-mails about location and arrangements. They were staying in a hotel in Leeds city centre and wondered what we were doing on Saturday. They would be heading south on the M1 to Southampton and hoped to stay somewhere close so they could access a cruise ship on the Sunday and wondered if they could stop to meet us on the drive down.

He would call later in the morning to firm up arrangements.

Nothing would have stopped us from making this meeting. We'd have moved heaven and earth to make this meeting! We began planning what we should do. Whether to meet them at the Hilton Hotel off Junction 24 of the M1 – would they be comfortable with this, a public place – or whether they would like to come here to have lunch with us at our house. We preferred the latter but wondered if they could make the time for such a detour and would this be too intimate?

Sometime before 1.00pm the phone rang and I heard his voice for the first time. American, he sounded quite young somehow. I know I sounded breathy with nerves. He was probably nervous, too. They preferred to come and meet us where we lived at about 1.00pm. Before he rang off he asked me if I was dark. I told him I was and had dark eyes. This was like Melanie. He wasn't dark at all. He was like his mother. I felt a pang of disappointment. I expected him to look like Zygmunt with the same eyes and colouring. I asked him a question. How did he pronounce his surname? Rosiak, he said, pronouncing each letter, using the pronunciation Kathleen had used and which we said before the lady from the Ministry of Defence called it Roshak softening the 's' and the 'i'. I explained this to Michael.

'You can say which ever you like,' he said. 'You have a right.' I felt privileged. And thrilled to have spoken to him. Coming off the phone, I emailed the directions to our house and went shopping for food. An earlier email told us they had been to a pub in Leeds where they had been given a recommendation for a good Italian restaurant. Drinking excess wine was making them feel a little worse for wear. Sounds like us!

*

I didn't sleep properly for two nights. Saturday morning arrived and as I had prepared everything the evening before, I went to a step aerobics class at the gym to work off the excess energy. It seemed preferable to sitting anxiously waiting.

The phone rang at 12.45. No surprise, they were stuck on the M1. I gave them alternative directions to use the A38 and after about forty-five minutes the phone rang again. Did we know the butchers shop? It was in our village. They were parked outside it.

'Stay put,' I said, 'we'll come and get you. You're two minutes away.' We piled into the car and set off for the butchers. 'I didn't ask him what car he was driving,' I told Brian. But it didn't matter; there they were. I waved to a woman standing on the pavement and Yoli waved back. A man wearing a black shirt and blue denim jeans was walking towards the car. It was Michael. He was tall, slim and has fairish hair. There some grey in his hair which was the same colour as a short beard and moustache. I jumped out of the car and shook his outstretched hand then we hugged each other. Stepping back we looked at one another scrutinising each other's faces.

I felt I recognised him. Did he look like some movie star or someone famous? No. I was probably looking at an image in the photo I had of Zygmunt. In the meantime Yoli and Brian stepped forward and introductions were made. We drove ahead and led them to our house through the traffic jam outside our church. A wedding was taking place and a large number of guests milled around on the lawn outside the church. Completing the picture was joyous peals of the church bells. There could not have been a more English country village scene. Having got out of the cars Michael and I walked together down the path as Brian opened the front door.

Chapter 25

The Visit – More Revelations

'I expected you to look like Melanie,' he said in his west coast American accent, 'because I look more like my mom.' And he must do as he has blue eyes, which surprised me. Fair to light-brown hair and clear blue eyes.

'But you look the same,' said Yoli

'You look like your father,' I told him. 'You look similar to my picture of Zygmunt.'

'You have the same long faces,' continued Yoli drawing her hand down her own face. And I felt pleased she had said this and a little ashamed that I had felt that disappointment earlier on the phone that he wouldn't be like Zygmunt. Because he was.

Sitting down in the kitchen with a glass of wine we started to talk. Some small talk to begin about the journey broke the ice but right from the start it was easy. I began by telling them the story of my search for Kathleen and they guessed we had been a long time on this.

'It's three years since I first met her,' I said.

'Do you see her?' asked Yoli.

'Oh, yes. Five or six times a year. She lives in Sheffield. She's lovely. Very funny. Quite a quirky sense of humour. She's cared for in a nursing home now as she has dementia.' I told them I had two half-brothers, John and Paul, younger than me, of course, as Michael and his sister were, and that I had met them. I revealed how difficult it had been for

Kathleen to tell them they had a sister and the circumstances of my birth.

Interested in the timing of his father's meeting with Kathleen Michael concluded that he would not have met his mother until after I was born. I was something that happened in Zygmunt's war-time life. Michael knew nothing of Hucknall but was amused to tell us when he was tired of driving after the flight from Los Angeles he had got off the motorway at Nottingham on his way up to Leeds a week before. He wanted to know if the relationship was a one-night stand. I said it wasn't and proceeded to tell him what I knew about Kathleen taking Zygmunt home to the house in Sheffield where her sisters and mother lived. He knew where his father had flown from in the war and wanted to see if he could match up the dates and locations of his flights with the dates of my conception and birth.

'Do you have these details?' I asked. He had.

'Are they in English or Polish?' They were in English and I informed him that we had them in Polish, too.

'At least that's what I think we have. As I don't understand Polish, it's a bit of guesswork but there are English RAF records which seem to match the dates of Polish records. Do you read Polish?' I asked. He didn't but, 'I have a cousin who is Polish who could do anything like that.' And he told us of a part of his family who now lived in the States. Zygmunt had an older sister, Irene or Irena, who lived in Poland during the war. She had one son, Jerzey, Polish for George, who married Halinka or Helena. He was unsure of the spelling of these names. They

341

had two daughters Isabella who married Piotr and Beata whose husband is Roman. Isabella and Piotr have two children, a son, Kusa, a daughter Nina, a red-haired angel whose hair is a mystery and a third baby due very soon. Isabella and her family now live in the States helped in their application by Michael.

Michael began to tell us his own story. His mother's family came from Lancashire. The family then moved to Leeds before the War. Grace had a brother, Doug and a sister called Sally and after the war their father decided it was time the girls left home. He was hoping they would meet servicemen, of whom there were so many after the War. Sally was the first to meet someone. Lucien was his name and he was French Canadian. He returned to Canada after a while and within six months Sally had joined him in Montreal. In the meantime Grace had met Zygmunt in the Mecca dance hall in Leeds. They married and had baby Melanie. Still living in the family home, the father was even more anxious to have them leave so they followed Sally and Lucien to Montreal where Michael was born. He was four years old before they left and what he remembered most was the cold weather there. Deciding to go to America, to California, where the weather was warmer, they all set off to start a new life.

So many people were doing that at the time,' said Michael. 'It seemed like the land of plenty. 'Now,' he laughed,' they can't get away fast enough.'

They lived in the house at Barker Avenue, the address given on Zygmunt's death certificate.

'It was the first house he bought,' remembered Michael recalling his childhood there. His aunt and uncle lived fairly close by.

'When I was eighteen,' Michael continued, 'I was in school at UCLA and my mom got sick.' He was struggling to tell us this and looked at Yoli for support. He took hold of her hand. 'I don't know what I'm looking at you for, you won't remember. You weren't there.' But his eyes were filling with tears. 'There are some things I wasn't going to tell you...' he began then quite suddenly he got up and left the kitchen where we were sitting looking across the garden with the French windows open to let in the breeze. It had become warm in the kitchen as the bolognaise sauce was heating in the oven. I knew we wouldn't be eating straight away so I had prepared something which would wait.

He returned after a moment wiping his eyes with tissue. He apologised as we insisted there was nothing to be sorry about and he started again.

'What I wasn't going to say was that the relative I was visiting in Leeds this last week was my mom.' Brian and I looked astounded.

'She lives in the UK? Not in the States?' we asked.

'No. She moved back to England after my dad died,' he explained.

'When you were eighteen?' We were incredulous. He made up his mind then that he was going to have to tell us the full story or we wouldn't be able to make sense of things. He took a deep breath.

'My mom got sick when I was eighteen.'

We realised this was costing him to explain.

'She wasn't able to cope and the drugs they put her on didn't help. Melanie and I were both in school. She was two years ahead of me. And soon after we learned about mom...' He was overwhelmed again and left us to try and get a hold of his emotions before he could continue.

Yoli explained, 'He has had quite an emotional morning. When we have left his mom in the past after a visit she has been very good and not got upset. Today was different. And it has upset him a lot. So he began the day feeling emotional and now he's finding it difficult to talk about her.' We understood, of course we did. I felt sorry he was putting himself through all this for us. He returned after a few moments.

'I haven't talked about this for years,' he explained. 'When I was in school...'

'University?'

'Yes, I went on a camping trip with some friends. We stayed till New Years and when I got home my dad told me he was very ill. I knew he had been suffering with this blistering under his arms and in the groin area and the doctors had been treating it with cortisone. It didn't seem to be making any difference and he was in a lot of pain. He passed on the following month. He passed away at home.'

'Were you there?'

'Yes. It was terrible really.' He looked drawn at the memory. 'He choked on his own vomit and that's what killed him. I haven't seen the death certificate before.' He and Yoli studied it. He hadn't heard the term septicaemia so Yoli told him it was

344

blood poisoning. He considered the seepage into the lungs referred to the fact that the blistering of the skin was also symptomatic of internal difficulties as well. We remarked how death certificates often did not reveal the full story as pemphigus was the illness which killed Zygmunt but the moment of death was as a result of choking.

'Well, after that, mom had to go back to England to live with her parents so she could get proper treatment for her illness.'

'You and Melanie were left on your own?'

'Yes, but my mom made arrangements for us to be cared for by her sister, my Aunt Sally. They had no kids so Melanie and I stayed with her and Lucien. As soon as my dad passed away I quit school because he had a milk delivery business. Do you remember Carnation?' We did. Carnation milk was famous when we were growing up. Everyone had it on tinned fruit at Sunday teatime in 1950's England. 'Well, he had the Superior Dairy and there was no one to deliver the milk so Lucien and I took it on until it could be sold. The house at Barker Avenue had to be sold as well. Dad had two businesses. He, with a partner, also ran a window screen business. Do you have them here?'

'Do you mean screens which keep out the sun and the flies?' We have a caravan which has them. He did.

'This had to be sold, too. But I went back to school and finished my education. I had about seven jobs while I did this.' Another industrious Rosiak. 'While she was there, Melanie met Julian and after they were married he got a professorship at the

345

University of Nebraska so they went off to Ardmore. They have two children: Ian and Elizabeth. They aren't married so no grandchildren yet. 'You'd like Julian. He's great.'

'We've seen his picture on the website for the University,' we told him. He looked amazed. We seemed to know so much more about his family than he had given us credit for.

I jumped up suddenly at the thought of this picture. I hadn't shown Michael my photo of Zygmunt with his training group. I grabbed it from the desk and rushed in again pushing it proudly into his hand. No need to cover the name up here. Michael looked at the faces.

'Here he is,' he told Yoli pointing at the bottom right side. 'Oh,' he said suddenly realising, 'they've all got their names on. I haven't seen this before,' he said to me.

'It's good, isn't it?' It was a statement rather than a question really because never having seen him before I didn't know whether it was a good likeness or not. What I meant was it was good for me to have it and he certainly looked like a handsome man to me. And it was wonderful that I could be the one showing it to his son. As he peered more closely at the picture I asked him, 'This may seem a funny thing to ask you, but do you mind if I look at your ears?'

He looked a little taken aback. 'I have a pointed ear, just one,' he began, 'which one is it, Yoli?'

As she began to examine him I said, 'It's the right one, isn't it.' And, of course, it was. 'You have the Polish ears,' I told him. He appeared non-plussed.

346

'That won't make much sense,' I blurted but we've been looking for the Polish ears for years! Did your father have them?' I felt I already knew the answer to this question because, fanciful or not, I had seen them on the photo when we had first received it. 'Nick has your ears. Because I hadn't nor anyone in Brian's family had them we always called them his Polish ears. When his son, Joseph, was born he phoned to tell us he and said: oh, by the way, mum, he has the Polish ears. Then when Robert's second son, Ben, was born in Dumfries Rob rang, told us all about the birth, then he said I'm sure Lisa won't mind my saying but Ben has the Polish ears! One pointy, the right one, and folded over a bit at the top.' We were all laughing at this point and Michael was holding the side of his face but I felt the need to explain that if you are an adopted child and have no one to look back at to explain various distinct characteristics it's wonderful to see yourself, or elements of your children and even your grandchildren in others.

Still referring to the photograph of Zygmunt, I said to Michael that it had been accompanied by a two sided document written in Polish in Zygmunt's own handwriting about his time in Russia and that I had sent it off for translation. He said he would certainly love to know what he had written about that time in his life. We looked then together at other documents I had received from the Ministry of Defence.

Michael read closely the document which told him Zygmunt had been keen on swimming and tennis.

'He never told me he played tennis,' he said incredulously.

'Do you play?' I asked.

Yoli replied for him that he played regularly. He commented from the same form that he had spoken French. 'He was fluent in French,' he said and I beamed thinking of my own small efforts. 'He was very bright. He could speak seven languages including Russian. Polish and English, of course but I can't remember what the other three were.

'After dad passed away I visited my grandparents in Poland and could only speak French to my aunt as she couldn't speak English and I hadn't a word of Polish. That was very testing. I met with Jan and Maria,' he told me.

'Zygmunt's parents,' I indicated that I knew their names. 'They'd managed to survive the War, then?'

Oh, yes, they were fine. But it's funny, you know, after dad passed away they only lived a short while. My grandfather was in his nineties.' He paused a moment to think out what he had said. 'Can that be right? It seems too old.'

'My dad was forty when they got me,' I told him.

'Right. Well, it's probably right, then. But he didn't live more than six months after and then my grandmother died. It's like that with lots of people, isn't it? When one goes, if they're quite old, the other one goes quite soon after.' I considered the tragedy of their losing a son before his time. Fifty-two is no age to die.

We continued to look at some of the other documents.

'This is what I treasured the most,' I said smiling and pointing at the document headed Alien

Identity Certificate completed at interview with the Polish Resettlement Corps at the time of his release for employment in 1949. It was on the top of this piece of paper that a note had been added that we had deciphered as 'Emigrating to Canada.' 'That was the only indication we had,' I said, 'but more importantly, there are details of what he looked like.'

He scrutinised the document. 'No,' he said, 'that's not right. He had black hair, so dark brown as to look black. And he wasn't five feet seven, he was five feet eleven!' Brian and I looked at one another.

'That makes more sense,' said Brian. 'It accounts for your height far more than five feet seven.'

'How tall are you?' asked Michael.'

'Five feet eight,' I told him.

'Melanie's five feet seven and I'm just over six feet. Warren, my son, is six feet four.'

A son? Warren?

'Our boys are six feet,' we told him. Definitely the Polish genes.

'You have a son,' I ventured hoping he would tell us more. And he did.

'Warren isn't Yoli's son,' he smiled at her. He isn't the son of my wife either, actually.' He looked awkwardly. 'I was married before but he's the son of another relationship that's gone now.' He didn't elaborate further. 'He's getting married in 2010 to Lauren.'

'How old is he?' I asked. Thirty four was the reply. Four years younger than Nick.

'I told him I was coming to see his aunt Margaret.' I laughed.

At this point I produced some photos of our boys and they exclaimed over them likening them both to niece and nephew, who were Melanie's children, and cousins and their children. 'We'll show you Warren if we can dial up Facebook,' Yoli volunteered.

It was time to eat. The meal had been waiting for almost three hours. But I still had photos I wanted to show them so I produced photos of Kathleen and Bill's wedding and the other photos of her sisters getting married where she was a bridesmaid. I wanted him to see the handsome woman who had caught the eye of his father. Eventually we sat down at the kitchen table and I produced the food.

Michael sat at the table with the papers I had researched from the internet of the Polish 300 Squadron. He had no knowledge of their exploits and made a note of the website so he could pursue it when he got home.

'I learned to fly, you know,' said Michael. Yoli laughed. 'She won't fly with me. It scares her to death.'

'Only the once,' she admitted.

'This was your father's influence?' I asked.

'Of course,' he said. 'He talked about it so often. Although he wouldn't talk about his war-time exploits to us. I have often wondered about that. I guessed he could have had a sense of guilt at the bombing raids over Germany where civilians were killed or been involved in some scary stuff. But you never know he could have wanted to conceal that he'd had a relationship. Do you know if he knew about you?' I didn't.

Brian and I had often speculated about this and it had never seemed the right time to ask Kathleen. Now it was too late as it might upset her. There are various scenarios we speculate on:

Kathleen met Zygmunt after Bill had gone to war in the Middle East and finished the affair when she knew Bill was coming home. She then realised she was pregnant, had to tell Bill and put me up for adoption.

Or Kathleen met Zygmunt. After a year or more (guesswork) became pregnant. Told Zygmunt and he finished the relationship.

Or Zygmunt knew Kathleen had become pregnant and offered to stick by her if, when Bill came home, he rejected her and the unborn child.

If the third scenario had been the truth we would all have had a very different life. At least one of us in the room wouldn't have been there!

'He might have known but what could he have done about it? We're only guessing aren't we?'

'Could you ask your mother?' wondered Michael.

'It's not very likely that she would want to talk about it. And I couldn't even broach it if John were there...'

'John?'

'My half-brother on my mother's side,' I answered. 'He is fine with me but my existence upsets his equilibrium, his peace of mind, as it forces him to see his mother in a light he doesn't think sons should be seeing their mothers in.'

'Right, I see,' he said.

'I'm the result of his mother's 'bit of a fling' he thinks, so not good. Naturally, he doesn't like to dwell on it,' I said smiling.

'Of course.'

Yoli asked, 'But there's another brother,' isn't there. What does he think about it all?' Brian, telling her about Paul, mentioned the fact that he was tall and at first had seemed accepting of me but since our first meeting he had become ill with dementia and, sadly, his health was gradually deteriorating. We both think he would have come round to the idea of having a big sister and been quite welcoming.

Over lunch Michael talked of his work. He and Yoli work for a company which provides aerospace and electronics systems. Brian had heard of them and mentioned the B2 stealth bomber. I didn't know anything about it but thought there could be an influence from his father that made him go into the line of work. We continued to eat our way through the pasta and bolognaise sauce and then I produced a trifle. I like to make it with black cherries and laced with plenty of sherry; it's easy and usually quite delicious.

Michael took a mouthful. 'That's good,' he said, 'even better than my Aunt Sally's and that's saying something.' He was on his second helping when he told us about his aunt. Coming from Yorkshire, she knew about trifle. He had lived with his aunt after his mother returned to the UK for her treatment. It was many years later that his aunt had met a tragic death in a road accident. She had been walking along a road and turned left into another road. As she did so a car came around the corner and knocked her over. She hit her head on the ground and was taken to hospital where she died later in the day. Michael had sent for Melanie.

'I saw her in the hospital and her face was bruised. Her left hand where she had reached out to try to stop the car was all grazed and bruised. We have looked after Lucien ever since. They have no children so Melanie and I are like their children.' It was a waste of life. He went on to tell us of how his mother lives her life in Leeds. She, like Kathleen, is in sheltered accommodation. She has a room of her own and can go to town in Leeds, shopping or meeting people as many as three times a week. At eighty-one she is doing very well especially as she might not have lived nearly so long had she stayed in the States at the time when her illness was first diagnosed. The treatment in the UK has been very successful. She is able to take her meals in the dining room with other people and there is a lounge, too, where events take place. 'She has four meals a day,' Michael told us, 'breakfast, lunch, dinner and supper as well.' He pronounced supper with a short 'u' in the way Yorkshire people do and it sounded familiar. Brian and I commented that his description of the place sounded like Kathleen's residential community.

After the meal was over we went outside into our small courtyard garden to take some photos. I stood with Michael with a backdrop of late-flowering deep pink clematis whilst Yoli and Brian snapped away. Then it was Yoli's turn to join us for Brian to take and Brian then for Yoli to take. Using Michael's blackberry, Yoli took our picture so he could send a photo of us by email to Melanie. He had a mischievous grin as he pressed send and I could imagine Melanie peering closely, looking for family likeness even as we were still standing in the garden.

Coming back into the house Yoli remembered she had promised to show Warren to us so using my laptop in the study she brought up his Facebook page. We all stood around her, watching. The page opened rapidly and there looking back at us was a face so like Nick's we gasped. 'Bloody hell!' I swore, 'look at that Brian,' and together we looked at the face on the laptop then over our shoulders at Nick's wedding photo on the study wall behind us then back to the laptop. Before our heads swivelled off, I pulled the photo off the wall and set it beside Warren's so we could better see them. His girlfriend was standing with him. She was a good-looking girl with long dark hair.

'That's Lauren. He's marrying her next year. They'll make beautiful children. Warren and Lauren'

'More good-looking Rosiaks?'

'Ah, yes,' he agreed.

I reminded them I had accessed the picture of a Melanie Leland on Facebook when I had Googled Grace Leland. I repeated the process and there she was again. 'It was the Leeds connection that triggered my memory of the Upper Wortley address and led my friend to find the marriage details.'

'We had dinner with these people yesterday evening. Melanie's my cousin,' Michael laughed.

He was quiet for a moment and then he said, 'When you come to California I'll show you the house on Barker Avenue where we used to live and the place where dad is buried. I'm sure you'd like to see the photos we have of him.' Would I? We walked back into the kitchen and sat down to have coffee.

'He's in Forest Lawn's Memorial Park, isn't he?' He nodded. 'Among the Hollywood stars. Michael Jackson's going in there, isn't he?' He laughed.

'I don't know about that,' he smiled, 'but it would be good for you to see.'

'We'd love to see it,' we told him not missing the pointed invitation. I felt so happy to hear what he said. 'We'll certainly come to California,' I said and Brian, said without missing a beat, 'Oh, yes, we'll be there.' He felt it, too. A welcoming, all embracing sense of being included. It was wonderful.

'I live in a five-bedroom house with an ocean view, he continued. 'It sounds grand but it isn't really as four of the bedrooms are really small. Yoli won't live with me but her daughter does and so does her granddaughter but she won't come.' Yoli laughed. 'You know that in a few months they'll have finished school and it will all be different.' It looked as if they would become a couple after being together for ten years. Yoli explained her two daughters were from a previous marriage and, of course, weren't Michael's even though they found it useful to live at his house. They admired the arrangement we had in our kitchen in that one long wall was all windows; the middle panels were a French window that opened onto the garden. We keep our old conservatory furniture, a settee and two easy chairs all of which are supremely comfortable, in the kitchen and can soon fall asleep there on a warm summer afternoon such as today was. But it was this that he would like to emulate in his home as a fireplace occupied the middle of his view on the ocean with two windows either side. I liked the idea of an ocean view and said this so Yoli explained that the Los Angeles area was a mixture of ocean, mountain and desert all within about two hours' drive of the other. Sounded good to me, especially for a holiday. I could see Brian planning; cogs ticking over.

Reluctantly, at last, they said they had to go. Still in the kitchen we hugged goodbye. I felt a sadness that we were losing them so soon but I promised to send a copy of the translation of Zygmunt's account of his time in Russia in the early 1940s when I had received the translation. We knew we would be meeting again. He had said earlier that Melanie and Julian were coming to England and we discussed dates but we will be in France when they come and won't be back before they go back to the States. This is a great shame but there is nothing we can do about it. Michael thinks Melanie should meet me some time and left it in the air as to when that might be.

*

I have a brother. I really feel that. And the difference between this brother and John is that I feel he wants to be my brother; not that I am his half-anything but his sister. For John it's very different. My appearance in his life has changed the way he looks at his mother and he has every right to feel that way. His life would have just continued very well without the knowledge of his mother's indiscretion. Michael is a warm person, inclined to be emotional and tactile. I feel he wanted to make our meeting work once he was convinced I was the genuine article and was delighted when it did.

Zygmunt was a dancer, meeting my mother in a dance hall in Nottingham and Michael's mother in the Mecca in Leeds. We concluded he was quite a dancer! Somehow it was more socially acceptable for a man to be meeting women and having affairs than it was for a woman. There is the social stigma for John to contend with that isn't present for Michael.

Chapter 26

Invitation to Lunch

I rang John the following day to find out whether he would be at the residential community the following Thursday as we were planning to visit before we went to France. Unrehearsed, carelessly, I told him I had a photo of Zygmunt.

'Do you want to see it?' I asked him.

'No,' he said quite abruptly. 'If you don't mind, I don't want to see it.'

It should have occurred to me how inappropriate it was for him to see his mother's war-time lover. Why didn't I think of him before blurting it all out? I didn't think it would be right to tell him of my meeting with Michael yesterday. As he had said in the past, all this is nothing to do with him.

Telling him that we were preparing to go to France the following Sunday I mentioned how we would spend some time in northern France having a little sightseeing break before going to our house. He told me that he and Lynn, as she was feeling well enough now, were going to France themselves this week to celebrate, belatedly, their fortieth wedding anniversary and he may not be seeing our mother. I told him Brian and I would be there on Thursday morning anyway and it would be good to see him if they hadn't set off. 'But,' I concluded, 'I'll be keeping my photo in my pocket.'

I went back into the kitchen to continue preparing lunch. Yesterday, I had put the camera memory card into the digital photo frame and there was a constant scrolling of the pictures we had taken of Michael and Yoli. I gazed at them intently scanning our faces. I printed off two of them to keep by me and find it hard to stop looking at them.

I sent an email to Michael telling him we'd had an amazing afternoon with them. 'I
felt excited about your coming here and I'm still excited,' I wrote. I told him about the photo frame. He replied that all was well with Yoli and him.

He concluded:

'We sooo...loved our visit with you. Tell Brian from both of us, he was so nice and seemed genuinely interested in your family exploits.' He finished off the email with 'Love, Michael'.

*

I received a delightful phone call this morning. It wasn't from Michael, nor from John, but from Lynn, John's wife. She had learned from John that we would be in France in a few days and would be stopping off for a while. Would we like to come for lunch? How wonderful was that? They had decided to go to France as Lynn feeling well enough.

'I knew you must be in Normandy,' I told her, 'because John wasn't there when I went to see mum on Thursday. Half of me thought, oh that's a shame but the other half thought good, oh, because you'd be well enough to travel and enjoy some time away at last.' Lynn explained her health problems and how she was feeling at the moment and seemed fairly upbeat about things even though she was feeling tired.

'It wasn't a good visit for us,' I remarked. 'Mum wasn't at her best at all.' I'd hoped from what

John said about his last visit that she would be lucid and able to hold a conversation but it wasn't so. I explained how things had been. Lynn was sympathetic and practical at the same time because there was nothing she or John could do about it.

We made arrangements to arrive for a late, light lunch, nothing too taxing if she was feeling at all tired. We are both looking forward to seeing them. Must drink less red wine than when we went before to see them!

*

No such luck but this time it was rosé, a Cinsault, in fact, several and a red or two. Lunch was delightful, very French with a selection of cold meats, pâté with salads and cheese.

We'd spent the morning wandering around the Caen Memorial to the Second World War. The tourist information suggested a minimum of two hours but that was conservative as we left after four and still felt there was more to see. Watching a film showing preparations on both sides for the Normandy Landings using a split screen technique, we both agreed we had rarely seen a more effective anti-war presentation. Lynn spoke of it, too, as she and John had been to see it some years earlier.

We spoke of Kathleen and her current state of health; their experience had been better than when we had seen her in the previous week. Much seems to depend on the medication being administered. After a while, when we had finished eating, we talked again of how I had traced my mother and how I had made my first approach through social workers. The matter of the hedge-cutter came up again.

'That was Hugh, wasn't it?' I told John. His and Lynn's son cutting grandma's hedge was in my imagination.

'God, no,' was the reply, 'You wouldn't see him with hedge trimmers in his hand. No, that was Stephen, our Paul's lad.' Seeing this tall boy and speculating about whom he could be seems such a long time ago now.

Lynn and I talked about our education. She had been at school at the grammar school next door to mine but she is younger than I am so would not know people I knew who went there at the time. We laughed about the strict adherence to uniform and the punishments metered out at the non-wearing of our berets out of school. Lynn assumed that I had been a teacher throughout my working life but queried this assumption when Brian and I talked about how we had met whilst working for the Inland Revenue in the mid-sixties.

Suddenly John said, 'I think you have had better chances in life through being adopted.'

'Oh? Why do you think that?' I asked surprised at this view.

'You had a better education than me.'

'Not so,' I countered. 'You've got an Open University degree.' We had seen the photographs very recently in Kathleen's room. 'You achieved it later in your life. I didn't go to university until I was thirty-three.'

'Well, you had more material benefits than I did,' he shrugged.

'What I had was a loving, caring upbringing, from parents I knew loved me. How was your upbringing any different? Upbringing isn't about how many things or privileges you have; it's about values your parents give you through their attitude to you. If you are confident in their approval you are likely to become a confident person. There was no one loved more than me. How was that different from you?'

'It wasn't. I had a great upbringing with good parents,' he agreed. 'They did their best for me and our Paul.'

'I recently asked my cousin, Margery, you know the one I brought with me to meet mum,' he nodded at the memory. 'I asked her what she had felt when she first saw me.' What John didn't know was that my parents had been at the youngest end of their largish Victorian families and married for fourteen years when they considered adoption. On my dad's side there were older cousins who I never saw as they were in their thirties when I was born and on my mum's side there were four cousins, two boys born to one of my mother's brothers who we never saw and two born to one of my mother's sisters who were Margery and her brother Les, who we visit in Toronto.

There had been no babies for a generation. Margery and Fred never had children and Les and Audrey's children were in Canada. No babies. So what did they think of me?

'What did she say?' asked John.

'We all fell in love with you the minute we saw you.' I gestured expansively with my arms, laughing.

'Oh, open that window,' he said. Lynn and I looked to the window. She smiled. He said, 'We just need to let the ego out.'

We returned to education. Not whose had been the better but about the later study he had undertaken with the OU in French. I want to continue learning French having just taken a GCSE French exam after a distance learning course and was interested in his experience. I told them about some of my experiences as a teacher dealing with unruly year nines in an incident of chair-throwing.

'I could never be a teacher,' said Lynn. I hear it all the time but I enjoyed my time in the class-room. Brian talked about his work with A.C.A.S., the advisory and conciliation service.

'You're a union man,' said John.

'Not exactly,' said Brian and went on to explain the work he did with companies during disputes and in advisory work. Having arrived at half past two and talking non-stop it was suddenly half past seven and we had to drive to Le Mans.

As we were leaving, there was hugging and handshaking all round. We walked to our car.

'You look like my mother from the back,' said John.

Chapter 27

The Connection Continues

Whilst at the French house visiting Rob, Lisa and the little boys, Michael and I exchanged emails during which he said the details of their continuing holiday in the UK would be appearing on Yoli's Facebook entries. Seeing Joseph before we came away, whilst at Diane and Steve's house, I had shown Di the Facebook entry for Warren Rosiak and watched her reaction. She thought his face was like that of Nick's. She told me Nick was on Facebook, too, and Debbie. 'Would you like to be?' she's asked me. And without further ado she created a page for me and used a photo of her own of me with Brian and Joseph taken last Christmas morning.

Because of this, I was able to access Yoli's entries as she 'had me as a friend.' I looked at them fairly regularly and joined in with their exploits around the coast of the UK and France on their P&O cruise ship. No communication from Melanie, though, even though she and Julian are in the UK.

Hoping to receive it before I went on holiday, I had been anxiously waiting for the translation of Zygmunt's time in Russia. I emailed my translator and she said she had been delayed by a visit to Poland but would do her best. I went away without receiving it. However after a few days it came through by email. She had done it in haste and had to admit to not being able to read it all. It revealed a terrible time for Zygmunt.

He had been ill-treated and seen the ill-treatment of others. With a rider that he would need to find a quiet moment to read it, I sent it as an attachment to Michael. What follows is Zygmunt's testimony written in Polish in his own hand in 1943 on his arrival in the UK:

'I was drafted to the military service on 11 November 1938 in Wloclawek, 14th division under Lieutenant-Colonel…… Having completed my initial first training I was sent to Niemenczyn Battalion of the Border Protection Corp in Niemenczyn, whose chief of command was Major Mierzejewski. On the 20 November I crossed the frontier to Lithuania, where I was stationed in Rokiszki and then to Kowno. When the Russians invaded Lithuania I was taken to the camp in Juchniowo.

When Polish Army was created on Russian soil I joined 5th Technical Communication Company under Lieutenant Wilk. The first camp I was interned in had its base in the outbuildings belonging to the manor of Count Przezdziecki. Food was adequate, hygiene very poor. During our protest against the decision to move us to a different block where living conditions were inadequate due to health reasons one of the Polish standard-bearer's (Chorazy) was killed.

After the camp in Rokiszki had been closed I was sent to the camp based 3 km away from Kowno – to the 5th Fort Shaulists' (Special Security Police Squad) – attitude towards Poles hostile, attitude of local people rather favourable. After having been taken from Lithuania by the Russians I was placed in a camp in Juchnowo on 15 July 1940. Food and health care were adequate there.

In April 1941 I was transported to Kola Peninsula to work helping to build an airport, where living conditions and food were just appalling. We were given 80g of bread a day and one bowl of soup. We were treated in a brutal way. I was then taken to Suzdala, where I soon joined the Polish Army.

After I had arrived to the Juchnowo camp, I was interrogated by NKWD. They wanted to find out if I was a threat to a communist propaganda in Poland and whether I worked for the 2ⁿᵈ Division.

In a Russian camp in Juchnowo we were subjected to regular 'talks' regarding all the advantages of the communist system, Polish political system was criticized and we were told that Poland will never be created. We were also obliged to watch a film showing Polish authorities mistreating the Ukrainians. A newspaper in Polish called "Kurier Wilenski" was delivered to the camp that showed the alleged benefits of the Russian economy on the territories invaded by the Russians in Poland.'

Michael did not comment on it in his next email. It was a very moving account and probably difficult for him to come to terms with. He didn't say either whether Melanie had commented on the photo he had sent to her of us on his Blackberry. I suspect an element of caution.

*

Taking my treasured photos to France, my intention was to show them to Rob and see his reaction to the photo of his biological paternal grandfather. Knowing his reluctance to engage in this I showed the Polish Institute photo of Zygmunt to Lisa first. She picked him out in a second. 'Is it this one, bottom right?' But of course. She loved the photos of myself and Michael and peered hard to find a family likeness but whether for her to find it for Robert or for me, I didn't really know. The following afternoon when Robert returned from work, I was sitting on the bench outside the back door sunning myself.

'Let's have a look at Sigmund Freud,' he suddenly said.

'Oh, you're ready to look are you? Did Lisa say you should?' I smiled encouragingly at my son.

'Maybe.' Non-committal. I fetched the photos from my room. He looked for a long time. I didn't cover anyone's name up; I didn't offer any clues. But he knew it was him. He knew it was an image of himself.

'Well, now,' he said. I didn't press him. I showed him the two pictures of Michael. He smiled and handed them back. I'm not sure what he's thinking.

*

Out of the blue, Warren Rosiak has asked to 'be my friend' on Facebook. I said yes, of course and so have access to all his photos. More and more he looks like Nick. And why shouldn't they resemble each other? They are, after all, cousins.

Michael and I kept up our e-mail correspondence when we arrived back from holiday. I told him that Colin Mitchell-Smith from RAF Faldingworth was interested in Zygmunt's testimony which had now been posted back from the translator with an updated version of the e-mailed one. I had already e-mailed him the earlier version.

This version had more details as she had managed to decipher some of the earlier lines where she had previously drawn a blank. Colin was interested in the photos of the No. 30 Course in RAF Newton taken in 1944 as so many of the Polish Air Men were named on the photo. He was thinking he could perhaps put them on the Polish 300 website. I had told Colin I needed to ask Michael if they could be used and that the copyright belonged to the Polish Institute. To Michael I attached a poem called 'Siberia' *see appendix, which Colin had sent to me suggesting the testimony could be set alongside it at the memorial service in September.

Michael wrote straight back.

The poem is amazing…I had to focus not to get all choked up again. It's odd (and then again perhaps not) that the things you are dealing with make me emotional. I don't say that in a bad way at all…just fact. Zygmunt died a terrible death and my Mom has been through hell…and yet made the best of it. These things are so deep inside me and I suppose they need an occasional outlet.

Margaret, I'm honored that you even asked me about the proposed postings. Those are Yoli's words, and I believe her intuition about you is strong. I'm proud of dad's achievements, and even prouder that you are now part of that heritage. You have done an amazing job with the research, and I so appreciate it. Yes, you may use your very good judgment to give permission to the postings or use of dad's history as you see fit. You are as entitled to enjoy it as we are.

As I read these words, I could feel the tears pricking at the back of my eyes. I blinked a lot before reading on. He added that he would be looking out some photos to scan and e-mail to us so I could see how Zygmunt looked when he and Melanie were growing up. I was excited at the prospect of seeing those.

I replied to his e-mail:

I feel very touched by your sentiments and because we are remaining in touch in this way, feel close to you. You have accepted my existence so well...I'm pleased you were moved by the poem, just as I was, although I'm sorry I keep making you feel emotional. Isn't it amazing to think that Zygmunt's words (his account from Siberia) which were written in 1943 could be read to others from Poland over sixty years later, in September 2009?'

On the same day Michael forwarded another e-mail which wasn't to me but to Melanie. There appears to have been some correspondence between them regarding Zygmunt's flying record which Michael has, passed on to him after his father died.

'Hi Melanie...checked the log books tonight...here are the service records. Note that some of them overlap which I believe means for different types of training he would go to different areas/airports.

He then listed with dates, beginning with 23 February 1944 at Hucknall, five references to RAF stations from where Zygmunt had flown. About an entry for 'Newton' he said he had been unable to locate a 'Newton', England. However, he also included the types of plane Zygmunt had flown: the 'Tiger Moth', the 'Oxford', the 'Wellington', and two references to the 'Lancaster'. The final date was 6th January 1945 from RAF Faldingworth. He told Melanie Faldingworth is in Lincolnshire. He noted:

'There is no 'through' date for Faldingworth' and his last daily flight log entry was 25th November 1946.'

Also, she could look at:

'some interesting websites and memorials to the 'squadron 300' which was the unit from Faldingworth dedicated to the Polish Air Force personnel. The last official flight of squadron 300 was 1 day later, on 26th November 1946 and the unit was disbanded in January 1947.'

His e-mail to me to include this correspondence with his sister begins:

'Hi Margaret...Melanie is still playing this very cautiously, and wanted to know where dad was 'hanging' out during his RAF/PAF days...enjoy...

P.S. When exactly is your birthday?...'

I understood the caution very well. John still has it a little. Melanie has a mum who is still alive and needs to be protected. John, too. I suspect the birth date will have Melanie counting on her fingers in relation to where Zygmunt was at the time of my conception and birth. They don't stack up well. Zygmunt would have been in Lincolnshire during both periods and it may be difficult for Melanie to realize how easy it would have been in post war-time to transport service personnel from Lincolnshire to Nottinghamshire which are adjacent counties.

Before replying to Michael, I accessed a website he had recommended which was like Google Earth in that you could zoom in with a bird's eye view on various airports current and disused. On the one for Faldingworth Brian and I could see, as well as all the various outbuildings, the part of the disused runway where the memorial stood. I told him:

'We had been standing there and at the other end of the strip, too, in a howling November gale with snow on the ground only last year. You get a feel, looking down the runway, of how it might have been

371

for the flyers in the war. It was spooky and a bit overwhelming.'

I had looked up the flight schedule that the MoD had sent and the dates tallied but mine were more extensive including postings to RAF Brighton, Blackpool, Morecambe, Finningly, and Lindholme. I told Michael about these and explained that 'Newton' was RAF Newton in Nottinghamshire not ten miles from where Brian and I lived before moving from Nottingham and not far away from Hucknall. I continued:

'The war in Europe ended on 8th May 1945 but flights continued to drop supplies all over Europe and to try and repatriate the thousands of displaced people. You'd be pleased to know that at Faldingworth, at these memorial events, they have a flypast from a Lancaster bomber (there is only one left that is able to fly, as far as Brian knows) over the village. There will be a lot of deaf people in Faldingworth. I was conceived in July/August 1945 (I was born 10th April 1946) when Zygmunt was in Lincolnshire. I can only assume the RAF provided transport to Hucknall for the dancers. Looking at his schedule, I'm surprised he found the time to dance. Until recently, Kathleen had a photo of him, apparently, but it has been lost. She remembers him in her head.
Her husband was demobbed in December 1945 and came home from the Middle East so the Relationship would have ended before then I guess. All the Polish 300 Squadron was based at

372

Faldingworth and was demobbed from there as the unit was disbanded on 9th January 1949. He would have gone to Leeds then to become a presser in a tailor's, Sassoon's Ltd. I've just looked that up again and the form where that information is printed is dated 15th April 1948 so he may have moved to Leeds then but his final discharge from the PAF is 9th January 1949.'

Shortly after this the photos began to arrive, in thirty separate e-mails. What a truly amazing experience. Michael had sent, first of all some of Yoli from their recent holiday in the UK. Then followed some of Warren as a young boy, Michael with Warren's mum then later came some of Warren as a young man. There were pictures of Michael and Melaine growing up. One picture of Melanie at aged eighteen had her smiling at the camera. It was of her graduation from high school.

Her eyes and hair are dark. I fetched my passport photo of me aged twenty. We have some similarities, not just because we were children of the late sixties/early seventies but the dark eyes show up and surprisingly the teeth – crossed left over right at the front. And finally came:

'some old photos of dad. The quality won't be so hot (since they're scanned) but I hope you'll love them as I do.

I adored them. The wedding photo from 1949. Both bride and groom look handsome. Michael's mother was very lovely as another photo of her in a 'glamorous' pose shows. Zygmunt with baby Michael in a pram with Melanie standing by looking a little as I did as a child. Zygmunt on a bench with the children of school age. Lots of family photos with them all together at Christmas, on holiday or at home. In one Melanie is wearing the kind of smocked dress that I wore as a child. I felt a rush of sadness when I looked at one with just Zygmunt and Michael at about five years old. I tried to understand why I should feel so sad, so bereft not to be in their company.

I sent some of my family to him. They included photos of our boys and Brian and me on our wedding day. He told me via an e-mail:

'When you are young, I see what must be 'Kathleen features'... When I look at you today, I see 'Melanie features'... Yoli sees 'Michael features'...doesn't matter really...I don't even look like my own sister of the same mother/father...'

'The difference for me,' I e-mailed in return, *'is I've spent over sixty years not knowing who I looked like! It's like a detective novel – following clues that twist and turn at every point.'*

Chapter 28

A Polish Connection

Included among the photos were two of Michael's cousin, second cousin actually, Iza who he had helped immigrate to the States a few years ago. The photos are of her wedding to Piotr. Included on them were her parents, Jerszy and his wife Helenka, and her grandmother, Irena. She was Zygmunt's sister (Michael's and Melanie's aunt). I'm not sure she is still alive. Michael had talked about Iza and her husband Piotr when they were at our house. Two days after I was looking at these photos I received another e-mail from Michael.

Michael asked if I had the Polish version of Zygmunt's testimony about his time in Russia. He reminded me of when he had mentioned his cousin Iza. Both Iza and Piotr, being Polish speakers would like to have a go at translating the document to see if the missing lines could be deciphered. When Michael had told Iza about our meeting and about who I was she told Michael that she remembered her parents telling her that 'some woman' had written many letters to Poland saying she was in love with dad. And it definitely was not Grace.

'Wouldn't that be fun?' he wondered. *'I don't know the details...Iza will have to check with her parents back in Poland.'*

I felt desperate to know if 'some woman' was Kathleen. I hope Iza's parents could recall who it was. I suggested if she wanted to know more she should e-mail me directly and I would answer any questions.

'I appreciate hearing from you.' I told Izabela. *'I have just seen a delightful photo from Michael of you getting married. Zygmunt was very handsome but then I always knew he would be. I knew he was Polish and that he was an airman as my adoptive father told me so but the rest I had to imagine for myself. So from being in my 30s when I first had this knowledge, in my imagination he was tall, had brown eyes and was good looking. My sons share something of these characteristics and the younger one is uncannily like him.*

Some of the original papers supplied by the Ministry of Defence suggest he was educated in France in Aubevilliers, near Paris, for at least two years but this wasn't really made clear as it is in Polish. You have just confirmed it. Michael said he spoke fluent French. I'll wait for more information on the besotted English woman in the hope that it could be my mother. She is now too confused for me to ask if she wrote letters to Poland.'

The next day an e-mail came from Iza.

'I have to ask my parents what they remember. I have a vague memory of a conversation that took place in my family about a lady from UK who was writing letters to my great grandma. I remember she was emotionally involved with him. He must have passed contact information for my great grandma to

her. I do not remember the name. I have to verify with my parents how accurate this is. I am not sure if those letters still exist. That would be the best way to check.

I am not sure who was translating the letters. At that point in time in Poland there were not many Polish/English translators so we could see if it was guessed or true information. I will know something tomorrow afternoon. I will keep you updated. Zygmunt could not return home, even for a visit in those times, so he became a sort of legend in my family. My great grandma really missed him as he was the apple of her eye, it seemed, a straight A student even in France where they lived before the 2ⁿᵈ World War, and a handsome guy.

Take Care, Izabela

A further e-mail from Michael advocated caution.

'I think what would be best is if someone kept the letters! It might be Kathleen, might not, yes? Seems like dad liked the dances...'

Well, that may be so. But the letters are a whole different dimension. Later that day he wrote:

'Hi Margaret...the 'story' is about to get much better. Iza will be sending you an e-mail when she can get to it that will fascinate you. '

I prepared myself to be fascinated. This had all the ingredients of a romantic novel. The next day Izabela wrote:

Hi Michael and Margaret

I spoke with my mom on Skype today. She said I was partially correct. This is her side of the story, based on her conversations with my great grandma who had lived with us. Grandma Marianna and Grandpa Jan were getting letters from Zygmunt during and after the war. At some point Zygmunt wrote about his girlfriend, Kathleen, whom he met in England. He was mentioning her for quite a while and it seems my great grandparents were getting used to the idea she might be their future daughter-in-law. She was sending them parcels with clothes, supplies or non-perishable food. Then they stopped getting those letters and parcels. Next letter from Zygmunt, my mom does not remember the time span of those events, was with his wedding pictures. He married Grace, apparently my great grandparents were surprised by the news, but he mentioned that he met her in Leeds and was very happy. My mom said that the period of non-communication was worrisome for them, as they were worried about what had happened to him, so perhaps it was a while. My mom said those letters might still be in the attic in their house, she will look, but she is not sure if she can still find them, it has been a long time. She will also talk to my dad and check out what he knows about this case.'

This news filled me with sadness. All so long ago and so much information missing that no one could supply. I returned Izabella's e-mail saying:

Hello Izabela and Michael

Isn't this so sad! Oh dear. You will know from Michael, Iza, that I have met Kathleen so the letter writer is real, alive with a story of her own to tell. The gap between Kathleen's letters from Sheffield and Zygmunt's marriage to Grace in Leeds could have been between three and four years, which is a long time for your family to be out of touch. There is so much missing from the story that we'll never know about; some of it's locked in Kathleen's head. We never imagined there was a Poland dimension to her story; everything so far has taken place in Sheffield (where we know Kathleen took Zygmunt to her mother's house when he was stationed in Nottingham) and Nottingham (where she met him). The letters, if they still exist, could reveal much more about them personally and about conditions faced by them at that time. Let's hope they are still around.

I appreciate your writing as Michael tells me you are moving house which is a stressful enough time without having any extra burdens. I'll put Zygmunt's documents into the post. Perhaps, too, you'll have a better copier. Michael, you have stuff from the MoD which is in Polish which I have not had translated. There are various forms and detailed flying records that perhaps Izabela could look at when life is less hectic.'

We have stopped looking at the post on the mat for letters from America. Instead my e-mail inbox is hot from repeated logging on. I put Zygmunt's testimony into an envelope and registered it, and posted it to Isabela's address in Colorado.

*

I showed Nick the new pictures of Zygmunt. Standing in his kitchen with a glass of his best Rioja in my hand whilst watching him cook Sunday dinner, I plugged in the laptop and held the photo of Zygmunt kneeling beside a three year old Michael and mentioned he might want to look at it. I watched him give it a cursory glance, saying nothing as he busied himself with testing the carrots in the steamer. We spoke of how the golf was going. Aimee came into the kitchen to say hello. She glanced once at the screen, looked away and glanced back.

'Is that your dad?'

'Yes.'

'Cool.' She wandered off.

Nicked stirred the gravy. Debbie came downstairs and into the kitchen, spotted the laptop straight away and gasped, 'Good God, Nick, this is how you'll look when you're older.' He continued to stir. A busy man. I took Debbie through the slide show pointing out Michael flying, Warren, Melanie and Grace. She looked mildly interested but became more animated and continued to comment on Zygmunt and showed surprise as some appeared to her as a likeness of Nick or sometimes Robert.

We ate dinner with the family. When Joe and Aimee had left the table Nick was ready to look at the

380

photos. Debbie looked over his shoulder and made comments about who she could see in the shots of Zygmunt. He conceded there was a strong family likeness in many of them. 'Who's Warren?' He asked after a while, 'Your cousin?'

'No. He's your cousin. Michael's son.'

We looked at his page on Facebook. One of the pieces of information he gave about himself indicated he supported Leeds United. He posted that he thought they would gain a higher division in the football league this year. Nick sent a message through my Facebook page that he thought they were related. Cousins, he believed? 'And,' he continued, 'Leeds United are right where they were supposed to be!' A reply was not long in coming asking Nick to be his 'Facebook friend'. Nick accepted this paving the way for them to correspond.

Nick wondered aloud why he felt it was the right thing to do; to connect with this Polish part of his existence when he had felt nothing when I had told him that I had found and met Kathleen. He said he had thought a lot about his Nan and Granddad but, when all was said and done, they had been dead for many years now; Granddad for thirteen years and Nan for ten, and it wasn't as if he were looking for some kind of replacement.

There is something romantic in the notion of a handsome Polish flyer having an affair with an English woman during the war but it was more than that. He had now seen pictures of this part of his genetic family, both photographs of men, and had been able to see a family likeness on my side for the first time. He has always looked something like both

Brian and I. He and I were sitting together one time not so long ago in the pub and a woman, a friend of his, leaning across the tables, said 'Ooo, Nick, I can tell that's your mum!' Pleasing for me although so not cool for him. And there were these Rosiak men quite amenable to making connections with me so why not with him?

He phoned the following morning. Warren had replied. He took the joke about Leeds United on the chin and wrote about what he did for a living, that he was engaged to Lauren and planned to marry in Florida next year. He wanted to learn more about 'his new extended family.' Nick told him that he was married to Debbie now but had been married before and had a son, Joseph. Debbie had a daughter, Aimee and they had a West Highland White called Billy. He thought his place in the pecking order in the household was somewhere just below Billy. He wrote, too, about working for a health insurance company. I felt very pleased they had made contact and said so in an e-mail to Michael.

*

Still waiting for contact with Isabela with news about the war-time letters, I check the e-mails daily. Still nothing but a wonderful surprise today, however. An e-mail from Melanie Holdsworth. Just a short one but making contact, nevertheless. She said she had been meaning to make contact since they had arrived back from their holiday in the UK but events had overtaken her. She would be on holiday from work on Monday and would like to talk on the phone with me. This is great news and I e-mailed back to say so and ask her to name a time. Awaiting events yet again. How exciting. Sunday at 3.30pm our time; they're six hours behind us.

*

I filled the morning with domestic stuff; some ironing and helped Brian in the garden. We ate lunch at about half past two, washed up, and I meandered around the kitchen waiting. Precisely at 3.30pm the phone rang.

Chapter 29

An Expression of Doubt

Melanie said hello in an American accent. We spent several minutes on small talk –how are you? It's good to talk and sorry we missed you when they were in the UK. They had been over in the UK to see relatives and it had been something of a whistle-stop tour. She wanted to ask me questions, she said, but first of all where was our house in France? I explained where the Charente was – no one seems to have heard of it; it's not as popular as the Dordogne. She and her husband had been on a coach tour, flying first to Bordeaux, to Sarlat one time for a holiday so she was familiar with the Dordogne and it was ideal as she was interested in ancient history so the area held great interest. I explained they would have been two to three hours south of us. 'Oh?'

Then began the first of her many questions. She was interested in how I had found out her father's name. I explained in great detail how we had begun to trace Kathleen, using the social services first in Nottingham and later in Sheffield. She understood how it was necessary to use social workers in such cases but confessed to knowing nothing about adoption procedures. Why should she know anything? I told her about my first meeting with Kathleen and how she had told me my father's name was Zygmunt and how she considered he would be dead by that time. She was right.

'It wasn't until the second meeting that she said his name had been Rosiak,' I told her. 'We'd no idea how it was spelled but it was important for me to know this.'

'How did your father, your dad, know what it was?'

'He didn't,' I said. 'What he did know was her name and where she was living at the time, although this proved to be a wrong address, and that my father had been Polish, Catholic and an airman.'

'But how did he find out about these things?' she persisted.

'I don't know. He should not have been privy to the information. I can only assume he and my mum were left alone in an office with papers on a desk and he took a look. Kathleen should not have known where they lived or their name but she did.'

'Oh, I see.'

'And that had been enough, first of all to trace Kathleen after I had sent for my birth certificate...'

'Is my father named on your birth certificate?'

'...and she told me...No, there was just a line under father's name...my name was given as Newcombe which was her name...which was her husband's name.'

'But she knew you weren't his child?'

Yes. He was away in Egypt at the time of my conception. When he came home she had to tell him and he said he wasn't willing to bring up someone else's child so she gave me up. They went on to have two more children, John and Paul, John born eleven months after me so they made a go of their marriage. In fact, they were married for sixty–four years before he died.'

385

'Did you send for my parent's marriage certificate?' she wanted to know.

'No. I didn't feel I needed to. Do you know when they were married? The records only refer to quarters; they don't give actual dates.' She didn't. 'My friend, Pam, who does the genealogy thing so well, suggested I send for it but for what purpose? I'd found you existed, that you were married in 1973 to Julian, where he worked...and so on...'

'How is it that you didn't know about Michael?' she wondered.

'For that reason. He wasn't born when you emigrated to Canada so didn't appear on the Internet records in the UK.'

'No...'

'So when I wrote to you I did say that there could be more of you. You needn't have been the only child. And of course you weren't.'

'Yes, your letter, you said in your e-mail to me that you forget things...me too.' She'll be sixty. She was born in 1949.

'Michael's e-mail out of the blue was astonishing and to meet him, and Yoli, too was wonderful.'

'Did you give him some papers you had of my father?'

'Yes, I did. I have so much.' I decided to explain to her at this point how I had managed to trace so much starting with my letter to the Polish Catholic Society in Nottingham and the reply nine months later from the Polish Air Force Association with the address at Goldsmith Hill in Leeds on it; their advice to apply to the Ministry of Defence for more information and how much of that I had; and finally to receiving the photograph from the Polish Institute and Sikorski Museum shortly before I met with Michael.

'How did you manage to get hold of all this material, all these records? Are they just in the public domain?' she asked.

'Well, not really. I have to have proof of kinship but of course, I now know I wasn't the next of kin.'

'No.'

'Your mother is still alive but I didn't know that at the time.' I felt defensive all of a sudden.

'Yes...what did you have that proved you were entitled to the records?' Oh, God, I couldn't remember. Was it the printout from the Internet? Had Pam found that he'd died before I sent off to the MoD. I told Melanie that and said whatever I sent they accepted but had to pay £30 to get them. Only war widows get them for free.

'When I applied to the Sikorski Museum they wanted to see what records I held on Zygmunt. Of course the majority was about his flying, his flight log, although in Polish and his time in Russia, but the most interesting to me were the details about him when he was interviewed before he was demobbed. There were too many to have copied so I registered them as they were. When they sent the photograph they didn't send them back so I rang and asked for them. When they arrived there were some missing so to cut a long story short they sent everything again so suddenly I had two complete sets and was able to give one to Michael when he came.' She hadn't seen any of these, she said and neither, it appeared had she seen the photo as when I asked her about it she said she thought she knew the one I meant. Michael hadn't e-mailed one to her.

'The most exciting moment was getting this photo as I could at last see the other half of me. He looked, too, so like our younger son.'

'It's not an exact science, though, is it,' she pronounced. 'People can see what they want to see, can't they?'

'Well, no, it's not but when you have never seen who you look like you look very closely for familiar features.'

'It would need a DNA test for absolute proof. I don't know how it works with half-brothers and – sisters, do you? Do you know about that?'

What did she mean did I know about that? Of course I know about DNA testing but never having thought about the need for any of that, having believed my mother's version of events, it would not occur to me to go into such issues.

'No.'

'Is there any documentary proof that you are their child?'

'No. But I have absolutely no doubt in my mind that I am their child.   But,' suddenly clutching at straws, 'if you look at the photo of you when you graduated and the passport photo of me at twenty that Michael has on e-mail you will see that we have a certain likeness.   You'll think this is odd but your teeth cross in exactly the same way as mine do...er...did. I haven't the same teeth now,'

'No? They looked straight on the photo I saw of you and Michael.'

'Yes, well, I don't want to go into the matter of my teeth here...' She laughed a little. '...but if you look at that photo...'

'When I graduated? Oh, from high school?' suddenly realising.

'That's the one. You're wearing something fluffy around your shoulders. You're eighteen...'

'I know the one you mean.'

'...Mine was taken in a studio, so like yours in that respect. I'm not saying we look alike. What I'm saying is that we have some similar characteristics. The crossed teeth, the brown eyes and brown hair although your eyes are a lot darker than mine. Mine are hazel, yours look chocolate brown.'

'The photo is black and white so it's hard to tell. But my eyes aren't that dark they are hazel, too,' she conceded. 'Are they? And then there's the Polish ears!'

'Yes, I know about that. Michael mentioned it,' she said. 'But I've never thought about it myself.'

'Of course not,' I told her. 'When you're in a family seeing everything day by day you don't spend time looking at what is after all familiar.' I told her how we had referred to Nick's ears as the Polish ears and how the characteristics had perpetuated through his son and Robert's younger boy.

'You have to realise, you know, how all this has affected the way I see my father. You may have a romantic notion of a war-time affair but I have a notion of how they, he and my mother were together.'

'Do you know how they met?' She didn't but I didn't comment on that. 'Kathleen and Zygmunt met in a dance hall in Nottingham, I'm convinced of that because my mother told me,' I said sounding a bit indignant. 'But what's to say that she didn't have other affairs? What was she doing going to a dance hall as a married woman? Do you see what I mean?'

I did see what she meant and felt resentment at what she implied. Melanie's implication is that Kathleen could have had more than one lover and photographic likenesses aren't any scientific proof of anything. She didn't want her romantic ideals of her parents' relationship sullying any more than I wanted her to imply that my mother wasn't all she should be. Her mother met Zygmunt in a dance hall in Leeds. And...she didn't know the date of her parents' marriage. Why not? She was born in February of 1949. Her parents were married between July and September of 1948. And what she failed to realise was that people behaved very differently in the War. Young married women, hastily married before husbands were shipped out to heaven knows where or to what experiences, left alone and lonely; young men flying daily into danger not knowing whether they would still be alive the next day. Life and moral values were very different then. Who are we, from our comfortable safe lives, to judge people then?

'Yes. But what I need to point out is that whatever happened, happened before your father met your mother. His relationship with Kathleen was over before they met.'

Zygmunt was thirty-three when he married Grace. It seemed wholly unrealistic to me to think he would not have had any sexual relations by that age.

'Do you think he knew about you?' she wondered.

'I've no idea. And I have no one to ask. I can't ask Kathleen. It would be too much for her. She said originally that he hadn't and that he'd gone home. But of course he didn't, did he? He stayed and met your mother and you were born.'

'You never know, my mother might be the one to know,' she speculated.

'Yes, but not the one to ask, of course,' I said. Melanie's quite rightly very protective of her mother and we both knew it wouldn't do to have a breath of this reach her.

'And then there's the matter of the letters,' I said. 'You know about the letters?'

'Yes. I have been talking to Isabela recently. I haven't spoken to her for over a year. Michael thinks Isabela and I look alike but I'm not sure.'

'You're both dark, though,' I volunteered then realised I'd given the game away that I'd seen her photograph so I mentioned the wedding photos I'd been sent by Michael. Melanie didn't know but went on, 'She told me about them but she has got it wrong.'

'Oh,' I wondered. 'How so?' A cold moment of doubt crept over me.

'The letters weren't written by Kathleen.'

I felt horribly disappointed. Were they written by another woman? 'They were written by my father. Kathleen sent the food parcels.'

'So Zygmunt wrote to his parents about Kathleen whilst she sent things over to them, food, clothing and so on.' What more proof did she want that there had been a relationship, an affair?

'My grandparents certainly thought someone called Kathleen was going to be their daughter in law.'

'But,' I went on, 'their next communication from Zygmunt was his wedding photo of himself and your mother getting married. He was very happy, he said.'

'Yes,' she conceded.

'Tell me what Isabela said to her parents. Did she prompt that the woman's name was Kathleen?'

'No, apparently not. I asked that question and she made it clear that it was her mother who had remembered the name.' I said nothing and a silence continued for a moment. I wanted to tell her that my mother was impulsive, loving and giving, warm and generous but said nothing. I wanted to say that she probably loved Melanie's father very much and had made a monumental mistake in becoming pregnant. It became clearer to me that she had probably not told Zygmunt at all that she was married and on learning, probably in September or October of 1945 that Bill was due to come home in December had ended the affair only to realise weeks later she was expecting a child. As she said, the worst thing she had to do in her life was to tell Bill she was expecting a baby. But perhaps having to tell Zygmunt the relationship was at an end could not have been easy either. On reflection, even if she had concealed the fact that she was married why risk taking Zygmunt to meet her mother and her sisters? Too many mysteries.

Suddenly into the silence, 'Michael said you had a manuscript, that you were writing a book.'

'Well, yes, I am.'

'A novel, he said.'

'Not a novel, a true account. The manuscript is with a friend of mine at the moment, someone who I have done some writing with, in the past. She is looking at it and her question to me was: 'who is your audience?' and my response is that I have written it for my own purposes.'

'If you published it, it would be for people like you to see how you'd gone about it, I suppose?'

'Yes,' I conceded, 'I guess so,'

It would need to be consensual,' she said. I could tell what she was getting at. 'My father wouldn't be there for you to ask his permission.'

'No. And it wouldn't do would it that your relatives in Leeds picked it up from the shelves in WH Smith and recognised themselves and all the while your mother was in ignorance. That wouldn't happen. You've no need to worry on that score.'

'No. I'm not worrying. I just want to get the picture.'

Well, yes, of course.

'One more question. What was your mother's maiden name?'

'James,' I told her. 'My birth certificate says Averill Newcombe but that was her married name. Her family was James.' I could hear her writing this down.

'I can hear you writing all this down.'

'Yes, well, I am,' she admitted. 'You know what it's like. You said you forget things.'

Remembering my two letters, of course.

'Julian will say when you get off the phone, 'what did she say?' and you want to remember the details,' I speculated. 'Yes.' I think Melanie had been busy writing down all my responses to her questions which she probably had written down on a piece of paper before coming to the phone. Very sensible. I had felt for a time that I had been in an interview. She suddenly noticed that we had been on the phone for the better part of two hours.

'I won't keep you any longer she said and I turned to see the time on the kitchen clock was almost twenty minutes past five.

'No problem for me,' I said, 'it's been good to have the opportunity to talk like this.' She agreed. 'Not letting her go immediately I asked, 'You have two children I remember.' She did and told me that Elizabeth had been working in another state and was now doing her masters in social work. Ian, her son had recently moved to Texas to live with his girlfriend so she was seeing less of him. Elizabeth was twenty-eight and Ian, thirty-one.

'You have an empty nest now,' I joked. She had but was still busy at work.

'Doing what?' I wanted to know.

'I'm an events' organiser across the campus. I'm very busy and, of course, my husband is a professor so we are both very caught up in university life.'

Of course they were. We agreed that if there were any more questions she wanted me to answer and anything that I wanted to ask her we could talk again or e-mail one another. Did I get the job? Did I even make the shortlist?

I came off the phone feeling deflated. 'She'll come round; she's in denial,' said Brian. 'It took John a while.' True. It occurred to me that whilst Michael had been all embracing in his acceptance of me he had been ruled by his heart. Melanie had intellectualised the experience and, ruled by her head still wanted answers.

Chapter 30

The Final Polish Connection

Before the phone call with Melanie, Michael and I had continued to exchange e-mails. Amongst the family photos he had sent me a photo of Zygmunt in his Polish flyers uniform wearing a lapel pin. Michael still has it and treasures it. Neither of us knew its origin so I e-mailed Colin Mitchell-Smith to see if he could throw some light on it.

Colin replied:

'The eagle is the diving eagle worn by Polish aircrew in the P.A.F. There are many variants depicting the various trades and dates ie: pilot or air gunner or navigator etc. This particular one is of a pilot 1st class 1933 or pilot 1919 to 1933. Cannot be absolutely sure because of the wreath. However the wreath is gold coloured which makes it one of these two. Information comes from a book Air Force Badges and Insignia.

I e-mailed Michael and we speculated on Colin's information as the dates didn't seem quite right.

'Hi Michael

I don't know whether this is helpful of not as 1933 doesn't seem to be the right date but it could well be that from 1933 the rank was changed to pilot 1st class whereas it had previously been pilot. Our

newspapers have been carrying articles on 1st
September about the Nazi invasion of Poland 70 years
ago and the brave efforts of the Polish forces to repel
them. 'The Times' carried an 8 page pull-out looking
at various aspects of Polish history. I've saved it.
Today has been the day 70 years ago when Britain
declared war on Germany. Quite a week of nostalgia
on the TV, as well.'

The television had carried scenes of memorial,
footage of the invasion of Poland and declaration of
war on every channel. Chamberlain's solemn voice
about the inevitability of 'war with Germany' could be
heard throughout the day. I read 'The Times' pull out
supplement whilst sitting up in bed one night looking
at photos of Polish soldiers with images of hope in
their faces. I felt a strange connection that I had never
felt before.

Michael thought perhaps the year Colin had
suggested for the pin was incorrect but it seemed to
him like a common bond the PAF had in wearing
these pins. He found it fascinating. He, too, was
feeling a connection and a deserved sense of pride that
his father had played his part seventy years ago.

Just below Michael's e-mail on the subject of
the pin was the e-mail from Melanie suggesting we
should talk. I e-mailed him:

'Well, in the same inbox as your latest e-mail,
Michael, is one from Melanie!! You'll probably know
that, though. And we are going to speak on the phone
on Sunday or Monday.

I'm soo... pleased. Is this your doing? If so, well done'.

He wouldn't take the credit for this. He said:

'It is fair to say I've been encouraging her to make contact, but it is not fair to say it is my doing. She is just progressing at her own pace. Once you and Brian meet up with Melanie and Julian, I believe you'll all get along famously, but for now, this is what she needs. Her struggle seems to be that it has somehow altered her mental picture of how it all happened between my mom and dad. From my vantage point, while there's some truth to that, it is a minor point within my framework. It's all so long ago, and all the people involved are still the same people, and I have an exciting new family to get acquainted with.

At the time I could have wept. Later, rereading it after the bruising phone call, that was what I needed to hear, what I wanted to be told. I was trying to understand. So often I am wrapped up in my own version of events that I don't give enough thought to how everyone else is thinking. After all I'm a bolt from the blue to John and Paul and to Michael and Melanie. Michael is so positive about all of this and I am grateful to him.

I have not e-mailed him to tell him about the phone call to Melanie but am sure he will know by now what the substance of the call was. Apropos of nothing came a little e-mail with an attachment.

'Warren and I visited Dad's burial site when he was last here. It's a sad photo, but I thought you might want it...

Love, Michael'

Attached was a photo of the memorial plaque placed in the grounds of the Forest Lawn Memorial Park. It reads:

'ZYGMUNT ROSIAK
LOVE ALWAYS
1916-1969

When we go to California, perhaps next summer, Michael and Yoli will take us to see it. They'll show us the house on Barker Avenue and there'll be more photos to see, I think. Perhaps, too, we will go to visit Melanie and Julian; Michael thinks we'd like them and if they met me, they'd like me. We'll meet Warren who will be married to Lauren by then and perhaps even Isabela and Piotr. These are my Polish relatives with an American connection.

Part 7

A Family Tapestry

Chapter 31

Reflections

Before Michael and Yoli came to visit I put together a hastily drawn family tree placing Newcombe's on the left and a sketchy Rosiak family on the right. Perched in the middle, linking the two, I placed myself and my immediate family. With Michael's help I have been able to devise a fuller family tree. It clarified my narrative and now I have a clear history of both my natural parents and know much about their other descendants.

I see Kathleen, Zygmunt and myself as a small unit at the centre of an extended web that has gradually been uncovered, revealing relationships and intriguing responses. Some of these have been unexpected and others have changed over time. Wondering if it would be helpful for others involved in such a search I have recorded my reflections on how and why the variety of characters in my drama have responded in different ways. My story has shown that not everyone welcomed the discovery of another dimension within family life whilst others embraced the addition of new family members.

Kathleen has responded wonderfully well. I recall Stuart, the social worker from Nottingham, in our first conversation telling me how some mothers had reacted to being found by their children (usually daughters) ranging from effusiveness, akin to killing the fatted calf at the return of the prodigal, throwing a party to include all the relatives, to absolute rejection taking the attitude that once given up, the child should be rejected a second time as the life of the mother had moved on. Somewhere in the middle of these extremes lies my mother. Her first reaction to me was cautious because she needed to protect Bill, then curiosity getting the better of her she displayed an openness of mind. Once in contact with me she bravely admitted her indiscretion to her sons and welcomed me into her life. I love her for that.

John, at first disapproving of his mother's bit of a fling – 'Tut, tut, Mother!' accepted I existed and set about dealing with the discovery in his own way. He would have been happy to exclude me from his life; I was, after all, an unnecessary distraction and in giving me his approval he felt all along that he was being disloyal to his father compounding his mother's betrayal. But he was prompted by his brother to stay in contact with me and was open to the suggestion of his wife, Lynn, to continue to see me. Both were welcoming and hospitable in France, for instance. I think he sees me as his sister and I want him as my brother.

For Paul things are different because of his health problems. He was warmly welcoming at our first meeting and encouraged John to keep in contact as much for his mother's needs as for himself or John's. I can only speculate that things would have been different had he been well. And Brenda, their cousin, what of her reaction? She was 'like a dog with two tails,' said her husband to discover she had a cousin but despite living in the same town I haven't continued the relationship except for the exchange of Christmas cards. What we have in common is a grandmother but our need for one another no longer has the initial intensity.

Then there's Michael. His response has been overwhelming. Whilst being mindful of protecting his mother he has been generous and emotionally all-embracing not just to me but to my family. He has been guided in part by Yoli who is so like him. Michael's e-mail in which he tells me he is proud of the fact that I am part of his family heritage and is willing...no...wants to explore his newly extended family is both gratifying and very important to me. His son, Warren, less emotionally involved, as his grandfather would have been dead some years before his birth, is interested in making contact with the next generation.

And what of my own 'next generation'? Robert's and Nick's reactions have been different. I think it's difficult for Robert. He sees himself so much as a Clarke. For years everyone who knows Brian's family knows Robert strongly resembles the men on Brian's mum's side of the family. He is so like his Uncle Norman, Brian's brother, not only in looks but in manner, too. Norman looks like his paternal grandfather. Robert resembles Norman so we always assume Robert is like his great-grandfather yet in a recent session of looking at family photos the resemblance seems less strong. But there is no getting away from the fact that a photo of Norman as a teenager could have been Robert. And now, suddenly, there is this other face, his biological grandfather, who he so strongly resembles. Like his dad he is naturally cautious and needs to think about things for a while before change occurs. Lisa is so supportive of me and

I appreciate her in this. She has gently prodded Rob to engage in my family search if not for himself then for me as I'm his mum. He may never do this and that is entirely up to him. There is no pressure on him to do it.

Both boys thought a lot about their Nan and Granddad and in Robert's view he doesn't need another set of grandparents so is not interested to know about Kathleen or Zygmunt. When Nick heard about my discovering Kathleen he too was non-committal and fairly disinterested. Recently he said he had felt no emotion at all when I had told him that I had found and met my natural mother. He has, however, reacted very differently to the discovery of Zygmunt and has asked himself why he was feeling it was alright to connect with the Polish element of his existence. He said that whilst he and Robert were very fond of their Nan and Granddad, when all was said and done, they had been dead for many years now and it wasn't as if he were looking for some kind of replacement.

There is something romantic about the notion of a handsome Polish flyer having an affair with an English woman during the War but for Nick it's not that. He has now seen pictures of this part of his genetic family, both photographs of men, and has been able to see a family likeness on my side of his family for the first time. He has always had characteristics from both Brian and me. He and I were sitting together in the pub not long ago when a woman said, 'Oh, Nick, I can tell that's your mum!' I felt pleased at the time. And now there were these Rosiak men quite amenable to making connections with me so why not with him? The trigger for his changed reaction has been seeing a different family likeness. He and Debbie would like to come to California with us.

My cousin Margery has been interested and supportive from the beginning even to the point of going to meet Kathleen. She is a blood relation of my mum but the fact of my adoption has never featured in our relationship. We are close because we have family ties and nothing has changed that. Brian's mum, however, has become interested only after I found Michael. This could be because she was staying with us at the time and saw my reaction in talking on the phone to him. But it's more than that, I think. She said to me when my mum died that she would be like a mum to me if I had a need. I am very grateful to her for this kindness but she might think the finding of Kathleen could have put this relationship in jeopardy. It hasn't but finding a brother does not present a threat. Mum in law is ninety-six and continues to be like a mum to me despite my new family

And finally Brian. None of what I have done could have been possible without him. All our married life he has supported me. When I went to university in the 1980s when the boys were young he encouraged me all the way stepping seamlessly into the domestic shoes as well as having a pressured working life. Over my need to find my biological parents he has been an equal partner taking on the responsibility of searching for, meeting and getting to know my new relatives. As ever his skill is putting on the brakes when my enthusiasm threatens to swamp events. He also has the social skills to make whomever I met feel comfortable, unthreatened and important. If I had one piece of advice to offer anyone setting out on such a search, it would be to have someone close to go through it with you. Kathleen had to make decisions on her own about making contact with me and we both felt it keenly for her. When I was at work supporting teachers in schools in the early 2000s a colleague who had got to know Brian once said, 'Everyone needs a Brian in their lives.' It makes me smile but it's the truth and I'm so glad that I have the original and the best.

I set out on my search to discover my roots. This I have achieved. I have seen in the flesh and through photographs or in the faces of others, the two people who gave me life. My relationship with Kathleen is a reality and on-going, whereas what I know about Zygmunt can only be a construction from records and the views of others. Nevertheless, I have found my sense of self and it is strangely fulfilling. What remains, as well, is having something that I hope will be a continuing and developing relationship with my discovered half-brothers and if she wishes my half-sister.

Appendix

Siberia   *by Anne Szczoanska*

Was it so many years ago, that I was ousted from my home?
Yet still the happening is still engraved upon my consciousness
Crudely and without warning, not fully understanding
I became a refugee.
All around bewildered and distraught groups were herded cattle-like
And soldiers with bayoneted rifles, escorted these disheveled souls
The wooden train windowless foul smelling
With a hole in the floor
Where humanity ceased to exist, and my only thought was to survive
Little families clung tightly, gaining comfort from familiar embrace.
I did not know and perhaps the unknowing was the worst
For all the travelers could only guess what their fate would be
Each of us was hungry, thirsty and ill clad
But the fear in our minds was even more terrible than the physical
What was my crime? I was Polish.
And the invaders feared my culture.
So my fate was sealed, and with thousands of others
We sped on our way to Starvation, illness and malnutrition
A living hell that was called Siberia.

Made in the USA
Charleston, SC
29 April 2015